TABLE OF CONTENTS

Preface
Foreword: USA TODAY editorial
The Trump Clones and Predecessors

[Type text]

The Early Trump Doubters: Polls, Trolls and Democratic Goals

Trump as White Male Prototype: Race

- The "Get 'em Out" Message: The Key to Colorlessness
- The Lambasting of Chicago
- Trump Derides Mexicans and Native Americans

    o *Gonzalo Curiel, Mexican-American judge*
    o *Forcing Mexicans to "Pay for the Border Wall"*
    o *Elizabeth Warren, part Native American ("Pocahontas")*
    o *Trump Maligns the Native American "Code Talkers"*

- Disdain for (Colored) Immigrants
- Trump and Recurring Racist Insults
- Trump Dumps Omarosa Manigault Edwards

Trump as Master Warmonger
Trump and the Violence at His Rallies
Donald Trump's Homoerotic Love Affair With Russia's Vladimir Putin
Trump's "Attraction" to Other Men: Obama, etc

- Trump as Rejected Ho: Ten Examples

Trump as White Male Prototype: Gender Bias/Misogyny

- Donald Trump: A Misogynist Overview
- "To the Victor Goes the Spoils"
- Trump and "Menophobia"
- Trump's Attacks on Carly Fiorina
- Melania Trump as "Trump Card": What Gives?
- Trump v. Mika and Joe of MSNBC's "Morning Joe"
- Trump Goes After Heidi Cruz, Wife of Sen. Ted Cruz
- Trump's Attacks on ESPN's Jemele Hill
- Punish Women Who Have Abortions
- Trump and daughter Ivanka: Innocence or Incest?

[Type text]

PREFACE

> *"To expect bad men not to do wrong is madness"*
> *--Marcus Aurelius, 167 C.E.*

I saw this quote at the beginning of a movie called "Acts of Vengeance" which starred Antonio Banderas. I found it most fitting as I was winding up this book on perhaps the most corrupt President that this already corrupt nation has ever had, Donald J. Trump. He was a ne'er-do-well long before he even thought about running for President, he was a racist administrator of a large corporation, and he won the Presidency despite being a foul-mouthed asshole who obviously despised people of color and women.

Hence, this book.

On November 8, 2016, Donald J. Trump became the 45th president of the United States. What prompted the writing of this book began many months before, when I saw this peckerwood lie time and time again in front of scores of politicians, news people and pundits, and literally get away with it. I realized then that he was saying what the white American public believed and was willing to stand behind. Therefore the problem was much deeper and bigger than just a white man who tanned his skin orange; it was about teaching the first African-American president, Barack Obama, a lesson for his "arrogance" and then to take that ire out on as many people of color as possible.

On Friday night, August 11, 2017, MSNBCs Joy Reid was sitting in for Lawrence O'Donnell on his show, "The Last Word." One of the segments dealt with President Trump's "obsession" with Barack Obama. The thesis was that anything that Obama did, Trump was bent on tearing down. Quoting six foreign diplomats, they informed interviewers that the first question Trump would ask them was "What did Obama say about this"? If they answered affirmative, he would immediately answer in the negative. Joy Reid concluded that Trump continually tries to "measure up" against Obama's track record, from the attendance of the inaugural (where Obama had thousands more) to legislative actions.

Alberto Nardelli, a guest on the show, said that Trump's "only real position is doing the opposite of Obama." Nardelli, who is the European Editor for BuzzFeed, added that "European diplomats see Trump as a laughing stock." He (Trump) seems to believe that the world started when he took office.

This is prototypical behavior on the part of this white man. White men are jealous and hateful of black men, and it stems from their belief that black men's penises are larger. From that petty stereotype stems the white man's historic actions, from lynchings and castrations to rapes of black women and stereotypes of black men as lazy, worthless and as rapists.

With an on-going bitch-like pique, Trump continues to get away with lies, insults and grandiose statements that no other person would have. The white press showed their commitment to white nationalism by allowing an idiot to gradually gain power and, while on stage with 16 other people who had an equal disdain for black people (including African-American candidate Ben Carson), set the stage for the gradual "re-energizing" of white racists all over America, male and female. Trump has come closer to destroying the American system of government than any threat past or present. A buffoon in charge of a nuclear arsenal, a dickless curmudgeon with forty million followers. You do the math

It should have been predictable for the most part.   For instance, a February 19, 2016 *Bloomberg News* article titled, "Donald Donald Trump can ride the wave of anger all the way to the White House" by Shirley Anne Warshaw offered that, "Trump offers no solutions, but he speaks for those who see little future." Continuing:

> What is noticeable about the Republican primaries and caucuses so
> far is the pent-up anger within the base of the Republican Party
> that Donald Trump has nurtured. (Warshaw, 2016)

[Type text]

And as we know, it worked. White people are angry about the fact that they have had to experience just some of the things that black people have had to endure for centuries. Spoiled rotten and knowing that much of what they have they did not deserve, their take their frustrations out on the same groups that Trump exploited and denounced: immigrants, Blacks, Latinos, women, the handicapped and veterans. And, like President-to-be- Trump, none of them take responsibility for being responsible for "the hate that hate produced."

Moving on:

> They are angry at their state of affairs, not the country's state of affairs. They aren't really angry at any particular thing; they are just frustrated that they aren't moving up the ladder. More than half of Trump's supporters didn't finish college and many didn't finish high school. According to one poll, only 11% made more than $100,000, with the overwhelming majority making less than $50,000. (Warshaw, 2016).

That is bullshit. These white people were mad at people of color, and they were made because a black man became president. They were mad because they were ignorant and therefore couldn't qualify for jobs that really paid well. It was time for a change, and these white people wanted to return to the way things "used to be" – a time when white people had absolute control and the laws backed them. The saw that in Trump, and that's why he voted for them.

Put another way,

> The Republican base has not benefited from the massive turnaround of the stock market that many Americans have profited from, especially the establishment Republican who profited significantly in the last six years. The divide in the Republican Party now is an economic divide, fueled by the divide of the haves and the have-nots. Once the party of Lincoln, often overseen by the White Anglo-Saxon Protestant (WASP) elite, the new Republican Party is the party of the working-class whites who see a shaky economic future. Into this perfect storm marches Donald Trump. (Warshaw, 2016)

I've seen and studied this trend before. It was George Bush and his rise from a Yale University screw up to the governor of Texas and then on to the presidency. Like Trump, he was viewed as a womanizing joke. In college he was an alcoholic (Trump claims he doesn't drink). His father was in Texas dominating politics and his brother Jeb was dominating Florida. George decides he's going to change his ways so the first thing he does is get into big business – just like Trump. But instead of real estate, this hick buys the Texas Rangers baseball team – and he was off.

Ann Richards was the governor of Texas and was much loved by black people – just like Hillary Clinton was in 2016. And Bush ran against her and destroyed her and became the new governor of Texas. He coined the phrase, "compassionate conservatism" and the people, including Texas Latinos, fell for it. By the time he ran for president he had created an empire in Texas and had that family heritage going for him. Like Trump he was unpopular but still won the presidency with the second one being as controversial as Trump's as he squeezed by Al Gore. Bush was not a smart person and made an ass out of himself numerous times, phrases and mis-statements that came to be known as "Bush-isms."

At one point during his bid for presidency, it was found out that twenty years earlier he had been busted for DWI (Driving While Intoxicated). It went public and the media was all over him. Just like Trump got busted talking about grabbing women's pussies and degrading them – the white people didn't give a shit. The politics of race are the undergirding and oftentimes hidden theme of these white men and as a result, the white voter is not going to tell the truth during a telephone survey when asked, "Who are you going to vote for"? Secrecy is a key to the white supremacist system because most of them are cowards. Like Bush before him (twice) Trump won by being his brazen, buffoonish self.

Donald J. Trump is eloquent (by white standards) but even more flawed than Bush. The masses of rednecks voted for both of these men, which is a direct statement against people of color. And from what I can see, like a weak-minded young girl whose playa boyfriend is fooling around all over the place but she still clings on to him, black people continue to have a police dog-like loyalty and commitment to this system, most recently coming up with this "Black Votes Matter" bullshit.

Why, in hindsight, are the American people therefore acting shocked at the election of Donald Trump? Bush had no positive relationship with black people and defeated men who claimed they did. Neiher did Trump. Trump had Donald Cheney, a racist warmonger as his vice-president and Trump has chosen Mike Pence, anti-women's rights Indiana governor. White men and their silly wives voted both of these men in despite knowing what they stood for. *Trump is therefore no exception – he is the racist rule.*

And that's why I started writing this book in August of 2015. I saw the writing on the wall because I have always been a student of history and the

Master's degree I received in December of 2000 was just a matter of credentialization. I was in a "no-lose" situation when it came to the 2016 election: I knew Bill Clinton's history and unlike most black people I was not a fan because I remember what he did to all those black boys he locked up with his Federal Drug Guidelines bullshit. I remembered when his blonde wife, Hillary, called black males "super predators." And unlike most of you I do not forget or forgive very easily.

The major thrust of this book is to quell the shock that people are feeling as time and time again Trump said things that we all know white people truly believed. This society has long held a low regard for women and it shows in their institutionalized actions. It has always been steeped in racism and it shows in Trump's claims about deportation of so-called "illegal aliens" and of course, the black and brown "inner cities." He was saying what cowardly white people (read: most of them) always believed and felt. But for fear of getting their asses kicked, they feigned liberalism, hid behind buzz words like "diversity," "inclusion," "equity" and "cultural competency" and kept their lipless mouths shut.

Far too many people don't pay attention to history which is why so many people, especially in America, fall prey to it. Had they been paying attention, they would have seen "Trumpism" alive and well throughout presidential history. I have documented a few examples but there are many more, believe me. This system could not have remained so racist, misogynistic and xenophobic for so long had there not been a system and a plan to hand the "baton of oppression" off from one cracker to the next.

Donald Trump's escapades and cacophonies of emotive labeling are not the first time the white male ego paved the way for the eventual undermining of the nation's political system. I am a scholar in political science and have kept close watch on these white men and their egos. I sicken when these cry babies whine and ask about, "did you see/hear what Trump did today"? I am a history scholar and therefore I've read about and studied tens of thousands of Trumps throughout American history, and millions of examples of actions generated by these Trump-like individuals. I don't whine and cry – I preserve a record so that those who come after me will not continue to continual complaining and crying about that which I view as a white male norm.

I have put together what I call "Trump Prototypes" as one part of this incredible analysis because so many presidential candidates before Trump committed the same kind of asinine mistakes that Trump has made, especially when it comes to their treatment of women, people of color and others. And let me add one more note.

[Type text]

The media is involved in aiding and abetting Trump in his lies, his crimes, his perfidy, his cowardice and so on. As a journalist I know what the protocols and priorities should be, and in my view, for the sake of an ad sale, television and print have taken what should have been a slam dunk case of treason and sedition and stretched it out so that they could create more "special reports" and the like. In doing so, they covered Trump's ass, provided reasons and rationale for his lying tendencies and because he's a white male, they looked the other way in one case after the other.

This fact is a key component of Trump as a white male prototype. The media is the voice of the American system. Look at how they came after us; how they castigated and critiqued the civil rights movement, the black power movement, the black arts movement, anti-segregation efforts and so on. There were no quarters given when it came to Black people and Latinos. But this is a white system with its own rules and in such a system bad guys make the news, if it bleeds it leads and "the hand that feeds, controls."

FOREWORD: USA Today Editorial

On October 16, 2016, Vice-President Joe Biden was on "Meet the Press" being interviewed by host Chuck Todd. Biden looked into the camera and claimed that Donald Trump's behavior toward women, his admitted sexual assaults and on-going insults, constituted things that "most men don't agree with." When I heard that, I had but once response:

Bullshit.

On September 30, 2016, the USA Today editorial board did something that it had never done before: it took a position on a Presidential candidate. The following editorial lambastes while accurately describing Republican Presidential candidate Donald Trump. My comments will filter in and out, but I felt it was an accurate opening for a book that postulates that Donald Trump is not an exception to the egotistical, racist ranting of presidential candidates but indeed, he is the rule.

If most men didn't agree with sexist behavior, there would be no sexism, plain and simple. This is a point that these talking heads don't want to deal with because it is their goal to make people like Trump: sexist, egotistical, racist and xenophobic – appear to be the exception, not the rule. These people don't see these white boys and black men in the clubs or the bars or the locker rooms. And this shit from these professional athletes about "we don't talk about assaulting women" is only half-true: they don't have to. They can flat out BUY pussy from a woman sitting in the stands. It is the college athlete who is taking pussy, assaulting coeds on campus, in dorm rooms, the frat house, in bars and anywhere else – that is the group where the "locker room" talk reflects boasting about assaults.

Back to the *New York Times* editorial, which begins with the opening claim: "The Editorial Board has never taken sides in the presidential race. We're doing it now." Let's take a look at what the New York Times had to say and now, with the benefit of hindsight, compare and contrast their views with what actually took place before and after Donald J. Trump was chosen to be President of the United States.

The editorial begins, thusly:

> In the 34-year history of USA TODAY, the Editorial Board has never taken sides in the presidential race. Instead, we've expressed opinions about the major issues and haven't presumed to tell our readers, who have a variety of priorities and values, which choice is best for them. Because every presidential race is different, we revisit our no-endorsement policy every four years. We've never seen reason to alter our approach. Until now.

They should have kept their damn mouths shut. What they did was allow emotion to rule them. That newspaper is no less racist than any other, and the Jews that control it have expressed selective reporting for at least a century. I still consider them the best newspaper in the world, but when they attempt to become moral leaders with their editorials because they stand against something someone did or said, one is remembered of the old saying, "People in glass houses shouldn't throw stones."

The editorial continues:

> This year, the choice isn't between two capable major party nominees who happen to have significant ideological differences. This year, one of the candidates — Republican nominee Donald Trump — is, by unanimous consensus of the Editorial Board, unfit for the presidency.

When these white people make these kinds of assessments – and a great number of them, from radio and television to newspapers and magazines – surely did that, they are implying that the office of the Presidency is without its own set of immoral, corrupt and racist standards. Nothing could be further from the truth. As I write in this book, Trump is the rule, not the exception; the only difference is that he had some knowledge of marketing and promotions and he knew how racist

America was and channeled that redneck mentality into a viable voting bloc. This has been done by people like Patrick Buchanan, Barry Goldwater, Richard Nixon, George Wallace and a host of others. But for some reason this time around the New York Times decides to take exception.

Their justification is then outlined:

> From the day he declared his candidacy 15 months ago through this week's first presidential debate, Trump has demonstrated repeatedly that he lacks the temperament, knowledge, steadiness and honesty that America needs from its presidents.

What about his predecessors? What about Gary Hart and his cockhounding and lying ways? What about John Edwards who was fucking an assistant while his wife was at home dying of cancer? How about John F. Kennedy who was screwing Hollywood starlets like Marilyn Monroe, as was his brother Robert? How about Bill Clinton who lied before he got into office, lied while in office and since he's been out has basically stood by and jinxed the hell out of Hillary? Trump was picked on because he was an asshole. But my point is that he was just one more white man who was an asshole who got into a position to be president. How is that any different than the way it's been for the past 200 years and among the other 44 men who became president?

What is the real fear? It was Trump's on-going refusal to insult Russian president Vladimir Putin. And because Trump also insulted American president Barack Obama on numerous occasions, the Times used all this to paint Trump as some kind of "communist sympathizer." Here is what they wrote:

> Whether through indifference or ignorance, Trump has betrayed fundamental commitments made by all presidents since the end of World War II. These commitments include unwavering support for NATO allies, steadfast opposition to Russian aggression, and the absolute certainty that the United States will make good on its debts. He has expressed troubling admiration for authoritarian leaders and scant regard for constitutional protections.

Vladimir Putin is just another white man with a different ideological outlook. What do he and Trump have in common? They both hate niggas. And that is the common denominator that Trump had with all those other presidents that the Times is making reference to. If the relative relationship between the white man and the black man is the same as it was during enslavement, then how much "change" can you really expect? So when Trump talks about "making America great again," he is implying that Barack Obama fucked it up and its up to him – the great white hope – to usher in some change and get these niggas back under control! This is a message that a whole lot of white folks could relate to and that's why Trump is now the President-elect!

How is the threat of "Russian aggression" any worse than the white American aggression that has been heaped upon black people on the streets of every major city by racist cops? By judges who want to teach black people a lesson? By racist social workers, high school principals and missionary-minded college deans? How could Russia treat black people any worse than the white American has done for the past three hundred years?

What these white men at the Times and "negroes" who supported the editorial and the "dump Trump" movement are implying is that the presidency is some kind of pristine palace of piety and morality. How can an egotistical, racist, misogynistic asshole be an insult to a position when all of those who have held that office, and most of the people who competed for it, had these characteristics? Just because they didn't get caught or exposed didn't mean that they didn't share in that mentality and attitude.

As I describe Trump later in this book, "You would think that Donald Trump would be able to "relate" to women since, in my view, he's a bitch himself. He has all the characteristics of a scatter-brained old woman who has been jilted by a lover and now just lashes out at everyone within hearing distance. He is, in the view of this writer (who by the way has several Master's degrees, one of them being in Political Science), a thin-skinned, name-calling, cosmetically covered, orange-tanned woman in a man's body and with a typical male mentality.

The key here is that he is typical; he is the white man stripped bare of the usual protocols, corporate facades and masquerades that so many of them adopt when they have some semblance of decision making authority. But don't get it twisted and don't be fooled. As the 960s group The Undisputed Truth warned in their song, "Smiling Faces," when it comes to the white man, "Beware of the handshake/It hides a snake."

THE TRUMP CLONES AND PREDECESSORS

In this book I have documented most of these egotists, womanizers or not, and they are: John Anderson (1980), Gary Hart (1984, 1988), Rev. Jesse Jackson (1984), Lenora Fulani (1988), Ross Perot (1992)Ralph Nader (1972, 1992, 1996 and 2000), Pat Buchanan (1992, 1996 and 2000), John Edwards (2004, 2008), Gary Johnson (2012 and 2016), and even the ultra-popular Bernie Sanders (2016).

Take note that there is but one woman and that is Lenora Fulani and in reality, she was not a "hound" but was indeed, the victim of several Presidential candidates who allowed her to tag along, one who even got romantically involved with her. But her ego and willingness to ally herself with any group out there is the reason why she appears in this book. I could have also added Geraldine Ferraro, who I viewed as an Italian nationalist, but she was a vice-presidential candidate alongside Walter Mondale (on a failed ticket).

The point that I want to make is that there is something really different about people who have the gall to vie for the highest office in the most racist nation in the history of the world. They know what they are undertaking and the question to ask is,"why"? Do these people really think that they are going to usher in the kinds of changes and make the type of difference that they claim they will? One thing is for sure: a person like that has to have an immense ego because just look at what is being implied: this person is saying "I feel so good about myself that I think that I can make decisions that influence, not only every single person in America, but the entire world." Now that's some narcissism for yo'ass!

Let's take a look at my sampling and you'll acquire a more profound understanding of the nature and extent of the type and degree of egotism that I am talking about.

John Anderson (1980)

When these white boys decide to make these runs for president, it is based on pure ego. They raise all that money and get to keep it at the end. They fly all over the country telling lies and duping stupid people into thinking that they are going to "make things better" or "bring about change." Like Trump, this is what John Anderson, a former United States Congressman, did when he decided to run for President.

He had already served ten terms as the U.S. Representative from the 16th District of Illinois – from 1961 to 1981. It was clear that he craved living off the government dole, which is what those Congressmen and Senators do. But then, although a Republican, he decided to run for President as an Independent candidate in the 1980 presidential election.

According to the research, which clearly shows how these ego-drive, party-switching, go-whichever-way-the-wind-blows white men have a tendency to be:

[Type text]

> Initially, Anderson was among the most conservative members of
> the Republican caucus. Three times (in 1961, 1963, and 1965) in
> his early terms as a Congressman, Anderson introduced a
> constitutional amendment to attempt to "recognize the law and
> authority of Jesus Christ" over the United States. The bills died
> quietly, but came back to haunt Anderson in his presidential
> candidacy.(Wikipedia, 2017)

See? He starts off as a conservative: a conservative is someone who wants state's rights and for the most part, doesn't give a damn about how each state treats the people of color in their state. They want limited government because without government oversight, these racist peckerwoods would have a field day discriminating and otherwise abusing black people.

And look at the religious zealot component – which a majority of conservatives appear to endorse. He introduced a constitutional amendment "to recognize the law and authority of Jesus Christ" over the United States." So that means that you believe that the bible gives white people the right to do whatever they want to people of color. It is this kind of thinking that has these white people continuing to believe that God is on their side. That is where the doctrines of "Manifest Destiny" and "White Man's Burden" hail from. And that is why to this very day in 2016, Sunday is the most racially segregated day of the week. As I see it, conservatism plus Christianity equals racism.

Moving on:

> As he continued to serve, the atmosphere of the 1960s weighed on
> Anderson and he began to re-think some of his beliefs. By the late
> 1960s, Anderson's positions on social issues shifted to the left,
> though his fiscal philosophy remained largely conservative. At the
> same time, he was held in high esteem by his colleagues in the
> House. In 1964, he won appointment to a seat on the powerful
> Rules Committee. In 1969, he became Chairman of the House
> Republican Conference, the number three position in the House
> Republican hierarchy in what was (at that time) the minority party.
> .(Wikipedia, 2017)

Like a whole lot of white people, the reason why he began to "re-think" his positions was because his country was getting its ass kicked by way of the black power movement. On the other end of the black ideological scale were the civil rights folks who were marching, protesting and getting all kinds of media play and in doing so, were exposing and embarrassing the living hell out of America. Being the political opportunist that so many of these white men are, they decided that in order to avoid getting their asses kicked, they'd better change some of their beliefs. And Anderson was one of them.

And as a result of the logic that was being displayed and spewed forth by black leadership, as a result of the rise of the Black Panther Party for Self Defense, the Revolutionary Action Movement, the Deacons for Defense down in the South, the Southern Christian Leadership, Stokely Carmichael and the post-King assassination rioting going on, Anderson began to criticize the Vietnam War, and a few other things:

> Anderson increasingly found himself at odds with conservatives in his home district and other members of the House. He was not always a faithful supporter of the Republican agenda, despite his high rank in the Republican caucus. He was very critical of the Vietnam War, and was a very controversial critic of Richard Nixon during Watergate. In 1974, despite his criticism of Nixon, he was nearly swept out by the strong anti-Republican tide in that year's election; he was re-elected with 55 percent of the vote, what would be the lowest percentage of his career. His spot as the chairman of the House Republican Committee was challenged three times after his election. And, when Gerald Ford was defeated in the 1976 Presidential campaign, Anderson lost a key ally in Washington. .(Wikipedia, 2017)

Just as Trump continues to flip-flop on issues and lie to cover his ass, John Anderson was doing it first. He started criticizing Nixon and as a result, began to lose favor with the Republicans. But this ego-driven politico was a long way from being done:

> In 1978, he formed an exploratory committee … finding little public or media interest. Anderson postponed his decision to run, lost his campaign manager, and struggled to raise money, but in late April 1979 he made the decision to enter the Republican primary anyway, joining a crowded field that included Robert Dole, John Connally, Howard Baker, Harold Stassen, George H. W. Bush and Ronald Reagan. .(Wikipedia, 2017)

These men are power mongers. Like the present-day Howard Trump, they come from money and they use it to acquire power. Once they have power they use that to generate even more money. Almost every one of them is a white supremacist, stripped of the pillow case, robe and swastika. Their job is to keep the way of life that got them their fame intact. And that way of life is white, through and through. People of color are only kept around for blue collar jobs, entertainment and comic relief.

But the key is not to appear to be the "same ol' same ol' as whomever you're running against. Trust me: in 2016, Hillary and Trump are the same when it comes to maintaining white power. Bernie Sanders talks a lot of shit, but his lines were lifted from 1960s black radicals. He doesn't want a revolution because if he did – and if the stupid ass American public understood what a revolution was – he'd be calling for his own ouster!

As for Anderson, you can see the beginnings of his ego-driven candidacy:

> The turning point for Anderson occurred in the first political event of 1980, a Republican candidates debate in Des Moines, Iowa on January 5. On stage Anderson successfully showed that he was very different from the others in the GOP race. He was alone in supporting Jimmy Carter's grain embargo against the Soviet Union as a reaction to its recent invasion of Afghanistan, an unpopular position in an agricultural state. Anderson also took issue with the other candidates who criticized his 50/50 plan, whose only new strategies for dealing with the energy crisis were deregulating the industry and mining more coal. .(Wikipedia, 2017)

So then he won through default – he got backing because of the lackluster presentation of other candidates. He was, in essence, the best of the worst. And in America, that is enough to catapult a candidate into the news media's priority operations. That's what Trump is about: he's an obvious asshole who keeps generating the attention of the media who are doing stories because stories mean more advertising revenue for the networks and respective stations that they work for. Anderson is of that same ilk.

More evidence can be found regarding the "best of the worst" approach:

> When questioned about which episode in their career they most regretted, none of the other candidates would answer the question, except Anderson, who cited his vote for the Gulf of Tonkin resolution. Unlike the others, he said lowering taxes, increasing defense spending, and balancing the budget were an impossible combination. In a stirring summation, Anderson invoked his father's emigration to the United States and said that we would have to make sacrifices today for a better tomorrow. For the next week, Anderson's name and face were all over the national news

programs, in newspapers, and in national news magazines.
(Wikipedia, 2016).

More bullshit, and the American public just eats it up. So desperate was the voting public then, as now, that anyone who sounds different, or who comes up with a lie that they have not heard before, is good enough to get their vote. So Trump is not the first bullshit artist to drop names, make promises about lowering taxes and to admit that he may have made a mistake in the past. With Anderson it was the Gulf of Tonkin vote; with Trump it was Trump University and a host of negative statements about women, the largest voting bloc in the country.

Another similarity is the idea of "making sacrifices today for a better tomorrow." This is akin to Donald Trump's talk about "making America great again," which is a back door way of saying that America ain't shit. See? Trump's egomaniacal statements are hardly new or original.

Next come the "crossroads."

> Anderson was at a crossroads. He seemed to have three options: to continue as a Republican despite the fact that the calendar was not friendly and he had lost three consecutive primaries in states where he needed to do well; to drop out of the race; or to mount an independent candidacy. The third option had a huge amount of support. The presumptive major party nominees, Carter and Reagan, then engendered little enthusiasm (Wikipedia, 2016).

Doesn't this sound like Trump to you? The ego is the most important thing and it must be satisfied at all costs. Rather than just cut your losses and get another vocation, something else to do, these power hungry individuals only consider the options "of least resistance" (translation: least amount of real work). So like Trump, Anderson pondered and third about a possible third party run because the opponents seemed to have little to offer in terms of grandiosity – and that is what the American public wants. They want promises, personality and if possible, some kind of pledge about what to do about the niggas. And while they can't come and directly say what they'll do, they can hint around about it based on their positions on other issues.

For example, check out Anderson's method of operation and choice:

> The Republican platform failed to endorse the <u>Equal Rights Amendment</u> or support extension of time for its ratification.
> Anderson was a strong supporter of both. Pollsters were finding
> that Anderson was much more popular across the country with all

voters than he was in the Republican primary states. Without any campaigning, he was running at 22% nationally in a three-way race. With the support of one of the premier media strategists of the day, David Garth, Anderson decided to join the race. (Wikipedia, 2016).

So many parallels. Although the ERA was not an issue, there were other issues that Trump was in on that essentially made him different from the other candidates, namely his own competition such as Jeb Bush, Marco Rubio, Ted Cruz and the other fourteen. In addition, he was at odds with Hillary Clinton although he was a one time supporter. And as for Bernie Sanders, he was nothing more than comic relief and an "also-ran," relying on warmed over lines he ripped off from black militants from the 1960s to energize his followers, most of whom were too young to remember people like H. Rap Brown, Huey P. Newton, James Forman and Eldridge Cleaver.

Appealing to white male rednecks, Trump was able to carve out a niche rooted and rested on racism, misogyny and anti-immigrant themes. Anderson, on the other hand, was simply lucky to be running against two duds who couldn't excite the electorate.

So Anderson decided to run as an Independent candidate, or at least he threatened to – just like Trump initially threatened a third party run. Check out the following:

> Initially, Anderson did very well as an independent. He built a new campaign team, qualified for every ballot, raised a great deal of money, and rose in the polls to as high as 26% in a Gallup poll ((Wikipedia, 2016). But the summer was cruel to Anderson … The major parties, particularly the Republicans, basked in the spotlight of their national conventions where Anderson was left out of the coverage. Anderson made an appearance with Ted Kennedy and it too was a huge error. By the third week of August he was in the 13–15% range in the polls. ((Wikipedia, 2016).

Mistake after mistake, all of them driven by ego. Just like Trump: he continued to make mistakes about his party loyalties. He backed Hillary in earlier years and even contributed to Bill's campaign. He then became a Republican and is running for president as one, only after threatening to switch over to a third party. He was forced to sign a declaration that he would endorse whomever was nominated and lucky for him, he is now the one. Were he not, there is no doubt that Trump would have wormed his way into some other position, the same way John Anderson attempted to do.

Moving on:

> Anderson again recovered and went on a modest spree of successes. A critical issue for him was appearing in the fall presidential debates and he won an important victory when the League of Women Voters created a qualification threshold of 15% for him to appear. In late August, he named Patrick Lucey, the former two-term Democratic Governor of Wisconsin and Ambassador to Mexico as his running mate. (Wikipedia, 2016).

So many similarities. For one thing Trump would also go on "a modest spree of successes" once he got the Republican nomination. In vintage white fashion, the old boy's network got behind him because if he was to win, they didn't want to lose their favor with the most powerful man in the world. Furthermore, American history, from Nebraska to California, is filled with white politicians who switch parties, change their loyalties and their philosophies just so they can maintain some semblance of power – or access to it.

Trump and Anderson had so much in common in terms of their level of desperation. The more success they had, it seemed that the more desperate they became. For instance,

> Late in August, Anderson released a 317-page comprehensive platform, under the banner of the National Unity Party, that was very well received. In early September, a court challenge to Federal Election Campaign Act was successful and Anderson qualified for post-election public funding. Also, Anderson submitted his petitions for his fifty-first ballot. Then, the League ruled that the polls showed that he had met the qualification threshold and said he would appear in the debates. (Wikipedia, 2016).

The concept of a "national unity party" sounds an awful lot like Hitler and his references to "national unity," the "German national state" and "National Socialists." Americans didn't pick it up because most Americans are ignorant of their own history, let alone the history of the world. But it was right there – as are the similarities between Trump and Hitler, many of them being addressed elsewhere in this book.

Anderson's support faded and Ronald Reagan was at his conservative and charismatic best. During the Presidential debate, Anderson

[Type text]

.... needed a break-out performance, but what he got was a modest victory. In the following weeks, Anderson slowly faded out of the picture with his support dropping from 16% to 10–12% in the first half of October. By the end of the month, Reagan debated Carter alone and Anderson's support continued to fade. Although Reagan would win a sizable victory, the polls showed the two major party candidates closer (Gallup's final poll was 47–44–8[31]) going into the election and it was clear that many would-be Anderson supporters were now supporting their second choice. In the end, Anderson finished with just under 7% of the vote. (Wikipedia, 2016).

And so we had another megalomaniac bite the dust, losing to another ego tripper, Reagan, who was a former Hollywood actor no less.

Gary Hart, (1984, 1988)

Despite the immense ego, all the books and traveling and the on-going positive publicity, it was pussy that brought down Gary Hart when all is said and done and he went out with a whimper.

In a nutshell, Wikipedia (2016) informs us of the following:

> Gary Warren Hart (born Gary Warren Hartpence; November 28, 1936) is an American politician, diplomat and lawyer. He is perhaps best known for being the front-runner in the 1988 Democratic primary until he resigned over allegations of a romantic affair with Donna Rice.Hart served as U.S. Senator from Colorado from 1975 to 1987 and as Vice Chairman of the Homeland Security Advisory Council from 2008 to 2011. Since 2014 he has been the U. S. Special Envoy for Northern Ireland. He is also an author, professor and commentator. He has been married to Lee (Ludwig) since 1958 and has two grown children.

All those credentials and great ideas, and he got taken down by some pussy. The same could probably be said for the next fellow that I analyze, Rev. Jesse Jackson, because Hart and Jesse did run at about the same time. But more on that later.

Rice had an impressive resume and had an affair behind his wife's back.

This talk about these "southern gentlemen" and "Midwestern values" is all bullshit. A man with power is going to abuse it and every single president has done that without reservation. In light of this, Trump would be the rule, not the exception. Look at some of Gary Hart's "down home" background:

> Hart was born in Ottawa, Kansas, the son of Nina (née Pritchard) and Carl Riley Hartpence, a farm equipment salesman … As a young man, he worked as a laborer on the railroad. He and his father changed their last name to "Hart" in 1961 because "Hart is a lot easier to remember than Hartpence."⋯ He won a scholarship to Bethany Nazarene College in Bethany, Oklahoma, in 1954 ⋯ and graduated in 1958. He met his wife, Oletha (Lee) Ludwig, there, and they married in 1958 … He also graduated from Yale Divinity School in 1961 and Yale Law School in 1964 … (Wikipedia, 2016).

Everything was going his way. He was, as they say in their racist way, "Free white and 21." He got a great job in law, a prelude for a political future, and it seems that Gary Hart was on his way:

> Hart became an attorney for the United States Department of Justice from 1964 to 1965, and was admitted to the Colorado and District of Columbia bars in 1965. He was special assistant to the solicitor of the United States Department of the Interior from 1965 to 1967. He then entered private law practice in Denver, Colorado, at the firm of Davis Graham & Stubbs (Wikipedia, 2016).

He was making money and the more he made, in typical white male fashion, the more selfish he became. He then got hooked up with the Democratic Party in 1968 and ended up aligning himself with George McGovern. As is the case with white people, they promote from within, based on race, and the resumes of those being promoted continue being padded, to be used for future aspirations and positions:

> In the 1972 primary elections, McGovern named Hart his campaign manager. Along with Rick Stearns, an expert on the new system, they decided on a strategy to focus on the 28 states holding caucuses instead of primary elections. They felt the nature of the caucuses made them easier (and less costly) to win if they targeted their efforts.[6] While their primary election strategy proved successful in winning the nomination, McGovern would go on to lose the 1972 presidential election in one of the most lopsided elections in U.S. history. Conservative Republican Senator Barry Goldwater remarked of Hart, "You can disagree with him

politically, but I have never met a man who is more honest and more moral" (Wikipedia, 2016).

But it appears that the political bug had bitten Gary Hart. Like Donald Trump his ego would not allow him to step away. Clearly it was not an issue of money, but of ego and power. So,

> In February 1983, during his second term, Hart announced his candidacy for president in the 1984 presidential election. At the time of his announcement, Hart was a little-known senator and barely received above 1 percent in the polls against better-known candidates such as Walter Mondale, John Glenn and Jesse Jackson. To counter this situation, Hart started campaigning early in New Hampshire, making a then-unprecedented canvassing tour in late September, months before the primary (Wikipedia, 2016)

And so another ego trip begins. Like Trump, Hart had a number of more qualified challengers. Like Trump, he didn't let that fact alone deter him from his goal. Like Trump, he was unorganized at first and his views were different from those of other candidates. And like Trump he was a habitual liar. Check it out:

> Hart's ideas were criticized as too vague and centrist by many Democrats ... Shortly after he became the new frontrunner, it was revealed that Hart had changed his last name, had often listed 1937 instead of 1936 as his birth date and had changed his signature several times. This, along with two separations from his wife, Lee, caused some to question Hart's "flake factor." Nonetheless, he and his wife have remained married for almost 60 years.(Wikipedia, 2016).

Like Trump, Hart was not afraid to falsify documents, knowing that as a white man he would always receive the benefit of the doubt. This speaks volumes about the system in America: white privilege works even when the actions being perpetrated are criminal or unethical. Indeed, he was a "flake," but not because he separated from his wife (the fact that he didn't divorce her implies that they just wanted some "quiet time "away from each other and time to "work things out"), but it was because of his going right ahead and doing things that he should have known were questionable. Just like Trump.

In the case of Hart, he just kept plugging away in that power hungry way that these kinds of men do:

Hart, already aware that the nomination was all but Mondale's after the final primaries, lobbied for the vice presidential slot on the ticket, claiming that he would do better than Mondale against President Ronald Reagan (an argument undercut by a June 1984 Gallup poll that showed both men nine points behind the president). While Hart was given serious consideration, Mondale chose Geraldine Ferraro instead. In his address to the convention, after his name was placed in nomination for president by Nebraska governor Bob Kerrey and he received a 15-minute standing ovation, Hart concluded, "Our party and our country will continue to hear from us. This is one Hart you will not leave in San Francisco."

Mondale, in my view, had the choice of the lesser of two evils. Ferraro was a feisty Italian who had no respect for black people whatsoever, as Mondale would find out. And we know about how "flaky" Hart could be. One can only imagine how much mileage he got out of that "left my HART in San Francisco" line. But the power monger wasn't finished yet:

After Mario Cuomo announced that he would not enter the race in February 1987, Hart was the clear frontrunner for the Democratic nomination in the 1988 election ... Hart officially declared his candidacy on April 13, 1987 ...

And this is where the rumors about a "mistress" started to circulate:

When Lois Romano, a reporter for *The Washington Post*, asked Hart to respond to rumors spread by other campaigns that he was a "womanizer", Hart said such candidates were "not going to win that way, because you don't get to the top by tearing someone else down ... The *New York Post* reported that comment on its front page with the headline lead in "Straight from the Hart", followed below with big, black block letters: "GARY: I'M NO WOMANIZER.'", and then a summary of the story: "Dem blasts rivals over sex life rumors ...

When these types of rumors rise up, there is usually a scintilla of truth. These white boys are constantly looking at young girls and women know it. The women in their immediate circle do what they have to do to get these guys in a position where they compromise themselves and then they (the women) can blackmail or bribe them. But it is the male's "weakness" that is almost a cultural universal and I've written a number of articles on the subject.

[Type text]

In other words Hart was a womanizer just like Trump. Trump admitted as much during his interview with Billy Bush. You may remember when Trump was caught on television saying:

> I'm automatically attracted to beautiful [women]. I just start kissing them. It's like a magnet. I just kiss, I don't even wait. And when you're a star, they let you do it. You can do anything — grab them by the pussy. You can do anything.

Few people would admit this publicly and neither did Trump – he just got caught. And it didn't make any difference: women still voted for him. And that's the point here. People like Gary Hart and the other men in this analysis are prime targets for women who know what men like. If you can pad that bra, wear a short enough dress, and bat an eye, you can seduce ANY man. The issue is to choose one who has some financial resources. This has been going on throughout world history (read: Delilah, Mata Hari, the Kardashian sisters and of course, Melania Trump). So Trump is a male prototype, not an exception. The case of Gary Hart proves this to be case.

Want more proof? Check it out:

> The *Herald* published a story on May 3 that Hart had spent Friday night and most of Saturday with a young woman in his Washington, D.C. townhouse. On that same day, in an interview with E. J. Dionne that appeared in the New York Times, Hart, responding to the rumors of his womanizing, said: "Follow me around. I don't care. I'm serious. If anybody wants to put a tail on me, go ahead. They'll be very bored" ...

The hole he dug got deeper and deeper, appearing to me that he wanted to get caught:

> The *Herald*'s reporters at some point learned that the *New York Times* was planning to feature the story with the quote on Sunday, incorporated it into their story, and the two articles appearing on the same day ignited a political firestorm ... On Sunday, Hart's campaign denied any scandal and condemned the *Herald*'s reporters for intrusive reporting ... Hart later noted that his "follow me around" comment was not "challenging the press with a taunt", but, made in frustration, was only intended to invite the media to observe his public behavior, and never intended to invite reporters to be "skulking around in the shadows" of his home ... "He did not think of it as a challenge," Dionne would recall many years later.

> "And at the time, I did not think of it as a challenge."... Nor did
> Hart's comment influence the Miami Herald to pursue the story ...

There are some people you can just look at and tell that they're scandal-prone. Check out the pictures of Gary Hard and you'll see one such person. When he made those statements to follow him around, he should have been astute enough that he was opening up carte blanche, free lance reportorial writes to the Fourth Estate. Kidding or not, they were going to jump at the chance to put this power monger in his place – just as the media today in 2017, on a more subtle level, is doing to the egotistical Donald Trump to this very day.
The scandal was now out:

> The next day, Monday, the young woman was identified as Donna
> Rice, and she gave a press conference also denying any sexual
> relationship with Hart … Hart insisted that his interest in Rice was
> limited to her working as a campaign aide ... However, "the facts
> floated on a sea of innuendo" ...

Just like Trump and Clinton. In the former case the claim was that when he said he would grab women's pussies that, "It was just locker room talk." In the former case, Clinton looked into cameras and claimed, "I did not have sexual intercourse with that woman," and later Hillary would write about how it hurt her heart to find out that he was lying, that he had claimed that Monica Lewinski came on to him, and made himself out to be a victim. And now we have Gary Hard claiming that the charges against him were "floating on a sea of innuendo."
But the media, pit bulls that they are (except when it comes to issues of confronting racist cops) were on the trail:

> The scandal spread rapidly through the national media, as did
> another damaging story about angry creditors of the $1.3 million
> debt Hart had incurred in his 1984 campaign … Media questions
> about the affair came to dominate coverage of Hart's campaign …
> but his staff believed that voters were not as interested in the topic
> as the media was … Hart's staff believed that the media was
> filtering his message … (Wikipedia, 2017)

And another one bites the dust. It has happened so many times in American history and Americans have short memories. They continue to believe the company line and vote for people who promise them the sky and the moon, get in office, become increasingly power hungry, write a bunch of bunk checks and then get caught in bed with some floozy who manipulated them by lying about how
[Type text]

"attractive" they are. This book is filled with examples proving that Trump is not the first nor is he the megalomaniacal exception: *he is the rule.*

Take note of the following:

> On May 8, 1987, a week after the story broke, Hart suspended his campaign after the *Washington Post* threatened to run a story about a woman Hart had dated while separated from his wife, and his wife and daughter became similar subjects of interest for tabloid journalists ...

The issue of being "separated from his wife" is just a cover. The first thing that the married womanizer does is create a situation where the wife asks for a separation. In that way you can keep her hanging on in the belief that "we can patch things up" and still be able to date on the side. The key is the separation, because a divorce means that the wife will get half of his shit. So it's a scam that these white women fall for. There is a trend in Hollywood, according to one source, that increasing numbers of women are intentionally marrying gay men so they don't have to worry about the sexual requirements and can be with a "companion" rather than a husband.

Like Clinton, even when caught, Hart kept up the bravado:

> At a press conference, Hart defiantly stated, "I said that I bend, but I don't break, and believe me, I'm not broken" ... Hart identified the invasive media coverage, and its need to "dissect" him, as his reason for suspending his campaign, "If someone's able to throw up a smokescreen and keep it up there long enough, you can't get your message across. You can't raise the money to finance a campaign; there's too much static, and you can't communicate...."

On-going cowardly denial just like President Donald Trump. Claiming to never break, just like Trump. Talking about other people throwing up smokescreens when, in reality, it is you who offers up gnarled and perverted manifestations of the facts – just like Trump.

And in vintage "blame the media' fashion, take note of Hart's outgoing alibi:

> Clearly, under the present circumstances, this campaign cannot go on. I refuse to submit my family and my friends and innocent people and myself to further rumors and gossip. It's simply an intolerable situation" ... Hart paraphrased Thomas Jefferson and warned, "I tremble for my country when I think we may, in fact,

get the kind of leaders we deserve" .... Hart later recalled, "I
watched journalists become animals, literally ...

Now all of a sudden he's concerned about his family. He wasn't concerned
when he was meeting Donna Rice at those secret rendezvous points. I even recall
seeing a photo of the two of them together on the back of his boat. He was acting
as if he was in love and lying about it all along. He wasn't "trembling for his
country"; he was trembling because he got caught with his hands in the cookie jar.
Just like Clinton and after that, Donald J. Trump.

<u>Rev. Jesse Jackson, Sr. (1988)</u>

Jesse Jackson was always viewed as an opportunity by many black people.
His Operation PUSH talked black but then leeched for money from the very
corporations that he was accusing of discrimination and racism. One source
provides a snippet containing background:

> Jesse Jackson's 1988 campaign for the Democratic Party's
> presidential nomination stirred the hopes of millions of blacks and
> working people. Most of those who supported Jackson did so as a
> protest *against* the fundamental injustice of the racist capitalist
> system. Yet, despite the illusions of his base, he ran as a candidate
> committed to preserving and maintaining the oppressive status
> quo. Jackson is not a leader of struggle *against* the bourgeois
> rulers--he is a Judas-goat *for* them. In the final analysis, "Jackson
> action" was a scam to fool those for whom the "American dream"
> is a cruel joke into getting out and voting Democrat
> (Bolshevik.com, 1988-89).

"Stirring hopes." "Keep Hope Alive." "Never stop dreaming." "I Have a
Dream." All this bullshit and niggas still don't get it. As the brother from the 1974
movie "Attica" made clear, "Don't nothin' come to a sleeper but a dream." Those
words have yet to be taken seriously by a black electorate that is following blindly
behind today's current egotists, Hillary Clinton and Bernie Sanders, and continuing
to believe that this is "our system" while spreading some bullshit message, "Black
Votes Matter."

Jesse Jackson preyed on this Christian-based naiveté. He knew he didn't
have a snowball's chance in hell of winning, but all the money that was raised is
money that he kept – after splitting it with and probably arranging for kickbacks

from his "backers" and "supporters." This was Donald Trump minus the swear words, the insults and the white skin.

According to the previous quote, "Most of those who supported Jackson did so as a protest *against* the fundamental injustice of the racist capitalist system." How are you going to support someone who has always been a part of the system and who believes in the system, to represent you against that system? Civil rights aficionados like Jesse Jackson, Andrew Young, Dr. Martin Luther King, Joseph Lowery, and those other poverty pimps made big money selling themselves as some kinds of "warriors." But in reality, they took bribes and in the name of "protest," extorted millions from corporations and big business. The scams that Trump ran with Trump University is akin to the way that Jackson duped black people with all that solution-less rhetoric he was mouthing off during the 1988 campaign.

The following paragraph hits the Jackson "nail" on the proverbial head:

> Jackson's candidacy was not a great "historic event" but a temporary interlude in the twisted development of the American working class' struggle for independent political action. The job of revolutionaries is not to promote illusions, but to tell the truth. And the truth is that Jackson's "Rainbow"is not a step on the road to the emancipation of the workers and oppressed-- it is a prop for the maintenance of the system of racism and exploitation. (Bolshevik.com, 1988-89).

And one more thing about that "rainbow" that I found out when I was working in Dallas, Texas: it is the symbol for the gay rights movement. During a raid at a gay club it was announced on television that the cops in Dallas had been especially abusive. The gays sued. But what was eye-opening to me was the rainbow sign that the club used as its symbol. Well guess what?

At the same time I was working at The Black Academy of Arts and Letters, the largest cultural center in the nation. It is attached to City Hall and the Omni Hotel, and is about 250,000 square feet. I built their record-setting archives by myself. At any rate, when you walk into the building the first thing you see is a big picture of Curtis King, the founding director, staring at you. And behind him is a rainbow. Now, Curtis King is gay, as are some of the other people that work at TBAAL, a factor that I overlooked because of the historical value of what was being done for black people. But I just wanted to share this because for all we know, that rainbow sign could have had the same meaning even back when Operation PUSH was in its heyday.

Trump as white male prototype is not just a negative view, but a realistic one. Recall earlier where the quote stated, "The job of revolutionaries is not to promote illusions, but to tell the truth." Today in 2016 Bernie Sanders is going around throwing the word "revolution" about like he's at a circus carnival. But recall that in the 1960s when black men were saying it – which is where Sanders stole most of his ideas – we were getting imprisoned, beaten up and murdered for it. Sanders is promoting an illusion because what he is saying constitutes "sedition," a crime they tried to charge both H.Rap Brown and Stokely Carmichael with back in the day. But he's an old white man with white followers so they cut him slack. But an egotist is an egotist and doesn't give a shit about the masses of people – just like Jesse Jackson.

Now bear with me: what if this black asshole had been elected president? Look at all the skeletons he had in the closet. Look at the dirt he's done since that election campaign. And look at how his namesake went to Congress and started engaging in similar shit. Just the fact that black people stand behind these clowns time and time again points directly to our political naiveté – the same thing that white rednecks are now showing in their blind allegiance to the egotist Donald Trump.

It's all about "hope" as far as America is concerned, and that is because this country realizes that it is down on its luck. The people around the world who are attacking and lambasting America right now are the orphans of those who America has killed, bombed, raped and massacred in years gone by. Those young orphans have grown up, and stories have been shared across national lines. The world of color views America as a white nation and recently, with the election and actions of President Barack Obama, they now consider black people in this country to be as "white" as any peckerwood. And with Jews financing and airing the television shows, movies and commercials that show us as happy go lucky "darkies" (which is what the Japanese call us), is there any wonder why, when the final war begins, black people in America will be viewed with just as much disdain-and-how-dare-you as the white boy.

Malcolm X saw this a long time ago when he taught us about the "house negro." In his 1964 speech, "Message to the Grass Roots," he laid out the kind of mentality that I just described and one that permeates black America to this very day:

> If the master's house caught on fire, the house Negro would fight
> harder to put the blaze out than the master would. If the master got
> sick, the house Negro would say, "What's the matter, boss, we
> sick?" We sick! He identified himself with his master more than

[Type text]

> his master identified with himself. And if you came to the house
> Negro and said, "Let's run away, let's escape, let's separate," the
> house Negro would look at you and say, "Man, you crazy. What
> you mean, separate? Where is there a better house than this?
> Where can I wear better clothes than this? Where can I eat better
> food than this?" That was that house Negro. In those days he was
> called a "house nigger." And that's what we call him today,
> because we've still got some house niggers running around here.

This can be seen in present-day terms, not only in the guise of "black Republicans" who carry water for the system, but even for the so-called leadership that continues to talk about black people and "our" system and talking about what we should do "as Americans." Is there any wonder why those people from other parts of the world who have it in for this country and its racist history now include US (black people) as a part of the problem? With the white-run media promoting images of us has happy and satisfied, the people of the world who suffer have begun to hate us as much as they hate the white man. They now lump all "Americans" into the same mold and it's because of that "house nigger" mentality that the black people who get on television continue to display. As far as the world is concerned, "the friend of my enemy is my enemy."

Malcolm's description continues:

> This modern house Negro loves his master. He wants to live near
> him. He'll pay three times as much as the house is worth just to live
> near his master, and then brag about "I'm the only Negro out here."
> "I'm the only one on my job." "I'm the only one in this school."
> You're nothing but a house Negro …

Can we deny this is the case even to this very day in 2016? And all this takes place despite restrictive covenants, lending discrimination of various types (including redlining and steering), and actual laws that forbade us from moving into areas where white people lived.

The feelings of impotence by white males ("the niggers are taking over the country ever since Obama got in office") has led to the rise of demagogues like Clinton, Sanders and Trump, just like the hopelessness of the 1980s, thanks to Reagan and Bush, did the same thing during that period. Just as a know-nothing like Jesse Jackson rose to run for the highest office in the land, Trump has done the same thing with a slightly different twist. More on the strategy later in this book.

The article that is being cited further posits that,

> The downtrodden and oppressed in this country desperately need
> hope for a brighter future, but not a sugary false hope. American
> workers and blacks need a party *separate* from their class enemies-
> -a party to lead the struggle to expropriate the landlords, the
> bankers, and the bosses; a party committed to fight for a workers
> government. Such a party, based on the unions--the mass
> organizations of the proletariat--can only be forged through an
> uncompromising struggle against *all* wings of the twin parties of
> the bourgeoisie. (Bolshevik.com, 1988-89).

The fact is, a "sugary false hope" is all the masses of people in this country are going to get from the powers-that-be. And the reason why they will continue to get it is because the sources and forces who provide it know full well that the American people, for the most part, are dumb and desperate. How else to explain how someone as crooked as Donald Trump, someone as old as Bernie Sanders, someone as two-faced at Hillary Clinton, could all be candidates for president of this, the most powerful nation in the world?

If you notice, even though the previous quote comes from a publication that might be considered "left wing," a white person is going to always be more committed to whiteness than to any "ism." Therefore their belief that they have the capacity to organize everyone, speak for everybody and do what's best for all is one reason why they lack credibility. Take note of where it is stated that, "Such a party, based on the unions--the mass organizations of the proletariat--can only be forged through an uncompromising struggle against *all* wings of the twin parties of the bourgeoisie." No, this cannot be done as long as white people, no matter what political orientation or stripe, are in charge. History has proven this to be the case in every single instance.

But Jesse came along and fed into the myth and made money as he did it:

> Jackson campaigned as a representative of the "left wing" of
> bipartisan bourgeois political consensus. He spoke to the
> dissatisfaction and desperation of large sections of the oppressed
> and exploited in American society. What really distinguished his
> campaign, however, was not his populist demagogy so much as his
> color--Jackson is the first black to mount a serious campaign for
> the presidential nomination. His candidacy thus acted as an
> emotional magnet for millions of blacks, for whom presidential
> politics has always been an exclusively white man's game.
> (Bolshevik.com, 1988-89).

Jackson did the same bullshit that Bernie Sanders is now doing, except Jackson used rhymes and hackneyed clichés whereas Sanders uses ripped off rhetoric from 1960s militants. Sanders can get away with talking about a "revolution" because he's a Jew, and they know that there is not going to be any overthrow of a system that they secretly control. Being a white man and to talk of "revolution" is alright because all it means is switching hands from white one political party to another. But just remember what happened to H. Rap Brown, Stokely Carmichael and other black men who used the word "revolution" back in the day: accused of sedition.

The previous statement that Jackson's "candidacy thus acted as an emotional magnet for millions of blacks, for whom presidential politics has always been an exclusively white man's game" is only partially true: it remained a white man's game despite the fact that Jackson was supposedly trying to become a part of it, just as it remained a white man's game even after the election of Barack Obama. It doesn't matter what the race of the captain of the Titanic is: the fuckin' ship is still going to hit the iceberg.

The system is so organized that people like Jackson and Obama can make it appear as if change is coming when, in reality, it is not. Parker (2016) recalls something about Jackson and it is most relevant to the present-day political contest among the Democrats featuring between Hillary Clinton and her husband, Bill:

> That black voters would prefer a familiar candidate such as Clinton over someone whose personal experience among African-Americans seems to have been relatively limited, notwithstanding his participation in civil rights demonstrations, is hardly surprising. For decades, the Clintons have worked for issues and protections important to the African-American community. But the Clintons, too, have been dismissive toward black voters when things didn't go their way. During the 2008 primaries when it was clear that Barack Obama would trounce Hillary Clinton in South Carolina, Bill Clinton remarked that Jesse Jackson also had won the state in both 1984 and 1988. No one needs a translator to get Clinton's meaning. His next hastily drawn implication that Obama would win because he was black. (Parker, 2016).

Jackson's bid was a smokescreen for the system and is aimed at showing the ersatz "inclusion" of American politics. Trump is working to cater to another large group: white redneck males and by the way, they are a group that far outnumbers the black rank and file that Jackson was appealing to.

[Type text]

Have things changed much? People have short memories just as they will in the case of the megalomaniac Donald Trump. As it relates to Jackson, let us fast forward to 2006.

Referring to what he calls "schemes to get paid," Kendrick (2006) wrote the following in regard to Jesse Jackson and Al Sharpton:

> In numerous conversations about alleged Black leaders a multitude of names usually surface. Among them are women, men, professionals, non-professionals, and businesspersons large and small, politicians, those appointed and those who anoint themselves. The white media did a survey a few months ago and although I have no idea who they interviewed, Al Sharpton and Jesse Jackson emerged as the most prominent Black leaders in the nation. These two are not favorites of mine. In fact, I view them as hustlers who get paid well but not for solving problems but addressing those with problems and saying whatever the listener wants to hear. They also receive certified checks prior to any speaking engagements …

The name of the article was "Are Al Sharpton and Jesse Jackson Poverty Pimps?" And the author was concerned about their 2006 attacks on large black churches, called "mega-churches" that weren't giving anything back to the black community. The reason I mention it here is because that is exactly what most black politicians have been doing for centuries: talking shit and not giving back anything. What is said about ministers preaching "pie in the sky" is the same thing black politicians do, and none was more pronounced that Jesse Jackson during his 1984 campaign for president.

Today the people who are ignorant of this nation's history – and that is most of them – forget about the ego-driven "work" that so-called "reverend" Jesse Jackson put in. He was fucking around behind Jacqueline's back a long time and finally got caught: he got some bitch pregnant and she saved his sperm, used it, and had a kid. It was all over the newspapers even as his young son was busy fucking up huge chunks of money when he (Jesse, Jr.) was a member of Congress. It appears that unbridled ego, tempered with a con-man's mentality, was a genetic hand-me-down.

And Jesse, having seen what Donna Rice had done to Gary Hart, should have known better. In my view what Jesse got caught doing with that woman that he would impregnate many years later had been going on his entire life – he just never got caught.

[Type text]

Just as Donald Trump appealed to and had mass support from working class white men (read: rednecks), Jesse Jackson had the same mass appeal from black people. As was the case with Trump, the faith was blind and Jesse could do no wrong. Even with his somewhat shaky track record, the fact that he claimed to be a "reverend" never once raised the question, among thinking people, about the so-called "separation of church and state" that was supposed to be a part of the Constitution and the Bill of Rights. Yet one religious nut after another has placed their hats in the political arena over the years.

Jackson, like Donald J. Trump, was no exception to the rule of perversion, perfidy and manipulation. *They are the norm.*

<u>Lenora Fulani (1988)</u>

Today's racist media talks about Hillary Clinton being "the first woman" to be a candidate for the presidency of the United States, but Lenora Fulani, in 1988 as a member of the New Alliance Party, achieved some "status" as well. She was the first black woman to achieve ballot access in all fifty states! And according to the research,

> … She received more votes for President in a U.S. general
> election than any other woman in history until Jill Stein of the
> Green Party of the United States in 2012. Fulani's political
> concerns include racial equality, gay rights and for the past decade,
> political reform, specifically to encourage third parties.
> (Wikipedia, 2016).

Lenora started out as a good sistah, in my book. Like so many, she was pro-black and involved. For one thing, despite her apparent pro-system ways and attraction to white men (read: Jews), she started off on the right foot. As one source informs us,

> While in college, she became involved in black nationalist politics,
> along with her then-husband Richard. Both had adopted the
> African tribal name Fulani as a surname when they married in a
> traditional West African ceremony. During her studies at City
> University, Fulani became interested in the work of Fred Newman
> and Lois Holzman, who had recently formed the New York
> Institute for Social Therapy and Research. Fulani studied at the
> Institute in the early 1980s. (Wikipedia, 2016).

Perhaps in her case, like so many others, she hooked up with the wrong person at the wrong time. As Africentric as the wedding was, maybe the brutha turned out to have married her for reasons other than love, Maybe he was kicking her off in her ass or something else. But being the free spirit that she was, there was no doubt that she was going to slow down her involvement in the community. And with that kind of energy and charisma, it was only inevitable that she would meet people, male and female, who would be attracted to her.

As for Fred Newman, I believe he was just a political hustler, yet another brutha in the mold of Jesse Jackson who could talk a good game and get people to believe that he knew what the fuck he was talking about. In the black community, this is no difficult task: with Jackson it was rhyming and timing ("The problem's not the bus – it's us!" or "Nobody can save us from us for us but us." Or how about the unforgettable general truism-based litany, "I am somebody …"). With Newman is may have been the ability to convince people that political strategy was the key to black unity – and by politics, I mean the white man's version of it

I also notice that in New York where you find a black man involved in politics, there seems to be a Jew not very far behind. And how do you "form" an Institute? File some articles of incorporation? Write a business plan and find a building? At any rate, Lenora was no idiot: she saw something in Newman and that Institute and was going to become involved with both.

Sure, she may have been a dyke and at one time she might have dated this guy, Dennis Serrette, who ran under the same party in 1984 and who I invited to Lincoln when I was director of the Malone Center, but the fact is that she put in work in the community, with young people and she wasn't afraid to talk shit. She did do some sellout type shit recently in around 2014 when she started hanging out with the police chief of New York, but for the most part she put in work in the black community – more than people like Jesse Jackson, John Anderson, Donald Trump or Hillary Clinton ever did.

Her problems, as I read about them back in the day, was when she hooked up with this nigga named Fred Newman, who was some kind of political pimp, running for office so he could get paid. Their relationship was strange, to say the least. According to one source:

> In her career, Fulani has worked closely since 1980 with Fred
> Newman, a New York-based psychotherapist and political activist
> who has often served as her campaign manager. Newman
> developed the theory and practice of Social Therapy in the 1970s,
> founding the New York Institute for Social Therapy in 1977.
> Along with psychologist Lois Holzman, Fulani has worked to

[Type text]

> incorporate the social therapeutic approach into youth-oriented
> programs, most notably the New York City-based All Stars
> Project, which she co-founded in 1981 (Wikipedia, 2016).

Whoever said "politics makes strange bedfellows" hit the nail on the head when it came to some of the people that Fulani teamed up with and some of the political risks she took. For instance, "In 1993, Fulani joined activists who supported Ross Perot for President in the United States presidential election, 1992, in a national effort to create a new pro-reform party. In 1994 she led formation of the Committee for a Unified Independent Party (CUIP). For years Fulani was active with Newman's version of the International Workers Party (IWP). More recently she has been active with the Independence Party of New York, which was founded in Rochester in 1991" (Wikipedia, 2016).

The key was her activism but it seemed like she was far more confused about who here alliances would be with (with the possible exception of John Anderson). She seemed to be flittering hither and yon. Ross Perot? That fuckin' nut? But that wasn't until 1992. Let's go back to her "involvement" with Fred Newman:

> Fulani became active in the Newman-founded independent New
> Alliance Party (NAP) and emerged as a spokesperson who often
> provoked controversy. In 1982 Fulani ran for Lt. Governor of New
> York on the NAP ticket but was unsuccessful. She has also been
> involved in the affiliated (or some say, secret) Independent
> Workers Party, the Rainbow Alliance, and other shifting groups
> led by Newman (Wikipedia, 2016).

So from the formation of an Institute that deals with psycho-therapy to a political party, Newman was a go-getter. And one thing about these kinds of men, they know a good woman when they see one. In my opinion, Newman used her to become spokesperson because he knew she was connected and could garner more support for what he wanted to get done. I remember her work with the Rainbow Alliance and back when I was editor of the Milwaukee Courier, I ran several of her syndicated columns. They were rather lengthy, but usually right on the mark. Little did I know that they had something to do with Newman who appeared to be the "puppet master" of this little "cross-racial" political approach:

> She helped recruit the NAP's 1984 presidential candidate Dennis
> L. Serrette, an African-American trade union activist. Although he
> was quite involved with the party for years, Serrette left and

published critical accounts of what he described as its cultic
operation. (Wikipedia, 2016).

Serrette, as I mentioned earlier, ran for the presidential slot before Fulani and Newman would later do. He was an integrationist and again, we find a black man and some Jewish woman hooked up as the ticket for the New Alliance Party. The fact is, as an historian, I know that the relationship between blacks and Jews is no "new alliance;" it is akin to the "alliance" between the farmer and the mule, with the Jew being the farmer. Guess what that makes us? Asses, that's what.

Continuing on, after Serrette's inability to get on the ballot in 1984, the next go-round would be Fulani's "time in the sun":

> Fulani ran for President in 1988 as the candidate of the New
> Alliance Party. She received almost a quarter of a million votes or
> 0.2% of the vote. She was the first African-American independent
> and the first female presidential candidate on the ballot in all 50
> states. In the 1990 New York Gubernatorial election Fulani ran as
> a New Alliance candidate. She was endorsed that year by Nation of
> Islam leader Louis Farrakhan. Fulani received 31,089 votes for
> 0.77% of the total vote (Wikipedia, 2016).

Lenora was "the first" in many ways as you just read. They were serious and she put in some major work. She was an energetic sister. The only problem in my view was her obsession with hustlers and Jews (in many cases, they two terms are synonymous). In 1990, take note that she even got the endorsement of Farrakhan – no easy task. But then again, Farrakhan kissed Jesse's ass, endorsed him and then turned around and dogged him later on. But let us get back to the late 1980s:

> Although in 1987 Fulani and Newman began an alliance with
> minister and activist Al Sharpton, in 1992 he ran for the U.S.
> Senate from New York as a Democrat rather than as an
> Independent. Since then, Sharpton has kept his distance from both
> Fulani and Newman (Wikipedia, 2016).

Sharpton was a crook himself. For one thing he got away with fucking that young girl, Tawanna Brawley. Secondly, he made an ass out of himself in court and got sued by some Jewish attorney that he slandered and he and Alton Maddox had to pay up. Like the true leech he was and still is, he got some famous "coon" to pay his part of the bill for him.

[Type text]

Game recognizes game and Lenora probably and Newman probably jointly recognized that Sharpton wasn't about shit. At any rate, the saga of Lenora Fulani continues:

> Fulani again ran as the New Alliance candidate for President in the 1992 election, this time receiving 0.07% of the vote. She chose former Peace and Freedom Party activist Maria Elizabeth Muñoz as her vice-presidential running mate. Muñoz ran on the NAP ticket for the offices of U.S. Senator and governor in California but was unsuccessful. In 1992 Fulani self-published her autobiography *The Making of a Fringe Candidate, 1992*(Wikipedia, 2016).

Lenora simply would not give up. Even with Latina affiliations she just couldn't get over the hump. But her perseverance is what should be appreciated because she stayed on the fringe and tried to elevate it the best she could. Even if it meant jumping from one bullshit political party to the next. Check it out:

> In 1994, Fulani and Newman became affiliated with the Patriot Party, one of many groups that later competed for control of the Reform Party, founded by Ross Perot. She also joined with Jacqueline Salit to start the Committee for a Unified Independent Party (CUIP), formed to bring together independent groups to challenge the bipartisan hegemony in American politics (Wikipedia, 2016).

These people all have these ideas, these grandiose names, these platform positions and some well-meaning intentions. But they don't want to change the white supremacist system: they simply want to SHARE it. Sistahs like Lenora are prone toward liberal pro-Jewish thinking, which is how they get financed. They may also be what some people call "bi-sexual" in their orientations. They are what we would have called "hippies" back in the 1960s. And that is why every election year there is some new-fangled fringe party that gets publicity for "challenging" the system, or some jive ass candidate like Bernie Sanders who takes black nationalist rhetoric about revolution and then when he says it (as a white man) the ignorant American public thinks it's unique thinking.

In simpler terms, the talk is always about taking down the "hegemony" that exists in American politics. But those who are involved in these parties don't want to take it down and smash it; *they only want to take it down and find a place where they can fit within it.* And Lenora kept on getting funding, kept on finding new alliances, kept on using her great oratory and writing skills to make a case that called for a new perspective, and all the while she knew what the real deal was: inclusion in the system, not dismantling of it.

Continuing:

> During the 2000 election, Fulani surprisingly endorsed Pat Buchanan, then running on the Reform Party ticket. She even served briefly as co-chair of the campaign. Fulani withdrew her endorsement, saying that Buchanan was trying to further his right-wing agenda. Fulani and Newman then endorsed the Presidential candidacy of Natural Law Party leader John Hagelin, a close associate of Maharishi Mahesh Yogi. Later, Fulani unsuccessfully sought the Vice Presidential nomination at the national convention organized by a faction of the Reform Party (Wikipedia, 2016).

Pat Buchanan? That racist muthafucka? Jillian Mayfield of Talking Points Memo (TPM) reviewed Buchan's book, *Suicide of a Superpower* back in October of 2011. She highlighted the key excerpts which clearly show that Buchanan is no multiculturalist and was surely a bad choice as a running mate of someone like Lenora Fulani. Following are some points made in his book and my brief analysis of each one before we move on.

> From the Preface:
> When the faith dies, the culture dies, the civilization dies, the people die. That is the progression. And as the faith that gave birth to the West is dying in the West, peoples of European descent from the steppes of Russia to the coast of California have begun to die out, as the Third World treks north to claim the estate. The last decade provided corroborating if not conclusive proof that we are in the Indian summer of our civilization. (Pat Buchanan cited by Mayfield, 2011)

Buchanan is not talking about faith in a deity or a spirit. Like most white men, his belief in religion is nothing more than a belief in an extension of his own power. He doesn't have to say it for me to know that he's talking about a belief in the white way of life, in white nationalism. In my view the concept of "patriotism" is a synonym for racism, plain and simple.

He's calling for white racial unity. He's using that old fear tactic that was used by Paul Ehrlich back in the 1950s in his book The Population Bomb. In short, he was saying that, "the niggas are eating up all the food!" No, he didn't put it in those terms, but a rattle snake need not bite me for me to know that since it's a rattle snake it is capable of such a bite! His concept of the "third world" is a reference to nations of color and "the estate" means the white nations. Then he concludes with the racist statement of America being "in the Indian summer" of our civilization.

What is an Indian summer? In this particular context it is defined as, "a happy or pleasant period near the end of someone's life, career." This is another tactic that the ego-driven white man uses when he gets his ass in a sling. When he gets caught promoting discriminatory policies, when his system of segregation gets international attention by civil rights groups, and of course when black people were burning the country down in the 1960s. He begins talking about "the beginning of the end" and the "Indian summer" of American civilization. In present day hi-tech America you see a spate of movies about America being post-apocalyptic or invaded: "Independence Day," "28 Days Later," "Invasion Los Angeles," and so many others: to divert attention away from his fuckups, he uses popular culture to spread fear and divert attention from his mistakes to some alien enemy, some outsider, some virus that is going to "kill humanity."

And all the white, white man's policies are doing just that.

Back to Buchanan's book:

> From the chapter, "The Death Of Christian America":
> Obama's White House thus enlisted in the long and successful
> campaign to expel Christianity from the public square, diminish its
> presence in our public life, and reduce its role to that of just
> another religion. (Pat Buchanan cited by Mayfield, 2011

So now he blames the Democratic president who just happens to be black. He makes these statements, as far too many of these white men tend to do, that he cannot back up. But if you can get on television or make the statement in a published book, they know that it will "stick" somewhere. And that's all it takes in America: you can always find a patsy because as P.T. Barnum once said, "There's a sucker born every minute."

This shit is called "scapegoating," and the white man and his egomania have used this tactic ad infinitum. They will blame the advances of women's rights, they will blame black militants, they will blame people having too many children, they will blame the welfare system, they will blame locked up inmates – anybody who they know that their fellow race members will also focus their hate on. By scapegoating these groups, you absolve the race-based policies of white decision makers of any responsibility for the fact that America is going to hell in a handbasket. Re-read the previous quote from Buchanan; it is but a snippet of the kind of racist drivel that has been pawned as an "intellectual thought" for the past several centuries.

Moving on:

> From the chapter, "The End Of White America":
> The white population will begin to shrink and, should present birth rates persist, slowly disappear. Hispanics already comprise 42 percent of New Mexico's population, 37 percent of California's, 38 percent of Texas's, and over half the population of Arizona under the age of twenty .....

Of course this demographic transition was inevitable. Time magazine saw it long ago in a 1978 article they did called "It's Your Time in the Sun." In other words, "The Mexicans are coming" in the same way the white segregationists used to scare America by warning, "the niggas is coming!" The end of white America will take place in terms of race, but the white system will remain intact. A lot of these pregnancies are white women having kids with men of color. The kids come out confused but still listed as being "minorities." But their minds are so fucked up they represent no real threat to the white-dominated male hierarchy. So while Buchanan states the obvious, he doesn't examine the racial intricacies of what will take place. All he need do is look around the stage during a taping of "The McLaughlin Report" and look at the way the white hosts interrupt and disrespect the comments of the only black on stage, Clarence Page.

He piles it on when it comes to the Mexicans:

> Mexico is moving north. Ethnically, linguistically, and culturally, the verdict of 1848 is being overturned. Will this Mexican nation within a nation advance the goals of the Constitution--to "insure domestic tranquility" and "make us a more perfect union"? Or has our passivity in the face of this invasion imperiled our union? (Pat Buchanan cited by Mayfield, 2011)

By calling the growth of the Mexican population in America and "invasion," you can plainly see where this racist bastard is coming from. Forget about the real "invasion" – the one engineered by his own people as they came here and began killing off the Native Americans. After securing the land, they now point fingers at people who were on the continent long before them and refer to them as "illegal aliens" and "unwanted immigrants."

Buchanan is a racist, pure and simple:

Also from the chapter, "The End Of White America":
Those who believe the rise to power of an Obama rainbow
coalition of peoples of color means the whites who helped to
engineer it will steer it are deluding themselves. The whites may
discover what it is like to ride in the back of the bus. (Pat
Buchanan cited by Mayfield, 2011).

This is a long time fear of the white male. So confused and guilty over what he has created by importing all those Africans here to enslave, he now spreads the myth that the black people are going to take over and do the same thing to them. As a form of scapegoating and hate mongering, this tactic strikes at the core of the white ego in many ways. One of those ways is that it brings out "the manhunt tradition" that these white men seem to obsess on. They want to use their police force and military to shoot down as many men of color as possible, and they glorify those who do it successfully. Witness the success of the movie "American Sniper" and the real life story of a white soldier who killed 160 people by sniping – in other words, hiding behind rocks and trees. And almost every single one of his victims – I'd say about 95% -- were men of color.

So they do their dirt and mask it in patriotism or "self-defense." And they get away with it. They use their language to consign everything "dark" or "black" to a category of evil, inferiority or filth. That same language teaches that white is right, angels are white, a white lie is only a little one and is therefore acceptable and so on. If there is "an end to white America," it should be clear that these people, based on all the dirt they've done all over the world, brought it upon themselves.

More from Buchanan:

On the group UNITY: Journalists of Color, Inc. pushing for more
diversity in journalism:
Half a century after Martin Luther King envisioned a day when his
children would be judged 'not by the color of their skin, but the
content of their character,' journalists of color are demanding the
hiring and promotion of journalists based on the color of their skin.
Jim Crow is back. Only the color of the beneficiaries and the color
of the victims have been reversed. (Pat Buchanan cited by
Mayfield, 2011)

The assumption behind asinine statements like the previous one is that white men have their positions and their jobs because of merit. As most of you know having encountered these types of men, nothing could be further from the truth.

[Type text]

You encounter idiot after idiot who have jobs because they were given to them by a friend, appointed to them by another white man or just stumbled into it. But when it comes to black people demanding to be a part of their system (unfortunate decision), here come ego-driven white men like Pat Buchanan once again fearing an imagined "black takeover," whining about skin color somehow being given priority over prospects and potential.

Jim Crow is not back because Jim Crow was legally sanctioned discrimination based on race, and it was de jure segregation. The de facto segregation that continues to exist has the same result (alienation of black people) but on the surface appears to be somehow "an improvement." Is it?

Sidney M. Wilhelm explains how the segregation reality script was flipped in his article, "Equality: America's Racist Ideology":

> As legal retributions seemingly remove racial segregation and discrimination in education, transportation, military service, housing, etc., whites turn to other measures to deprive the Negro people. The new efforts are designed not to subjugate, oppress or exploit the black minority, but rather to separate the two races ... White America, by invoking the equality standard, reverses the maxim 'separate but equal' to 'equal but separate.' The placement of 'equal' before rather than after the qualifying 'but' accords with the present myth of racism -- Constitutional equality ... and assures the identical outcome as the pre-1954 Court-sanctioned 'separate but equal' maxim -- Negro removal (1973: 140).

And,

> Unlike segregation, which prescribed an inferior status, separation divides the American population according to race in order to inhibit racial contacts. Whites established segregation to keep the Negro in place; they now wish only to banish the Negro out of sight and beyond empathy or understanding. With three-quarters of the Negro population living in cities and 80 percent of the black urban population settled upon ghetto-reservations, isolation solidifies still further the Negro's very lifestyle ... (Willhelm, 1974: 140).

And there you have the reality, and not the crazed notions of conservative curmudgeons like Pat Buchanan. So Congress is still overwhelmingly white as are all other national political bodies – what is Buchanan whining about.

[Type text]

And yet this is the kind of man that political obsession will get you to side with, even if you are a black woman of Lenora Fulani's caliber.

Ego then has always been a part of running for the highest office in the world and it appears that black people (Jesse Jackson, Dennis Serrette, Lenora Fulani) can be impacted by it too. In fact,

> In the 2001 election for Mayor of New York City, Fulani endorsed the Republican candidate Michael Bloomberg and organized city members of the IP to work for his campaign. Bloomberg, once elected, approved an $8.7 million municipal bond to provide financing for Fulani and Newman to build a new headquarters for their youth program, theater and telemarketing center. (Wikipedia, 2016). In the municipal election of 2003, Fulani was among those who endorsed Bloomberg's proposed amendment to the New York City Charter to establish non-partisan elections. Although Bloomberg spent $7 million of his own money to promote the amendment, voters rejected it ….

Loyal to a fault – to the white political system, that is. Lenora teamed up with this rich Jew and probably got paid for doing so. That's what most of these political consultants end up doing: joining the white man so they can pay their car notes. But the youth program was what was important, and at least they got a building out of the deal. Black people in places like Milwaukee and Omaha don't care about a building, all they want is the money. Then they'll go find some abandoned structure or a desperate church and run a "program" out of there. So at least Fulani and Newman saw the importance of a physical plant where they would have some semblance of "control."

Fulani's escapades continued:

> In September 2005 the State Executive Committee of the Independence Party of New York dropped Fulani and other members from the New York City chapter. This was part of a fierce power struggle that has brewed between members from upstate and Long Island, and Newman, Fulani, and the New York-based members. The majority of party members were disaffected by the ideology of Newman and Fulani. The party's state chairman, Frank MacKay, a former ally of Fulani, claimed the action followed Fulani's refusal to repudiate an earlier statement which many considered anti-Semitic ….(Wikipedia, 2016).

And there it is: the word that Jews use against anyone who doesn't tow their line: "anti-semitic." Even if you say something good about the Jewish people, if they didn't approve it beforehand, they will consider it anti-semitic. And why would they charge Fulani, who had a history of kissing Jewish ass, with being an anti-semite? It's because,

> According to the *New York Times*, "In 1989, Dr. Fulani wrote that the Jews 'had to sell their souls to acquire Israel' and had to 'function as mass murderers of people of color' to stay there." Fulani said she did not intend the statement as anti-semitic but wanted to raise issues which she believed needed to be explored. She has since repudiated the remarks, which she characterized as "excessive". She publicly apologized to "any people who had been hurt by them" (Wikipedia, 2016).

So she sold out, even though what she said was true. The Jews are known all over the world as thieves, especially when it comes to the land of other people. What she said was accurate but in New York, the Jews have a lot of sway and that includes the editorial board of the New York Times, which I consider to be the best newspaper in the world. At any rate, we can see that ego is at the fore of Fulani's agenda because she'll do whatever it takes to curry favor with the people who have power. Like Trump who himself used Jews to build what he's got (and even used a Jew to ghost write The Art of the Deal), Jewish people have the media sewed up, as they are in control of all four major television networks as well.

And they occupy a lot of major legal positions as well. Check it out:

> Citing the "anti-Semitism" allegations, Independence Party State chairman Frank MacKay initiated proceedings to have nearly 200 Independence Party members in New York City expelled from the party. Each case MacKay brought to the New York State Supreme Court was dismissed. In one instance, Manhattan Supreme Court Justice Emily Jane Goodman wrote that the charges were "more political than philosophical." (Wikipedia, 2016).

So once again, here come the Jews. Remember: what you say about Jews need not be negative; if you say something about Jews as a group and they don't approve it, then as far as they are concerned it's anti-semitic. The fact is, they simply don't want the attention "as a group." They know that if you bring attention to the group and observers begin probing them, those who are conducting the probe will inevitably dig up dirt because Jews are hated the world over for a reason. It's not about racism (are Jews a "race"?), but about their modus operandi:

[Type text]

hunker down, set up banks and give out loans charging astronomical interest (to non-Jews) and then foreclose and/or take property. Read world history and see for yourself.

At any rate, the Independence Party got past the initial Jewish salvo:

> Fulani formed a coalition to organize Independence Party support for the re-election campaign of Mayor Bloomberg. The local press described the coalition as composed of "union officials, clergy, sanitation workers, police officers, firefighters, district leaders and others who work at the grassroots level." Spirited defenses of Fulani have appeared in the city's black press; writing in the *Amsterdam News*, columnist Richard Carter wrote "there is little doubt that the main reason for the negative press, which, by the way, is not unusual for this brilliant, outspoken political strategist, is because she is a strong, no-nonsense Black woman. So strong she makes the city's political establishment and lockstep white news media nervous." (Wikipedia, 2016).

Although I never met him personally, Dick Carter and I have mutual respect for one another as journalists. He would often praise me for columns I wrote when I was the editor of the Milwaukee Courier. A former Milwaukeean himself, he used to tell me that I hit the nail on the head whenever I castigated the role of the Milwaukee power structure to black residents of Brew City.

With that having been said, it is clear that Carter and I also see Fulani in the same way. This "multicultural coalition" bullshit that Fulani keeps getting involved in looks good on paper but it continually being scrutinized by Jews and others who don 't like it and don't see the NAP as a serious political party:

> … Newman and Fulani's leadership, as well as various manifestations of the political party, such as the International Workers Party (IWP), have been strongly criticized by former members through the years, including party candidate Dennis Serrette and five-year member Marina Ortiz. In addition, Political Research Associates published a critical report on the NAP in 1987, and updated and revised it in 2008 on their website www.PublicEye.org. (Wikipedia, 2016).

This is ego, the same time that convinces Donald Trump that he can be president. And that's all it is. There are no real programs that make any sense. These third party candidates talk about getting the system to change, or fighting for green power, or for more racial inclusion, knowing full well that they don't have a snowball's chance in hell of getting any of that bullshit passed or even considered, for that matter. And yet Fulani, like the others mentioned in this book, just keep on making promises, keep on organizing rallies and meetings, keep on collecting and taking in money (that they don't have to refund) and in short, continue bilking the masses of people.

Moving on:

> After working with Fulani for several years, Serrette, who also had a personal relationship with her, has questioned his experience and publicly criticized Newman and Fulani's leadership of the party and its members. "[I]t was clearly a tactical ...a racist scheme of using Black and Latino and Asian people to do the bidding of one man, namely Fred Newman, that's my opinion, and to use other whites as well, you know through the therapy practices." (Wikipedia, 2016).

I met Serette when I was director of the Malone Center in Lincoln. Even then he struck me as a bitch-ass nigga, saying all the middle-of-the-road shit that wouldn't offend either black or white people. His positions on the issues were equally lukewarm; he was just a nigga with a full beard who appeared to be the type who chased white bitches. The criticism of Newman and Fulani was nothing more than ego once again – sour grapes that takes place when egotistical assholes have to compete with one another; the way that Cruz, Rubio, Cristie, and the other Republican candidates for President in 2016 did in opposition to Trump.

At any rate,

> After he raised his concerns internally, Serrette said his treatment by other NAP leaders worsened dramatically. He also questioned the way in which therapy was used in the political work: "...[T]herapy was a way of getting people to not only operate in an organizational way, but also a way of controlling every aspect of their lives...you certainly couldn't straighten anybody out. But it was certainly effective in terms of controlling a lot of people to do the kinds of things that were asked of them...they would do anything, just about, that he would ask them to do."

And that's the way "therapy" has always been: a way to bullshit people into thinking that they can and will solve their own problems when the real problem is the system that legitimizes therapy in the first place. It's as shallow as the 12-point program that alcoholics and drug fiends undergo: warmed over activities and sayings taken from some religious text that make you feel good but don't really

[Type text]

solve the problem – which is the system that keeps churning out the alcohol and the drugs.

But Serrette, like a rejected lover, continues to raise issues against his former allies:

> In an article published after he left the NAP, Serrette stated:
> "I knew when I joined NAP that it was not black-led, and I knew when I left it was not black-led. It took longer to understand that NAP was not even a progressive organization as it also pretends. Be that as it may, I probably still would not take the time to write about the organization. However, as a long-time activist who made the mistake of joining NAP, and who served on the organization's "Central Committee," I believe I have a responsibility to reveal the intense psychological control and millions of dollars Fred Newman employs to get well-meaning individuals in our communities (they target the black community), to viciously attack black leaders, black institutions, and progressive organizations for purposes of building Newman's power base."

Fronting as if he was ever pro-black. That's what they all do. They use the black community's "messiah complex" to set up a base of operation. The "messiah complex" is a belief that someone will rise up and lead the masses of people out of oppression the way Jesus is alleged to have done. That shit has been exploited for centuries by these "hallelujah hucksters" and these "pulpit pimps". Go to any black community and you'll find them, selling their lies and bullshit, passing the collection plate and pimping the shit out of people who are still waiting for the coming of a chariot called equality – which ain't comin'.

Serrette was no different. The same strategy was used by both he and Fulani. They talk and write black until a white man comes along to "adopt" them. And then off they go, forming a bullshit political party, lambasting the Republicans and the Democrats, garnering support from Latinos, Asians and hippified white folks. Along the way, sexual interaction with white folks at fundraisers – the same way the Black Panther Party used to do – take place but are kept quiet. It's the same ego driven game, and that is why *Donald Trump is no exception; he's the racist rule.*

And as is the case when these "interracial coalitions" are led by these "black political leaders" like Newman and Fulani, it is the black woman who receives short shrift. Just like with the Black Panther Party – the sisters are overlooked because these movements are overrun with white bitches. And they can't wait to spend money and give up head to the first black man they find who gives them the time of day.

[Type text]

And once they lose, get their asses kicked or get humiliated, there's always the opportunity for a talk show or a book. As was the case with Lenora Fulani:

> Fulani dismissed his charges as related simply to the end of their personal relationship. In her self-published autobiography *The Making of a Fringe Candidate, 1992* (1992), Fulani wrote that Serrette frequently fought with black women in the New Alliance Party and would "criticize and ridicule" them for their relationship to Newman.

And there you have it. The male ego dogs out women just the way Donald Trump is doing and will continue to do. The female exposes it only when she doesn't get what she wants. If what Fulani wrote is true, then she knew about it all along. But as long as Serrette was fucking her, she kept her mouth shut. This is the exact strategy that these white women do, even if they're not getting screwed. They can be paid to keep their mouths shut about the dirt that their ego-driven men do, smile when ain't nothin' funny and "look cute for the cameras" in exchange for a share of the throne of oppression. This has been going on for centuries in this country and even back in the days of Europe.

Ross Perot (1992)

Now this is a case of real unbridled ego. When you look like this man and still have the nerve to run for president just because you have a lot of money (read: Trump), then not only do you have immense ego but also a gargantuan amount of pure gall. This, in my view, aptly describes the motivations of one Ross Perot, who ran for President in 1992 as an "Independent" candidate. According to the research,

> Though he had never served as a public official, Perot had experience as the head of several successful corporations and had been involved in public affairs for the previous three decades. Spawned by the American dissatisfaction with the political system, grassroots organizations sprang up in every state to help Perot achieve ballot access following his announcement. James Stockdale, a retired United States Navy vice admiral, stood in as Perot's vice presidential running mate to ensure ballot eligibility (Wikipedia, 2016).

[Type text]

As was the case with Trump, Perot exploited the dissatisfaction of the American populace and jumped on it. Like Trump, he had no previous experience as a public official but, like Trump, he was involved in a number of successful businesses. Like Trump, Perot made it sure that he was eligible to run and also, like Trump, funded his own campaign. Like Trump, Perot relied on marketing and widespread grassroots support from rednecks - and he got it.

In the same way that Trump played on the racial and ethnic fears of white America, Perot used another tactics – a more "economic" one:

> Perot focused the campaign on his plans to balance the federal budget, further economic nationalism, strengthen the war on drugs and implement "electronic town halls" throughout the nation for direct democracy. His views were described as a combination of "East Texas populism with high-tech wizardry."[1] Supporters saw Perot as a nonpolitical and witty "folk hero", but critics described the candidate as "authoritarian"[2] and "short-tempered".[3]

When you hear the term "East Texas populism," that is just a polite way of saying "redneck." As was the case with Trump, the supporters viewed him as "nonpolitical" and even "witty." And as you just read, the critics viewed Perot in a way that sounds like the way today's analysts view Trump: as being "authoritarian" and "short-tempered."

Ego. The white man with money is always trying to find a way to use that money to acquire real power. That is why so many of them choose to run for office, and that's why so many members of Congress are millionaires. To be more precise,

> For the first time in history, more than half the members of Congress are millionaires, according to a new analysis of financial disclosure reports conducted by the non-partisan Center for Responsive Politics. Of the 534 current members of the House and Senate, 268 had an average net worth of $1 million or more in 2012 – up from 257 members in 2011. The median net worth for members of the House and Senate was $1,008,767. (Cody, 2014).

So "the rich get richer" while the poor continue getting poorer. And these do-good liberals who run around talking about "equity," "diversity" and "inclusion" see this taking place but are too desperate and unqualified for their own jobs (and therefore risk losing them) to actively and audaciously do anything about it. That's the way it is today in 2016 and that's the way it was in 1992 in the days of Ross Perot.

More on Perot follows:

> In certain polls, Perot led the three-way race with Republican nominee George H. W. Bush, the incumbent President, and Governor Bill Clinton of Arkansas, the Democratic nominee. He dropped out in July 1992 amid controversy, but reentered in October, participating in all three presidential debates. Despite an aggressive use of campaign infomercials on prime time network television, his polling numbers never fully recovered from his initial exit (Wikipedia, 2016).

Since you may have a short memory, let's stop here and first deal with those "controversies" that forced Perot to temporarily drop out because these are issues that have been repeated in and during the Trump campaign.

For one thing, the media found out that Perot had launched a private investigation of the Bush family back in the late 1980s. And when that hit the major newspapers and TV stations, Perot's response – like the "they did it first" responses of Donald Trump in 2016 – was to claim that there was a "Republican research team" and that since he (Perot) had such a clean record (the same lie that Trump told in the early going) that "They" were going to be out to destroy you." To this day in June of 2016, Trump is still making the same claim.

Flipping on issues was another reason for his having to temporarily put a hold on his campaign. Like Trump, Perot talked out of both sides of his mouth. In the Perot case, it was the issue of AIDS and gay rights. At first he said "no gays" in the military but once confronted, he changed and said later that he would allow gays to serve in the military. This was long before the "don't ask, don't tell "policies that came along later under Clinton.

Like Trump, Perot was also a racist. During one of his presentations, this one to the NAACP, he made the mistake of referring to blacks as "you people." Like Trump who claimed that Mexican immigrants were criminals and rapists, Perot got dogged by the media and a number of major political leaders, both white and black.

Like Trump, Perot was so traumatized that he said he wouldn't speak again without his supporters. Trump did the same thing, and his supporters – white rednecks – began showing up at his rallies and the result was bedlam and violence. Perot also made the claim that members of the New Black Panther Party were out to assassinate him." Like Trump, Perot attempted to paint himself as the victim and everyone who didn't agree with him was somehow "the bad guy."

Like Trump, Perot was an authoritarian and didn't like taking the advice of the people who were hired to advise him. Like Trump, the Washington Post reported that Perot wanted to be "in full control of operations" and indeed, went so far as to have his volunteers to sign "loyalty oaths" (Milwaukee Sentinel, 1992; St. Petersburg Times, 1992).

By the end of July Perot had called it quits after spending $12 million of his own money on the race. He then formed United We Stand to influence the presidential race just as Trump would threaten a "third party alternative" if he didn't get his way and if Republicans turned on him.

One thing Perot's ego did manage to get was a position on the stage during the Presidential debates, alongside Bill Clinton and George Bush. The problem was that he was the opposite of Trump in this regard: Trump talked off the cuff and the top of his head while Perot would produce a number of charts and graphs and then point out his positions using a pointer. Not only did he bore the living shit out of those watching, but he also tended to talk down the audience and at times, to talk over their heads.

As one source concludes,

> On Election Day, Perot appeared on every state ballot as a result of
> the earlier draft efforts. He won several counties and finished in
> third place, receiving close to 18.97 percent of the popular vote,
> the most won by a third-party presidential candidate since
> Theodore Roosevelt in 1912.

Perot, like Trump, had an impact on the election as outlined above. Trump has gone further, but it should be clear that both men were ego-driven and almost maniacal in the amount of control that they believed they were entitled to. And despite the amount of money they had and continued to make, their greed motivated them to leech for more.

Ralph Nader (1992, 1996, 2000, 2004, 2008)

Ralph Nader had great ideas and contributed a great deal to issues of consumer protection and the environment. Like Donald Trump as a crooked businessman, Nader had his own niche, one that was totally above board and he was putting in good work. Then he lost his god-damn mind. In Trump-like fashion, he decided to run for president, and on several levels, fucked up the system in the same way that Bernie Sanders almost did for Hillary Clinton in 2016.

First, some background:

> Ralph Nader was born in Winsted, Connecticut, to Nathra and Rose (née Bouziane) Nader, immigrants from Lebanon, who were Antiochian Greek Orthodox Christians … They raised the children in their homeland's culture with both their native Arabic and English, telling them proverbs and stories they felt would encourage independent thought, appreciation of things such as wildlife that cannot be "measured by the dollar," plus instill traits such as perseverance and inner strength … (Wikipedia, 2016).

So humble upbringings and an ethnic background. These combined to serve as Nader's moral base. But as you will see, the more he got into the system, the more success he achieved, the more "Trump-like" he would become in terms of ego and irrational bullshit. That "inner strength" that he had back in the days of advocating for the down and out began to wane.

At any rate,

> His father initially worked in a textile mill; later, he owned a bakery and restaurant, where he discussed politics with customers … which Ralph listened to along with their comments about conditions at the meat-packing plant, the chemicals they were exposed to, and similar issues that later featured in his activism (Wikipedia, 2016).

All this prompted Nader to get involved in the consumer protection movement, and he was successful. It was fairly new ground (as far as the majority population was concerned) and he was able to publish books and make a name for himself on the speaking circuit. It appeared he was on the right track:

> … Nader graduated from The Gilbert School, a private post secondary school in Winsted, Connecticut, in 1951. He then was accepted at Princeton University, and the university offered him a scholarship, but his father turned it away, saying it should go to a student who could not afford tuition … Nader graduated *magna cum laude* with a Bachelor of Arts from the Woodrow Wilson School of Public and International Affairs in 1955 … He then went on to Harvard Law School, where he obtained a Bachelor of Laws in 1958 … (Wikipedia, 2016).

[Type text]

And then – what happened? He was doing so well as exposing the system and its crimes but for some reason decided to become a part of it – just like Jesse Jackson and Lenora Fulani did. The publicity, the attention all goes to their head and they start looking in the mirror and they see a red cape and super powers!:

> … Nader is a five-time candidate for President of the United States, having run as a write-in candidate in the 1992 New Hampshire Democratic primary, as the Green Party nominee in 1996 and 2000, and as an independent candidate in 2004 and 2008.(Wikipedia, 2016).

Five times. *He ran for president five times*. What does this tell you? It tells me that there are a lot of stupid ass people out there who were probably the parents and grandparents of the same dumb muthafuckas who are backing Donald Trump in 2016. When you run for President people offer and give you money. You get to keep that money. Isn't that incentive enough? Even if you doubt your credibility or fear some kind of skeleton coming out of the closet in the days ahead, by the time it does, you will have gotten paid!

However, unlike the spoiled, bitch-like Trump who was born with a silver spoon in his ass …. Oops! I mean mouth, Nader started off humbly enough:

> Nader came to prominence in 1965, with the publication of his book *Unsafe at Any Speed*, a critique of the safety record of American automobile manufacturers in general, and particularly the first-generation Chevrolet Corvair. In 1999, a New York University panel of journalists ranked *Unsafe at Any Speed* 38th among the top 100 pieces of journalism of the 20th century (Wikipedia, 2016).

So Nader made contributions to public awareness. But though the polar opposite of Trump in terms of grass-roots oriented commitment and consciousness, that doesn't mean that he's not another prototype. Ego is the key, as I've postulated throughout this book. It is what drives these white men and "others" who are white mentally because they believe that they can change the system which means that they believe in it. If you believe in an oppressive system then you become a part of it. The talk about "changing" it is a sign of extreme naiveté since systems are designed to perpetuate themselves. You join it, you run for office in it, you become what it is.

If you don't believe it, look at what it did to Barack Obama.

[Type text]

At any rate, his campaign history is as scatter-brained as he would later become. Let's take a brief look.

In 1972 Nader's name was on the ballot as a candidate for the New Party, which split off from the Democratic Party (the way that Bernie Sanders' followers wanted him to do in 2016, but his ego wouldn't allow it). Nader backed out but accepted the nomination for vice president (with Benjamin Spock taking the presidential slot) and got one vote.

In 1992, Nader stood in as a write-in and appeared on a number of ballots including one as a write in for "none of the above" in both the New Hampshire Democratic and Republican Primaries. Four years later in 1996, he was drafted by the Green Party. According to Wikipedia, Nader refused to raise or spend more than $5,000 on his campaign, presumably to avoid meeting the threshold for Federal Elections Commission reporting requirements; the unofficial Draft Nader committee could (and did) spend more than that, but the committee was legally prevented from coordinating in any way with Nader himself.

During this stint one source says that, "Naderreceived some criticism from gay rights supporters for calling gay rights "gonad politics" and stating that he was not interested in dealing with such matters" (Wikipedia, 2016). He later came out in support of same-sex marriage.

In 2000, he ran as a candidate for the Green Party, which was supposedly formed in the wake of his 1996 campaign. He was excluded from the debates that year, but he and his running mate Winona LaDuke recieved2,883,105 votes, for 2.74 percent of the popular vote (third place overall), missing the 5 percent needed to qualify the Green Party for federally distributed public funding in the next election, yet qualifying the Greens for ballot status in many states (Wikipedia, 2016). See? Qualifying for "federal funding" seems to be what these egotists have as a major concern. And they get to keep that money, don't forget. But the year 2000 was where Nader really screwed up. According to Wikipedia:

> A common claim is that Nader's candidacy acted as a spoiler in the 2000 U.S. presidential election, in which 537 votes gave George W. Bush a crucial and controversial victory in Florida (Nader received almost 100,000 votes in Florida, from which a slight decrease in favour of Gore would have altered the outcome). Others, including Nader, dispute this claim.

As a result George W. Bush defeated Al Gore by 537 votes, meaning that Nader was responsible for Gore's defeat, since Nader had garnered 97,421 votes. And in 2004, Nader said he would not seek the Green Party's nomination for president, but did not rule out running as an independent candidate. One source says that, "Nader's 2004 campaign, ran on a platform consistent with the Green Party's positions on major issues, such as opposition to the war in Iraq. He has detailed the legal reasons George W. Bush and Dick Cheney fit the criteria for war criminals, and why they should have been immediately impeached.(Wikipedia, 2016). Nader ran and received 0.38 percent of the vote. In 2008, after dogging Hillary Clinton as a "panderer and a flatterer," he again came in third.

In 2012 he suggested that people vote for Jill Stein and in 2016 he didn't run but recommended that Bill Gates, Ted Turner and Oprah Winfrey make a run. And get this: he showed support for Donald Trump making a run as well claiming that Trump would "help break up the two party system." We now see how his "prediction" turned out.

The point is that he just can't stay out of it. Ego does that to people.

Pat Buchanan (1992, 1996 and 2000)

Although I gave Patrick Buchanan more space than he deserves elsewhere in this book, there are nevertheless a few more specifics that I would like to offer in order to make my point about the roles of ego, nationalism and greed and how they combine to clearly show that what America saw in the 2015-2016 Republican campaign bid of Donald J. Trump was surely no exception –it was the rule. And as you will see, the chameleon-like "morphing" that Buchanan underwent (from racist to more racist) is very similar to the overall image of Trump and many of his Reform Party positions sounded very Trump-like.

One of the more unheralded bombastic peckerwoods to contaminate the political system as a presidential candidate was one Patrick Buchanan.

As a former White House Director of Communications (1985-1987, he worked under former President Ronald Reagan. He was also a senior advisor to other racists – namely Richard Nixon and Gerald Ford. This means that much of what these white men did to the black community during their reign was co-signed (authored?) by Patrick Buchanan. More on that elsewhere in this book.

Buchanan was born in 1938, meaning that when he was born, racial segregation was still a matter of law all over the United States. In fact, since it was not "outlawed" until 1954, this means that he actually grew up living with and accepting racial segregation. He was 16 when the Brown v. Board of Topeka Kansas decision was rendered. This means that he was accustomed to white nationalist rhetoric (akin to what you hear from the supporters of Donald Trump, and from John McCain, Mitt Romney, George Bush, Ronald Reagan, Hillary Clinton, Bill Clinton and others).

Although a Republican in mentality he briefly joined the Reform Party from 1999-2000. He attended both Georgetown University and Columbia University and his religion is Roman Catholic (Wikipedia, 2016). He is now a regular on PBS' The McLaughlin Group and has been since the 1980s. But this asshole was bypassed during Watergate, even though at the time he was a special assistant to Nixon. According to one source,

> Buchanan remained as a special assistant to Nixon through the final days of the Watergate scandal. He was not accused of wrongdoing, though some mistakenly suspected him of being Deep Throat. In 2005 when the actual identity of the press leak was revealed as Federal Bureau of Investigation Associate Director Mark Felt, Buchanan called him "sneaky," "dishonest" and "criminal."[14] Because of his role in the Nixon campaign's "attack group," Buchanan appeared before the Senate Watergate Committee on September 26, 1973.(Wikipedia, 2016).

He worked for Reagan and got into a little trouble when he called into question the Jewish Holocaust. The Jews got involved and got some Jews to defend him when he said he wasn't anti-Semitic. But the tag stuck.

In 1992, Buchanan entered the presidential primaries, and showed a lot of ideas quite similar to those of the Donald Trump of 2016:

> He ran on a platform of immigration reduction and social conservatism, including opposition to multiculturalism, abortion, and gay rights. Buchanan seriously challenged Bush (whose popularity was waning) when he won 38 percent of the seminal New Hampshire primary. In the primary elections, Buchanan garnered three million total votes. (Wikipedia, 2016).

But that's as far as it got. Buchanan threw his support behind Bush, "and delivered an address at the 1992 Republican National Convention, which became known as the culture war speech, in which he described "a religious war going on in our country for the soul of America." (Wikipedia, 2016). Four years later he would try again:

> 1996 saw Buchanan's most successful attempt to win the Republican nomination. With a Democratic President (Bill Clinton) seeking re-election, there was no incumbent Republican

with a lock on the ticket. Indeed, with former President George H. W. Bush having made clear he was not interested in re-gaining the office, the closest the party had to a front-runner was the Senate Majority leader Sen. Bob Dole of Kansas, who was considered to have many weaknesses.(Wikipedia, 2016).

And this is how these egotists do it: they seek an opening and almost immediately form a group of people who can help them leech for money – not that they don't have money already. They need an opening based on the lack of charisma of the people who are already in the race. Dole was droll, to put it mildly, not to say that Buchanan was much better. But Buchanan had a way of saying enough dumb shit – similar to Trump – to capture the American imagination. So he went for it:

> Buchanan sought the Republican nomination from Dole's right, voicing his opposition to the North American Free Trade Agreement (NAFTA). Other candidates for the nomination included Sen. Phil Gramm of Texas, former Tennessee Governor Lamar Alexander and the multi-millionaire publisher Steve Forbes.(Wikipedia, 2016).

Whoever can sound the most racist can get the nod. And it's not just the Republicans. The ultimate question, though cloaked in discussions of the economy, taxes and the like, is what to do about the niggas. That is the ultimate question. And since the turn of the 20th century the concept of "niggas" has grown and expanded to include Mexicans, immigrants and now, middle easterners.

So the "racist race" was on, but his desperation and ego-driven needs were still high:

> In the Super Tuesday primaries, however, Dole defeated Buchanan by large margins. Having collected only 21 percent of the total votes in Republican primaries, Buchanan suspended his campaign in March. He declared however that, if Dole were to choose a pro-choice running mate, he would run as the US Taxpayers Party (now Constitution Party) candidate… However, Dole chose Jack Kemp and he received Buchanan's endorsement. After the 1996 campaign, Buchanan returned to his column and *Crossfire*. He also began a series of books with 1998's *The Great Betrayal*.

What you have to remember is that all the money that is "contributed" to these sheisters is money they get to keep. That campaign kitty is like a personal bank account. So you can pretend to give a shit about running for office (like Jesse

[Type text]

Jackson, Herman Cain, Rand Paul and others have done), knowing you don't have a snowball's chance in hell of winning, and just kick back and spend the dough as you see fit.

Four years later, Buchanan was at it again. After ditching the Republican Party in 1999 and dogging them out – similar to what Trump initially attempted to do in 2015 – Buchanan sought the nomination of the so-called "Reform Party." Now look at how the money mystically and magically "appears":

> Ultimately, when the Federal Elections Commission ruled Buchanan was to receive ballot status as the Reform candidate, as well as about $12.6 million in federal campaign funds secured by Perot's showing in the 1996 election, Buchanan won the nomination. In his acceptance speech, Buchanan proposed US withdrawal from the United Nations and expelling the UN from New York, abolishing the Internal Revenue Service, Department of Education, Department of Energy, Department of Housing and Urban Development, taxes on inheritance and capital gains, and affirmative action programs.(Wikipedia, 2016).

If you look closely, this is the same kind of bullshit that Donald Trump was talking in 2016. Remember? He was downplaying the relevance of the United Nations and charging that the member nations weren't paying their fair share. He (Trump) called for a "change" in the IRS and of course doing away with Obamacare, but look at Buchanan's madness: abolishing the department of education, energy and housing? This is the same thing that Texas governor Rick Perry tried to propose when he ran for President in 2012, just before he made an ass out of himself and "forgot" one of the departments he wanted to abolish.

Now it gets really interesting. This white man who talks all that shit about minorities being the problem decides that he's going to choose a black running mate! Check it out:

> As his running mate, Buchanan chose African-American activist and retired teacher from Los Angeles, Ezola B. Foster. Buchanan was supported in this election run by future Socialist Party USA presidential candidate Brian Moore, who said in 2008 he supported Buchanan in 2000 because "he was for fair trade over free trade. He had some progressive positions that I thought would be helpful to the common man" ... On August 19, the New York Right to Life Party, in convention, chose Buchanan as their nominee, with 90 percent of the districts voting for him.

Let me state at this juncture that when white people select black people as running mates, it means that the black person is mentally as white as the white person. Ezola Foster was certainly no exception. As one source documents it,

> Pat Buchanan selected Foster as his running-mate after several other candidates such as Jim Traficant of Ohio and Teamsters Union president James P. Hoffa declined his offer. Foster, who had supported Buchanan's campaigns in 1992 and 1996, quit her own speaking tour to join the race. While Buchanan was hospitalized during part of the campaign, Foster was the ticket's mouthpiece, campaigning through television and radio appearances. This was the first time in history that an African-American had been nominated for Vice-President by a Federal Election Commission-recognized and federally funding political party, and the second time a woman had accomplished this (Democrat Geraldine Ferraro being the first) … (Wikipedia, 2016).

Rarely have such "Jemimas" see the public in such a manner other than Hollywood. When a black woman is "trusted" enough to be a mouthpiece for a conservative white boy, you know she has to be a sellout, a water-carrier, a flunky – a willing thrall.

Check out Foster's "credentials":

> Foster was chosen because of her conservative credentials and speaking ability; she called Lyndon B. Johnson's Great Society social policy "Marxist". Buchanan critics saw her as an affirmative action selection because she had never held a political office and is African American …(Wikipedia, 2016).

Throughout our history as a people there has always been some crazy ass "nigger" who the white man dubs a savior of our people. The more insane or stereotypical the person was, the more whitey propped him or her up. In our recent history the names Ward Connerly, Clarence Thomas, Michael Steele, Alan Keyes, and Dr. Ben Carson come to mind. Ezola Foster is of that ilk. If you think that today's black conservatives are backwards, their predecessor was this black woman, Ezola Foster. Known for saying dumb shit, following are some of the positions she's held. To begin with,

- Left Democrats & GOP because of differences of belief. (Aug 29)
- In the race to win. (Aug 29)
- Encourages attending John Birch chapter meetings. (Aug 29)
- No rift in Reform Party; no change in platform. (Aug 29)

- Worker's Comp claim not based on real mental disorder. (Aug 24)
- Foster was president of California John Birch Society. (Aug 14)
- Calls black leaders "snake-oil peddlers". (Aug 12)
- Foster denies reports of divorce filing. (Aug 12)
- Ran for office as both Democrat and Republican. (Aug 11)
- Strongly defends "family values". (Feb 14)

It should be clear that this is one confused bitch. But it gets worse. Check out her record as it relates to civil rights:

- Homosexuality is biologically & psychologically damaging. (Aug 29)
- Racism is out of govt; now focus on people. (Aug 29)
- Supports display of Confederate flag in southern states. (Aug 12)
- Against racial preferences. (Aug 12)
- Confederate battle flag should be honored. (Aug 11)
- Against gay rights & women in military. (Aug 11)
- Accuses Jesse Jackson campaign of using fascist slogans. (Feb 14)
- Democratic party policies are motivated by racial hatred. (Feb 14)
- Reparations bill for descendants of slaves is socialist. (Feb 14)
- No pro-gay groups & no AIDS educaiton at RNC. (Feb 14)

Just like Trump had the sellout Ben Carson and then hired beautiful black female Amarosa Manigault (for window dressing), the point is that she joined a long list of white men and "negroes" who literally had been throwing herself at him ever since she appeared on "The Apprentice." Others like Herman Cain often come out of the woodwork, as did Paris Denard, Michael Steele and a number of sick reverends and celebrities like NFL Hall of Famer Ray Lewis, rapper LL Cool J and former boxer Mike Tyson.

These kinds of black people are the types that white men feel most comfortable around. Trump is no exception: he is the rule. In late 2016/early 2017, Trump was seen parading in front of Trump Tower with the likes of Kanye West, Steve Harvey, and even Mike Tyson.

John Edwards (2004, 2008)

Yet another overblown egotist with a great track record who couldn't keep his dick in his pants. His "mistress'" name was Rielle Hunter and like Gary Hart before him, tried to lie about the affair but the National Enquirer busted him out (I recall seeing the cover of that issue at the newsstands). But before we get into that Trump-like ego trip called the Presidential candidacy, let's take a look at John Edwards.

[Type text]

In sum, "Johnny Reid "John" Edwards[1] (born June 10, 1953) is a former American politician, who served as a U.S. Senator from North Carolina. He was the Democratic nominee for Vice President in 2004, and was a candidate for the Democratic presidential nomination in 2004 and 2008." (Wikipedia, 2016). During his heyday he was compared to the late John F. Kennedy and as far as I was concerned I saw two glaring similarities: both were white and both were cockhounds. I could read it in this guys eyes every time he did an interview. And his own greed and selfishness, along with his treatment of his wife, paved the way for his undermining and eventual destruction.

> Edwards defeated incumbent Republican Lauch Faircloth in North Carolina's 1998 Senate election. Towards the end of his single six-year term, he sought the Democratic Party's nomination in the 2004 presidential election. He eventually became the 2004 Democratic candidate for vice president, the running mate of presidential nominee Senator John Kerry of Massachusetts. (Wikipedia, 2016).

The power craving was there, as it had been with the other men who start off with some small time election wins and then climb the ladder. Edwards was working his way up and in 2004 was teamed with another white power monger, John Kerry, a user who had married mega-rich Teresa Heinz. Though born in Mozambique, this white woman was former married to U.S. Senator J. John Heinz III (R-Pennsylvania) and then she hooked up with Kerry. Ever heard of Heinz catsup? She owns it and has so much money that as a "philanthropist," she gives it away.

So he was a user with experience. But Kerry got his ass kicked by George W. Bush. So what does Edwards do? Check it out:

> Following Kerry's loss to incumbent President George W. Bush, Edwards began working full-time at the One America Committee, a political action committee he established in 2001, and was appointed director of the Center on Poverty, Work and Opportunity at the University of North Carolina at Chapel Hill School of Law. He was also a consultant for Fortress Investment Group LLC. (Wikipedia, 2016).

Still making money, but still has one foot in the political realm. But he was also playing around on his wife and was eventually busted.

[Type text]

> On December 28, 2006, John Edwards officially announced his
> candidacy for President in the 2008 election from the yard of a
> home in New Orleans, Louisiana, that was being rebuilt after
> Hurricane Katrina destroyed it ... Edwards stated that his main
> goals were eliminating poverty, fighting global warming,
> providing universal health care, and withdrawing troops from
> Iraq.(Wikipedia, 2016).

So he pimped the poverty that destruction that was rampant in New Orleans. He took a disaster like Hurricane Katrina and used it to promote his own cause. Edwards was borrowing from the Bill and Hillary Clinton playbook: he was using that greed and false need model just as they did. With ego as the basis, as was the case with Donald Trump, he wanted to pawn himself off as being a champion of the people. He may have well bought into his own lie:

> National polls had Edwards placing third among the Democratic
> field beginning in January 2007, behind Senator Hillary Clinton
> and Senator Barack Obama ... By July 2007, the Edwards
> campaign had raised $23 million from nearly 100,000 donors,
> placing him behind Obama and Clinton in fundraising. (Wikipedia,
> 2016).

Three people with the same type of approach to wooing voters, all promoting change and all working to use their track records of "community organizing" to demonstrate their true commitment to the poor. They had a lot in common; for instance, "Edwards was first to boycott a Fox News-sponsored presidential debate in March 2007.[68] Hillary Clinton, Bill Richardson, and Barack Obama followed suit. (Wikipedia, 2016).

At any rate, the race is on:

> On January 3, 2008, in the Iowa caucuses, the first contest of the
> nomination process, Edwards placed second with 29.75% of the
> vote to Obama (37.58%), with Clinton coming in third with
> 29.47% of the vote.[69] On January 8, Edwards placed a distant
> third in the New Hampshire Democratic primary with just under
> 17% (48,818 votes). On January 26, Edwards again placed third in
> the primary in South Carolina – his birth state – which he had
> carried in 2004, and he placed third in the non-binding January 29
> vote in Florida.
> '

Edwards was losing ground, or so it appears. He saw the writing on the wall. Therefore, "At the Musicians' Village in New Orleans, Edwards announced suspending his campaign. On January 30, 2008, following his primary and caucus losses, Edwards announced that he was suspending his campaign for the Presidency ... He did not initially endorse either Clinton or Obama, saying they both had pledged to carry forward his central campaign theme of ending poverty in America ... In April 2008, he stated that he would not accept the 2008 vice presidential slot if asked ... On May 14, 2008, Edwards officially endorsed Senator Obama at a rally in Grand Rapids, Michigan. Two years after that – in 2010 - Edwards had a child with his mistress though still married. But let us not get ahead of ourselves.

But four years before that there was more than enough reason for Edwards to have dropped out of politics altogether. After all, he had a strong law firm going and they were not a poor family. And he had a good reason to drop out – that is, if he gave a damn about his wife, Elizabeth. Because four years before he dropped out of the race, on November 3, 2004, his wife revealed to the world that she had been diagnosed with breast cancer and had been treated with chemotherapy and radiotherapy.

But Edwards had a good woman and she kept on backing his political beliefs. She also,

> ... continued to work within the Democratic Party and her husband's One America Committee. On March 22, 2007, during his campaign for the 2008 Democratic nomination for the presidency, Edwards and his wife announced that her cancer had returned; she was diagnosed with stage IV breast cancer, with newly discovered metastases to the bone and possibly to her lung ... They said that the cancer was "no longer curable, but is completely treatable" ··· and that they planned to continue campaigning together with an occasional break when she requires treatment ... (Wikipedia, 2016).

So Edwards had an affair and his wife was slowly dying. But the lack of character on Edwards' part came shining through. And look what he put that woman through in the process:

> In June 2010, Elizabeth published a book called *Resilience*. Her book is about the struggles of her marriage and how she was affected by her husband's affair. In the book, Elizabeth talks about how long she was in the dark about the affair and how many times her husband, John, lied about the details of the affair. She never addresses John's mistress by name but calls her a "parasitic

groupie" and claims that she is pathetic. Elizabeth also opens up
about how she tried to forgive her husband after she first learned of
the affair but struggled to find forgiveness when he continued to
lie. After Edwards' January 21, 2010, admission that he fathered a
child with his mistress, Elizabeth legally separated from him and
intended to file for divorce after a mandatory one-year waiting
period ... (Wikipedia, 2016).

Edwards had denied that the baby was his even after he had admitted to the affair. Now here is where we get into some serious Uncle Tomfoolery. Enter: Andrew Young:

He further said he was willing to take a paternity test, but Hunter
responded that she would not be party to a DNA test "now or in the
future" ... Initially, campaign aide Andrew Young claimed that he,
not Edwards, was the child's father ... Young has since renounced
that statement, and told publishers in a book proposal that Edwards
always knew he was the child's father; Young alleged that
Edwards pleaded with him to falsely accept responsibility ...
(Wikipedia, 2016).

By getting involved, Young was making this woman like even more of a slut and homewrecker than she was by playing around with Edwards. Now she's added a "nigga" to the mix, interpreted by white boys as meaning she'll screw anybody. Edwards was a dog and should have been exposed in the same way as Bill Clinton would be. Check out the following:

In the proposal, which *The New York Times* examined, Young
claims to have set up private meetings between Edwards and
Hunter. He wrote that Edwards once calmed an anxious Hunter by
promising her that after his wife died, he would marry her in a
rooftop ceremony in New York with an appearance by the Dave
Matthews Band.[104] ABC News reports that Young stated that
Edwards asked him to "Get a doctor to fake the DNA results...and
to steal a diaper from the baby so he could secretly do a DNA test
to find out if this [was] indeed his child ...

Such gutterish behavior on the part of young, but it wasn't the worst thing he ever did. So in answer to the question as to why Young was keeping such a low profile, let's take a short trip back to 1987.

From time to time people will ask me "whatever happened to Andrew Young"? I simply look at them because I had never known him to be anything more than an opportunist. If you're in the South and you have light skin, those black people will kiss your ass from dusk to dawn, a residue attitude and action from the days of slavery. Young capitalized on it, curried favor with Jimmy Carter and rose to the top. It went to his head and he and Julien Bond got caught snorting cocaine. In case you don't remember (black people tend to have selective amnesia when it comes to being betrayed by their "negro leadership"), let me remind you. As it was reported in the May 19, 1987 edition of the New York Times,

> What began as a distraught wife's visit to the police to accuse her husband of cocaine abuse has mushroomed into a broader scandal here involving race, politics and the reputation of black leaders who had inherited the legacy of the Rev. Dr. Martin Luther King Jr. As a result, Mayor Andrew Young, the former Congressman, diplomat and longtime aide to Dr. King, has emerged as the target of a Federal grand jury that wants to know whether he sought to hinder a police investigation into accusations of drug use involving not only Julian Bond, the former State Senator and civil rights activist, but Mayor Young himself. (Schmidt, 1987).

Like Jesse Jackson (who is dealt with elsewhere in this book), Congressman John Lewis, Senator Bernie Sanders (dealt with in this book), and so many other King "hangers-on," both Bond and Young drop that "King card" when it's convenient to curry favor with Atlanta black people or to beg for money from the white man. Along with King's widow Coretta Scott, these coons bled Georgia of all the grant money they could get. Their speaking fees were astronomical and their resumes used the name of Dr. Martin Luther King, Jr., every time they wanted to get a free pass into some event. They talked a lot of black talk when the time period dictated it, but after the FBI dogged out the Panthers and the black power movement was no more, they shifted to silent "go with the flow" type negroes, plain and simple.

Young fronted as a minister but he was never really nothing more than a political pimp. The charges about the cocaine, however, never stuck:

> The allegations were made in March by Alice Bond, the estranged wife of the former civil rights leader. According to confidential police memorandums given to Atlanta newspapers and television stations, Mrs. Bond said her husband was a habitual cocaine user. She also named several other prominent public figures, including Mr. Young and his brother, Dr. Walter Young, as having used cocaine on at least one occasion. (Schmidt, 1987).

[Type text]

See how these women are? If what she says is true and she knew about it, then she should be arrested as well for aiding and abetting. At any rate, I believe her because these black people live in these gated communities and are well protected. If the cops do come they have to get buzzed into the property first and that gives you plenty of time to hide the dope. Not only that, but when you're a political pimp, you are surrounded by temptation of various kind, including women and drugs. Look at Marion Barry (former mayor of Washington, DC) and Kwame Kilpatrick (former mayor of Detroit). Young was no exception, and by being light-skinned in a part of the nation where black people are still "color-struck" opened up a lot of doors.

Continuing

> Not only have Mr. Young and Mr. Bond denied ever using cocaine, but Mrs. Bond has since made a public retraction of her allegations, saying they were untrue and the result of stress brought on by her marital difficulties ... Dr. Charles H. King, who heads the Atlanta Urban Crisis Center, said the disclosures of the last two months have "virtually slaughtered black reputations built up over a lifetime." The story, he said, "was and continues to be a personal hurt to most blacks in Atlanta." (Schmidt, 1987).

Black people have too much trust in these black "leaders" who want to be preachers and politicians and tell black people what to do. This is called "the messiah complex," and these men – the ones that I discuss in this book – have some semblance of it. What is the messiah complex? Simply put, it is "A state of mind in which an individual holds a belief that they are, or are destined to become, a savior." They believe that they are above the law, which is why they obtain a small amount of power and then immediately begin to act like children. Civil rights leaders, as this book shows, are typical of this "complex."

As Schmidt (1987) wrote in regard to "leaders" like Bond and Young,

> At stake, finally, is the reputation not only of political luminaries like Mr. Bond and Mr. Young, who are longtime friends and colleagues, but of a local political leadership that has historically been associated with the highest values and aspirations of the struggle for black civil rights. "Over the last 20 years, there has always been a special affection across the nation for Atlanta's black leadership, in politics, in education, in business," said Stoney Cooks, a Washington political consultant who is a former aide and longtime friend of Mr. Young. (Schmidt, 1987).

[Type text]

And this is why Andrew Young did what he did when it came to another man with a God complex, John Edwards. When called on by Edwards to lie for him, there was good ol' "Uncle Andy" shuffling and putting his own reputation on the line. Check it out:

> On February 2, 2010, Young released a book detailing the affair. Young also began working with Aaron Sorkin on a movie about the affair based on the book *The Politician*. On February 23, 2012, an Orange County, NC, judge ruled that Young and his wife could not publicize the movie. The judge also ruled that an alleged "sex tape" of Edwards and Hunter be destroyed by the court. The judge also allowed only the materials already in the public domain to be used for public purposes. All other photos and materials not yet released, can be used for family purposes only ..... (Wikipedia, 2016).

See how these "black leaders" are once they get the whiff of power? And see how beholden they are to the white man – in the same way that Donald Trump is beholden to Vladimir Putin? Here's how it concluded with Edwards:

> In response to the scandal involving Edwards' extramarital affair and attempts to cover it up, he has stated "I am a sinner, but not a criminal" ... On December 7, 2010, Elizabeth died of metastatic breast cancer at age 61 ... (Wikipedia, 2016).

So John Edwards was carrying on with his mistress while his wife was dying of breast cancer. That's why in 2011, "a Federal grand jury in North Carolina indicted Edwards in 2011 on six felony charges of violating multiple federal campaign contribution laws to cover up an extramarital affair to which he admitted following his 2008 campaign. Edwards was found not guilty on one count, and the judge declared a mistrial on the remaining five charges, as the jury was unable to come to an agreement. The Justice Department dropped the remaining charges and did not attempt to retry Edwards" (Wikipedia, 2016)

What a loser.

Gary Johnson (2012 and 2016)

Of all the mistake-laden stories that these egotists over the years have given us to reflect back on and share, this guy was undoubtedly the most ignorant – some would say stupid.

[Type text]

In 2016 as missiles and gas rained down on Aleppo, a small country inside of Syria, this asshole was asked what he thought about the internationally conflictual situation. When asked, he replied, "What is Aleppo?" Later, he said he thought it was an acronym. Then, on the ABC talk show "The View," this asshole apologized and owned up to his error.

On September 29th he did it again. He was asked what international leader he most admired. He couldn't name a single one. Then he blurted out, "the former president of Mexico." When asked which one, he couldn't even name the person. And yet this man was a third party candidate, one whose ego would not get him to pull out of the race. Here is what was ironic: Johnson was at one time the governor of New Mexico and held office there from 1995 to 2003. Not only is this evidence of his own stupidity, but also of the stupidity of the voters of New Mexico. No wonder rumors of UFOs and flying saucers reign supreme in the state, especially in the small town of Roswell.

How could he not be a hick at heart? He was born in Minot, North Dakota, where there are about as many blacks and Latinos as there are Klingons on Earth. He is a member of the Republican Party back then, but now in 2016 he's running for office as the leader of the Libertarian Party. In 2012 he won the Libertarian Party nomination and received 0.99% of the popular vote, amounting to 1.27 million votes, more than all other minor candidates combined and according to Wikipedia, "it was the best showing in the Libertarian Party's history by vote count."

His background sounds somewhat interesting as we find out from Wikipedia:

> Johnson graduated from Sandia High School in Albuquerque in 1971, where he was on the school track team ... He attended the University of New Mexico from 1971 to 1975 and graduated with a Bachelor of Science in political science ... Johnson earned money as a door-to-door handyman ... His success in that industry encouraged him to start his own business, Big J Enterprises, in 1976. When he started the business, which focused on mechanical contracting, Johnson was its only employee ... His major break with the firm was receiving a large contract from Intel's expansion in Rio Rancho, which increased Big J's revenue to $38 million ... Over-burdened by his success, Johnson enrolled in a time management course at night school, which he credits with making him heavily goal-driven ... He eventually grew Big J into a multimillion-dollar corporation with over 1,000 employees ... By

the time he sold the company in 1999, it was one of New Mexico's
leading construction companies.

Like Trump he was a businessman, although Trump was born with a silver spoon in his ass … oops! I mean mouth. But it makes no difference: both men have the protections and blessings of "white privilege." So even when they screw up, they are white in a society that rewards whiteness.

With the business dimension out of the way, we now check out Johnson's political rise:

> He entered politics for the first time by running for Governor of New Mexico in 1994 on a fiscally conservative, low-tax and anti-crime platform … Johnson won the Republican Party of New Mexico's gubernatorial nomination, and defeated incumbent Democratic governor Bruce King. During his tenure as governor, Johnson became known for his low-tax libertarian views, adhering to policies of tax and bureaucracy reduction supported by a cost–benefit analysis rationale. He cut the 10% annual growth in the budget: in part, due to his use of the gubernatorial veto 200 times during his first six months in office ….

Johnson ran for re-election in 1998 and won but could not run due to term limits for a third term. So after leaving office,

> … Johnson founded the non-profit Our America Initiative in 2009, a political advocacy committee seeking to promote policies such as free enterprise, foreign non-interventionism, limited government and privatization. He endorsed the Republican presidential candidacy of Congressman Ron Paul in the 2008 election …

This is a clear-cut example of one nimrod endorsing another. Johnson endorsed Ron Paul, who was a Libertarian. Why? I'll tell you why: in 2000 The Libertarian Party tried to draft him for the 2000 Presidential election. But at that time he claimed he was a Republican "with no interest in running for President" (Wikipedia, 2016).

More lies – just like Trump. Remember, at one time Trump was a Democrat and was giving money to democratic candidates. But these white men can flip-flop because they understand their constituencies: a case of the blind leading the blind.

[Type text]

He couldn't even decide if he was a liberal or a conservative. Check out the following:

> In February 2011, Johnson was a featured speaker at both the Conservative Political Action Conference (CPAC) and the Republican Liberty Caucus … At CPAC, "the crowd liked him—even as he pushed some of his more controversial points" … Johnson tied with New Jersey Governor Chris Christie for third in the CPAC Straw Poll, trailing only Ron Paul and Mitt Romney (and ahead of such notables as former Speaker of the House Newt Gingrich, former Minnesota Governor Tim Pawlenty, Indiana Governor Mitch Daniels and former Alaska Governor and 2008 vice presidential candidate Sarah Palin) …

I cite the preceding to show you the company that this confused man was associating with: conservative curmudgeons like Mitt Romney, Newt Gingrich and Sarah Palin. So Johnson decides to run for president. He joined in the debates with the usual conservative crew -- Michele Bachmann, Herman Cain, Newt Gingrich, Jon Huntsman, Ron Paul, Rick Perry, Mitt Romney, and Rick Santorum. To show you the low level of thinking during the debate, two credible publications said that Johnson delivered the best line of the night: "My next-door neighbor's two dogs have created more shovel ready jobs than this administration." Again, similar to the asinine analyses, insult-riddled statements and shallow proposals put forth by Donald Trump.

Johnson was zany as hell. He ran again in 2015 and made an ass out of himself on a number of occasions. For one thing, during a television interview he was asked what he thought about "Alepo," a city in Syria that was being carpet bombed by the Russians. He said he didn't know what it was. Later he said he thought it was some kind of acronym. What he succeeded in doing was taking votes away from Hillary Clinton (as did Green Party presidential candidate Jill Stein). But he got votes, attention, and money – the same things that megalomaniacs like Trump thrive on.

Bernie Sanders (2016)

Bernie Sanders, a Jew out of nowhere, almost became president of the United States. Hailing from a lily-white state which Ebony magazine once featured as "the whitest state," one of the truly stupid articles that have ever been published in this senseless magazine (it is about as "black" as a snowball). At any rate I wrote a response to that article and it was so eye-opening that Ebony published it in the

[Type text]

March 1988 issue in the "letters to the editor" section. Following is the full text of my response:

In December of 1987, Ebony magazine ran a story about Vermont being "the whitest state in America," and I was so perturbed by it that I sat down and wrote a response to it. During the time I was teaching at Milwaukee Area Technical College, but this is once again more evidence that no matter what I am doing or where I am working, my concern for my people is a priority and I will use what I need to use to defend their interests.

In March of 1988, the following "Letter to the Editor" appeared in Ebony magazine:

The December issue of EBONY carries an article about the State of Vermont, referring to it as "The Whitest State in America." I beg to differ with your assessment, although much of what you had to say did have validity.

For example, there are only 1,200 Blacks in the entire state, which shows that Vermont is "White" in terms of sheer numbers. But on the other hand, I would think that a lot of Blacks who live there – isolated from any major urban area – would be somewhat "culturally naïve" themselves and would come out, in many ways, as "White" (mentally speaking) as the Caucasians who reside in the state.

But more profoundly the examples used to demonstrate the "ups and downs" of the state were not any major indications of "race relations," per se. When Blacks are few in numbers, Whites feel less of a threat by their presence; and therefore actions such as helping to halt a KKK rally are expected. Patronizing a Black mail order business that is prospering in Vermont is yet another familiar pattern. When Blacks have businesses in predominantly White communities, this shows a "system orientation" and, once again, reduces the threat of deviance. It should also be duly noted that Blacks in Vermont have the highest income of al Black families in the country, meaning that being so few in number our people there can benefit from a high tax base. In turn, this means that Black children can get a good "basic" education, perhaps live in decent housing and generally avoid the kind of "segregation" that is employed in cities like Chicago, Omaha and Milwaukee.

You think Vermont is bad? We here in Milwaukee have got a lot of nerve. We have a street that is named Martin Luther King Jr. Drive on one side and Third Street on the other side – yet we allow it, even though it is very possible that it's an illegal act. We sit back and watch the major newspaper have a virtual monopoly on the news, but still won't support Black publications; we watch the mayor appoint a nearly all-White committee to deal with fire problems in our community.

Vermont may be the "Whitest state" in America in terms of racial composition and percentages. And if it is, then it would only reason why there are so few Blacks in power there. But Karenga is correct when he writes, "White doesn't just represent a color; it represents a mentality that is anti Black." And if this is true, then don't judge Vermont because of the numerical manifestations of White power that one sees; look at places like Milwaukee and Omaha that have institutionalized racism to the point that Black population size is neutralized anyway.
MATTHEW C. STELLY
Milwaukee, Wisc.

In my view Bernie Sanders continually ripped off slogans and concepts from the 1960s radical fringe and was able to convince millions of white and black people that he was the real deal. Although more than 70 years old, his claim to fame was as a civil rights activist (as many old white men will now claim), but he also got over by talking general bullshit, attacked the establishment and cashed in on his white privilege to mouth the word "revolution" without being arrested one time for sedition or treason.

Some background is in order:

> **Bernard "Bernie" Sanders** (born September 8, 1941) is an American politician who has served as the junior United States Senator from Vermont since 2007. Sanders had been the longest-serving independent in U.S. congressional history, though his caucusing with the Democrats entitled him to committee assignments and at times gave Democrats a majority …(Wikipedia, 2017).

So he was born before the desegregation decision of 1954, and was therefore raised in a lily-white city in what Ebony magazine referred to as "the Whitest state" (1988), and became a successful politician. So far there is no evidence that Sanders is culturally competent or that he's some kind of civil rights hero.

> His father, Elias Sanders, was born on September 14, 1904 in Słopnice, Poland (then, until 1918, in the Austro-Hungarian province of Galicia) … to a Jewish family; in 1921 he immigrated to the United States at the age of 17 … His mother, Dorothy Sanders (née Glassberg), was born in New York City on October

> 2, 1912 … to Jewish immigrant parents from Poland and Russia
> … Many of Elias's relatives who remained in Poland were killed
> in the Holocaust …(Wikipedia, 2017).

So here we have someone who is a Jew, whose parents probably told him about the Holocaust, but who is nevertheless surrounded by lily-whiteness. He therefore grows up in a racially sterile environment and out of that begins to make his way into a career.

> Sanders became the ranking minority member on the Senate
> Budget Committee in January 2015; he had previously served for
> two years as chair of the Senate Veterans' Affairs Committee. A
> self-proclaimed democratic socialist or social democrat …
> Sanders is pro-labor and emphasizes reversing economic inequality
> … (Wikipedia, 2017).

Adopting socialist ideas that basically mean a system of white folks by white folks. There is nothing culturally expansive or racially inclusive about this man's background – this man who campaigned for President and had black people working for him and following him as if he was the Messiah, even as he ripped off slogans that came from the mouths of black power leadership from the 1960s. His civil rights work started when black people's activities opened his eyes, or so it seems:

> Sanders was born and raised in the Brooklyn borough of New
> York and graduated from the University of Chicago in 1964. While
> a student he was an active civil rights protest organizer for the
> Congress of Racial Equality and the Student Nonviolent
> Coordinating Committee. After settling in Vermont in 1968,
> Sanders ran unsuccessful third-party campaigns for governor and
> U.S. senator in the early to mid-1970s. As an independent, he was
> elected mayor of Burlington—Vermont's most populous city—in
> 1981, where he was reelected three times … (Wikipedia, 2017).

Bernie Sanders, like many Jews, got involved in the civil rights movement. But unlike many others it appears that Sanders actually put boots on the ground. Many Jews just donate money and in doing so, end up in control of black thinking and black planning. But politics was in Sanders' blood and he used his liberal bent to march into office:

[Type text]

> In 1990 he was elected to represent Vermont's at-large
> congressional district in the U.S. House of Representatives. In
> 1991 Sanders co-founded the Congressional Progressive Caucus.
> He served as a congressman for 16 years before being elected to
> the U.S. Senate in 2006. In 2012, he was reelected with 71% of the
> popular vote. (Wikipedia, 2017).

So Bernie was on his way as a "progressive." And he didn't forget the civil rights schooling that he had received and had been involved in. According to Wikipedia (2017, "Sandersattended the 1963 March on Washington for Jobs and Freedom, where Martin Luther King, Jr. gave his "I Have a Dream" speech … That summer, he was convicted of resisting arrest during a demonstration against segregation in Chicago's public schools and was fined $25." This must be the picture that he continually flashed when he was running for President, a photo of him being carried long ways by some cops to who knows where.

But egotistical Bernie wasn't through there:

> In addition to his civil rights activism during the 1960s and 1970s,
> Sanders was active in several peace and antiwar movements. He
> was a member of the Student Nonviolent Coordinating Committee
> and the Student Peace Union while attending the University of
> Chicago. Sanders applied for conscientious objector status during
> the Vietnam War; his application was eventually turned down, by
> which point he was too old to be drafted. Although he opposed the
> war, Sanders never criticized those who fought and has been a
> strong supporter of veterans' benefits … (Wikipedia, 2017).

Of all the people we've analyzed, he seems to be the most sincere. That could be one reason why he was allowed to shout "revolution" throughout the 2016 campaign, and never got arrested. He never mentioned Judaism but claims to be very spiritual, which is why,

> In 2016, he stated he had "very strong religious and spiritual
> feelings" and explained, "My spirituality is that we are all in this
> together and that when children go hungry, when veterans sleep
> out on the street, it impacts me" (Wikipedia, 2017).

Bernie Sanders ran for president and got millions in donations. Where does that money go? What did he do with it? And he's still at it, long after the election was over, and he's doing television shows, rallies, community meetings and so on, to push his "progressive" agenda.

[Type text]

So there you have it: ten megalomaniacs of varying degrees, ten people who will say whatever it takes to get what they want, ten people who crave power and ten people who have made money selling an "American Dream" that is more like an "American nightmare."

You have just read overviews and analyses of ten people – nine men and one woman – who have done to you what you now point your finger at Donald Trump for doing. Is there a difference when all is said and done? If there is a difference it is that Donald Trump has a more demonic and deadly goal: to destroy the American system that everyone else claimed to be about expanding, improving and defending. Trump grew up a thoroughgoing capitalist and he remains one, and what is capitalism? It is "the ceaseless pursuit of profit." That means that he will do anything for money and capital. He's for sale to the highest bidder, no matter where that bidder is located in the world

My purpose with this book is simply to show that if there is any difference between Trump and the ten people I've shared with you, it is merely by degree. It is like an older version of Jack the Ripper being compared with a younger, teenaged version who merely raped women without killing them. By comparison the younger version (the ten people I've described) appears to better, or more humane. But not to the victims of his crimes he's not!

The sampling I have just shared is filled with people who themselves share Trump characteristics: lying, ripping people off, taking money under the table, and making promises they can't keep. Look at the list: are any of them still active and visible and helping to make America great again? No, and neither is Trump. It's all a façade to satisfy the male (and in some cases the female) need for gratification, visibility status and wealth.

Now with all of these egomaniacs out of the way, there is one man who is at the center of this analysis. He is now known as "President" Donald J. Trump, and from his incestuous actions toward his daughter and his prostitute-looking wife to his orange-colored skin and maniacal tendency to lie, it should be clear that this man is cartoon material, plain and simple. But he's white in a majority white nation and because of that, he has the benefit of the doubt and of what is known as "white privilege."

What you see and hear each day from a misguided asshole like Donald Trump is no exception – it is a "type." Look at what I've just shared: people run for that office in the quest for power, they come into contact with powerful people, they raise huge sums of money and then, win or lose, they nevertheless show what low regard they have for the everyday issues that impact on the lives of people of color in general, and Black people in particular.

So without any further ado, let's look at "The Donald" himself and see if we can find out what makes this racist asshole tick.

INTRODUCTION

Arrogant. Bombastic. Rich, Racist. Cowardly. Bitch-like, Misogynistic. A general asshole when all is said and done. I'm accurately describing Donald Trump, the billionaire developer out of New York. *But more importantly, I'm describing most white men who have anything even remotely related to power or wealth.* The more power they gain, the more likely these white men are to adopt some or all of the characteristics I've just pointed out.

The extreme allegations against the moronic and bellicose statements of Donald Trump are not unique to him; white men have been lying and fantasizing about their accomplishments and plans for centuries. They have embellished their actions, they have falsified their plans and goals and values and have built a nation that is built on all of these fake folkways and mock mores. Donald Trump is a white male prototype and, like most of them, has benefited from white privilege and has used it to oppress others. He has been sued a plethora of times, run out on his debts, left debtors hanging in the wind, and moved on down the road to the next group of people he plans to bilk,

The recent rancor and rigmarole surrounding Donald Trump is nothing new or nerve-shattering; it is a prototypical extension of what white males have been doing, on varying levels, ever since the beginning of their takeover of this country. Having murdered off the native population, their bombast knew no bounds, and their megalomaniacal commentaries, histories and theories permeated the air in the same way their bullets often did.

Pointing the finger at Donald Trump for merely being the asshole that he is represents nothing more than a "scam" in my book. By singling him out, other whites who are just as racist for the most part, can make it appear as if "he bad, we good." The same shit is done when these white people shout out their so-called opposition to "white supremacists" like the Ku Klux Klan, Breinbart, the Nazi Party and the Tea Party. In doing so they are implying that the majority of white folks are not themselves believers in, beneficiaries of and proponents of white supremacy. It's the old "prestidigitation" of the magician or snake oil salesman.

And it works on black people (and gullible whites) every time.

[Type text]

Donald Trump: Ideological Views and Philosophy

From outsourcing to bailouts to gay relationships, Donald Trump has continued to contradict himself and offer up some of the most bizarre explanations ever in the history of American politics. When I speak about "ideological views," these range from Trump's worship of money and profit to his views on waterboarding and even the perspectives of one other famous racist asshole regarding the level or degree of Trump's "Christianity."

Following is some overview information that will be buttressed with specific examples elsewhere in this book.

To begin with, an article by Paul Singer in *USA Today* titled, "Trump's Old Blog Shows Very Different Views" nevertheless provide us with some understanding of his pre-Presidential views and values. The March 18, 2016 article appears below with my analyses filtering in and out.

> Ten years ago, Donald Trump had a pretty open mind about gay marriage. "If two people dig each other, they dig each other," he wrote about the marriage of Elton John and longtime partner David Furnish. "I'm very happy for them." (Singer, 2016).

I think it was much more than a "pretty open mind." In my view, Trump IS gay. I think he's been involved in gay trysts and that he has homoerotic attractions to people like Jefferson Sessions, Vladimir Putin and other men who are ultra rich. This is just a theory but I look at the actions of these men and I look at the way these men act around women and what they say about women. I've never heard a man say that he grabs women by the pussy before; to me, that is nothing erotic – it is an outright assault. And then there is how he acts around his wife in public. There is nothing intimate about how they treat one another. Compare how he treats Melania and then recall how Barack and Michelle behaved. I believe that his marriage is a façade and this guy s 70 years old – he's not screwing that mannequin-looking wife of his. More on this later.

After his previous comment on gay relationships, he seemed to alter his position: "For instance, on gay marriage, in June 2015 he told CNN, "I'm for traditional marriage." (Singer, 2016). How are you going to be for "traditional marriage" and still believe that gays should have the right to marriage? Dress a liar as you will, a liar is a liar, still.

[Type text]

That takes care of the gay situation. Now let's deal with his views on women, in general. Check it out:

> The December 2005 comment was posted on the "Trump Blog" that he maintained on the Trump University website, a kind of journal of Trump's thoughts on everything from why he chose various contestants for *Celebrity Apprentice* to why women struggle in the workplace: "I think women have a tough situation in the workplace because of the sexual undertones," Trump wrote in October 2005. "The business environment is so cutthroat that men and women learn to use whatever they can to get ahead, including their sexuality. Yet, when women do this, the perception of them changes. That's why women have to work harder to overcome obstacles." (Singer, 2016).

His simplistic explanation of what is known as "the glass ceiling" is so simplistic it sounds like something that a high school sophomore would say. He claims, ""I think women have a tough situation in the workplace because of the sexual undertones … The business environment is so cutthroat that men and women learn to use whatever they can to get ahead, including their sexuality. Yet, when women do this, the perception of them changes. That's why women have to work harder to overcome obstacles." Women do what they do because they realize the situation they are in, and the glass ceiling prevents them from moving up the corporate ladder. The glass ceiling is reinforced by people like Donald Trump who force them to screw them or give them some head in order to get consideration. That's what part of the problem is, Donald.

And another part of the problem is when over-aged lazy white men have to deal with their sexuality by surrounding themselves with women who will fuck or suck anything to get ahead. During the interview these men know who these women are, and they have people in the Human Resources Department who have been given orders regarding the "type" of women that these higher ups want to have working. "Are they single"? "Can they work long hours?" "Do they have family members who live nearby?" "Do they have any kids?" This is how it works.

So when he says that women have to "work harder," he's not just talking about the kind of tasks they perform at the workplace. He's talking about working harder to keep secrets and to be willing to screw around if they want more pay or they want advancements in the workplace. This is the way of the "glass ceiling," the "slippery pole", the "sticky cobweb" or the "greasy pole."

The two-faced white man agreed with then President Obama's bailout plans and bailouts in general:

[Type text]

> "The concept of bailouts is a two-edged sword. If they didn't do
> the bailout, we would be in depression No. 2, and maybe it would
> be just as big as depression No. 1, so they really had to do
> something. We don't really know if it's going to work for quite
> some time. If it's really wrong — and it could be wrong — we're
> going to really have a mess in two years." "We are in a situation
> that is trial and error. We've never dealt with this before. But I
> think Obama is doing the right thing and all of us must remain alert
> to what is happening." (Singer, 2016).

Not only did Trump agree with Obama's bailout plans and the implementation of those plans, he also agreed to Obama's subsequent stimulus package:

> In another post the same month, discussing his appearance on Neal
> Cavuto's television show, Trump seemed to break from the broad
> Republican opposition to President Obama's $800 billion stimulus
> package than most Republicans at the time. "Neal asked me about
> Obama's stimulus plan, and I said that something had to be done,
> but that there are no guarantees. We are in unmapped territory
> these days. We haven't encountered this kind of situation before,
> and it is complex. We can only hope for the best." (Singer, 2016).

Notice Trump's own words: "We are in unmapped territory," "We haven't encountered this situation before" and "We can only hope for the best." These terms are a sharp departure from the "I know everything" type of bullshit that he was spewing forth as the election grew near and the Republican debates began. This is a sign of someone who is suffering from psychosis, defined as, "Psychosis is an abnormal condition of the mind that involves a "loss of contact with reality". People experiencing psychosis may exhibit personality changes and thought disorder." Can you be in contact with reality when you flip flop 180-degrees on important issues on a near daily basis?

For instance, on the issue of "outsourcing."

Here is a guy that had a number of his products, from his vodka brand to his men's dress ties, made overseas a decade ago. As Singer (2016) explains:

> In a 2005 post, Trump defended "outsourcing," the practice of
> companies moving production overseas that he has railed against
> as a presidential candidate. In an August 2005 post titled
> "Outsourcing Creates Jobs in the Long Run," Trump wrote: "We
> hear terrible things about outsourcing jobs — how sending work
> outside of our companies is contributing to the demise of American

businesses. But in this instance I have to take the unpopular stance that it is not always a terrible thing."

And this is what he does: he walks the fence and when he's caught in yet another contradiction, he'll outright lie and claim somebody else said it. To this day in 2017 he continues this pattern of prevarication. Now that he is President he talks about "America first" and talks about bringing the jobs home. This is after he's made his money exporting jobs abroad.

Exporting jobs abroad means that there are fewer jobs for the people in this country. And in a nation where people of color are already at the bottom of the totem pole, to send jobs elsewhere means even more dire straits for us. And a lot of those jobs are paying wages that no sane American would ever accept. In other words, these decision makers chose profit over human life and when one looks at it, this is the prototypical definition of what "capitalism" is all about.

Continuing with the outsourcing issue:

> Trump noted a study "that showed how global outsourcing actually creates more jobs and increases wages, at least for IT workers": "The study found that outsourcing helped companies be more competitive and more productive. That means they make more money, which means they funnel more into the economy, thereby, creating more jobs." "I know that doesn't make it any easier for people whose jobs have been outsourced overseas, but if a company's only means of survival is by farming jobs outside its walls, then sometimes it's a necessary step. The other option might be to close its doors for good." (Singer, 2016).

Trump "notes" a study but with all the money he has, he should be commissioning his own studies be done. But he quotes these anonymous sources so that he can buttress his bullshit beliefs. Outsourcing jobs might increase competition but that doesn't mean anything to the American working people that he claims to love so much. His slogan, throughout his campaign, was "we're going to make America great again." How are you going to do that when you are sending jobs overseas so that every camel-jockey and his mama can feed their families while Americans join the unemployment line?

But then again, Trump is a two-faced sonofabitch. Want proof? Check out the following passage for yourself:

> In two blog posts at the end of 2008, he praised both President-elect Obama and Hillary Clinton. Recounting his appearance on a

New York radio program, Trump wrote that he had said: "Hillary
is smart, tough and a very nice person, and so is her husband. Bill
Clinton was a great President. They are fine people. Hillary was
roughed up by the media, and it was a tough campaign for her, but
she's a great trouper. Her history is far from being over." (Singer,
2016).

That was nine years ago when those blogs were issued – kissing the asses of
Obama and Hillary. But you can't rely on a liar and expect him not to change his
position like some kind of chameleon. An old saying taught me long ago that an
honest enemy was always better than a friend who lies. When it comes to people
like Donald J. Trump, we have to pay less attention to what he says and more
attention to what he does. After all, action speaks louder than words.

Peruse the previous quote from Trump where he says in 2008 he talks about
how tough Hillary is. She told him to his face in front of millions of people that he
was Putin's "puppet." Like a nine-year old girl on the playground all he could
counter with was, "YOU'RE the puppet!" The fact is, Putin was very much like a
bitch in his fear of Hillary and didn't want her in office because he knew she
wasn't afraid of him. So in my view he went out and got some dirt on Trump and
now the President of the United States is currying favor with this Russian asshole.
But what people have to always keep in mind is to not let the media over-
complicate the basic fact that both Trump and Putin are white men, meaning that
they have more in common than any differences that may exist.

Trump also said he had high hopes for Obama's presidency:
"Barack will need to be a great president, because we're in serious
trouble as a country. It hasn't been this way since 1929. So he
doesn't have much choice — he will simply have to be great,
which he has a very good chance of being. I saw him speak in
Berlin, and what he has done is amazing. The fact that he
accomplished what he has in one year is truly phenomenal."
(Singer, 2016)

The Native American bruthas had it right when they said, "The white man
speaks with forked tongue." That was the way it was been back then upon their
contact with this white man whose life they had saved time and time again, and
that is the way it is today in 2017 with Donald Bush kissing ass on one hand and
taking photos with a few token coons like Steve Harvey, Kanye West and the like
and then turning around and insulting and lambasting the city of Chicago and every
"inner city" in America. These points are addressed elsewhere in this book.

[Type text]

What he said above about Obama was an exaggeration until you interject the variable of race. As a black man, Obama did pull off miracles. With an entire Congress hating his guts, he still didn't fall down to their level and he still took the high road. And that is what is irking Trump so much: he comes in behind a two-term pregnant who brought young people into the electorate, whose wife looked like a model and had an intellect that had been previously unmatched (and whose speech Trump's wife, Melania, had to plagiarize), and who left with a high rating. Trump had none of these things and was and continues experiencing a political version of "penis envy."

This two-faced "orange man" (which is Trump's tanned color) has some serious personality issues. Singer, for one, writes:

> "After 9/11, this country had a lot of compassion from countries around the world. Within a short amount of time, we were hated. How did that happen? We had no dialog with other countries because they just plain hated us. I think we know who is responsible for that. What's different today is that we have a new chance, a new beginning. The world is excited about Barack Obama and the new United States. Let's keep it that way!" (Singer, 2016).

Trump's ideological views and philosophy changes with the weather. He's a spoiled coward who bloviates and boasts about things that he did not do and cannot do. He was kissing Obama's ass during the transition, and now talks behind his back like the coward that he (Trump) is. He contributed to the Democratic Party a decade ago and now he's fronting like he's a conservative Republican.

Singer (2010) writes,

> The blog also served as way to promote Trump's various brands and business ventures, many of which — like the university itself — are gone. In 2006, Trump wrote about his launch of a new travel website called "GoTrump.com" "I recently put my name on a new travel site, **GoTrump.com**. It has everything from the ultimate in luxury travel to the absolute best deals on everything from hotels to airfare." "It's a great site, check it out. It has to be, or I wouldn't have put my name on it." (Singer, 2016).

And now that he's in office, he continues to conduct business as usual, and these white people see him doing it in full view and don't do anything about it. He's doubled the price of the memberships to his Mar-A-Logo Hotel to $200,000 per year, he's got the secret service guardian his wife at over $120,000 per day, and his daughter Ivanka is peddling her cosmetics and fashions while having an office right there in the West Wing of the White House.

Finally, pay close attention to the following because times are going to get worse before they get better:

> "I've worked hard to make sure the Trump name is found only on
> buildings of the highest caliber and products of the finest quality. I
> won't even consider giving my approval to anything unless I know
> it's the top of the line because when people see or hear 'Trump,'
> they expect the best. That's just basic marketing and good
> business." The travel site appears to have shut down a year later.
> (Singer, 2016).

He never "worked" a day in his life. Other people construct the building and design them. All this lazy bastard does is put his name on them – he "brands" them. And then takes the credit and collects the rent. The fact of the matter is, Trump continues to build hotels overseas and continues to conduct business with foreign nations right there in what he calls "the Second White House," the Mar-A-Logo Hotel. He sneaks people in, conducts business and then ships them back to their countries. And he keeps getting away with it.

In sum, Trump's ideology and that of America's capitalist oriented white supremacy mesh hand in glove. America is now becoming a "kleptocracy."

<u>The Trump/Bannon Vision and "Dark Money"</u>

This whole "dark money" thing is about: as I said before its about funding people and movements that are going to serve as buffers between the shriveling white majority in this country and the world and the flood of people of color. It's about skin color and white people maintaining their pale domination of the world.

"Dark money" is defined in the following way by Wikipedia (2017):

> In the politics of the United States, dark money are funds given to
> nonprofit organizations—and include 501(c)(4) (social welfare)
> 501(c)(5) (unions) and 501(c)(6) (trade association) groups—that
> can receive unlimited donations from corporations, individuals,
> and unions, and spend funds to influence elections," The term was
> first used by the Sunlight Foundation to describe undisclosed funds
> that were used during the United States 2010 mid-term election

That, of course, is the white man's definition. But even in their definition of what constitutes money that may be abused for bad purposes, take note that they have to preface it with the word "black." This is what white people and their system are all about: the hatred they have for color is manifested in a myriad of ways. Just as Trump has issues with any person of color or country of color, just as America is "at war" with nations of color, the white supremacist system realizes that it is on its last legs. Russia and America are not enemies because both are white: stand a Russian against a wall next to a white American. There is no difference.

Trump and Steve Bannon are both racists and both are dedicated to white supremacy masked in some political ideology that they read about in a novel. Who gives a shit? The main point here is that America is in trouble and in its quest to rid the White House of the eight years of a black man being in there, the American population was willing to do anything. But their only choices were between a power hungry white woman, Hillary Clinton, and a power hungry white man, Donald Trump.

First, a word of explanation.

In a white racist culture, anything prefaced with words like "black," "dark" or related terms like "tainted" or "marked" will be negative descriptors. Even the term non-white" translates to mean "the absence of whiteness" which is about as negative as you can get in a white supremacist culture. Now we come to the meaning of the oft-used term "dark money," which is the frequent term used by Steve Bannon, Steve Miller and other members of the "alt-right" as they call themselves.

Therefore "dark money" is money that can avoid the light of day. It is used for means that may be considered other than legal. According to Wikipedia,

> In the politics of the United States, **dark money** are funds given to nonprofit organizations—and include 501(c)(4) (social welfare) 501(c)(5) (unions) and 501(c)(6) (trade association) groups—that can receive unlimited donations from corporations, individuals, and unions, and spend funds to influence elections, but are not required to disclose their donors … Dark money first entered politics with *Buckley v. Valeo* (1976) when the supreme court laid out Eight Magic Words that define the difference between electioneering and issue advocacy.

More on that later. At present let's go through an article about Trump and Bannon. In a Democracy Now! Video interview that was aired on March 23, 2017,

Amy Goodman and Nermeen Shaikh. They provide their views and I will analyze those views. And you will see what I mean when I stated earlier that America is in big trouble.

Goodman & Shaikh begin their video, thusly:

> We look at Robert Mercer, the man who is said to have out-Koched the Koch brothers in the 2016 election. The secretive billionaire hedge-fund tycoon, along with his daughter Rebekah, is credited by many with playing an instrumental role in Donald Trump's election. "The Mercers laid the groundwork for the Trump revolution" (Goodman & Shaikh, 2017).

Can there be any doubt that this is about white nationalism? These people don't give their money away; they "invest" it, to use the words of another billionaire, Warren Buffett. And with those donations come a list of demands that they want to see followed. And those demands including maintaining control over minority communities with more cops, the end of any kind of social services, and on-going commitments to international trade with America getting rid of its inferior goods and services while hoping to obtain imports that they can in turn profit from by jacking up the prices.

Continuing:

> Trump's chief strategist Stephen Bannon said. "Irrefutably, when you look at donors during the past four years, they have had the single biggest impact of anybody, including the Kochs." Before Bannon and Kellyanne Conway joined the Trump campaign, both worked closely with the Mercers. The Mercers bankrolled Bannon's Breitbart News, as well as some of Bannon's film projects. Conway ran a super PAC created by the Mercers to initially back the candidacy of Ted Cruz. (Goodman & Shaikh, 2017).

Now, with the benefit of retrospect, we know that both Bannon and Conway are key components of the Trump administration although they have been relegated to kind of "down in the basement" status. These are people who are ultra right wing, but don't get it twisted: white supremacy comes in many ideological colors, from far left to ultra right.

Again, let me quote from an old cultural nationalist who once wrote, "White doesn't represent a color; it represents a mentality that is anti-black." And the people who support Trump – mostly blue collar peckerwoods who had good jobs and were to short sighted to continue their education, believing that these good jobs were going to last forever – are the kind of peckerwoods who blame their lack of success on people of color. That is what launched Trump into the Presidency in the first place.

Dark money enables ultra-rich white people to fund Klan-type groups and get away with it. Simply put, the white folks with the money support the people who they believe can keep black people and minorities "under control" and in doing so, continue to promote white supremacy on a global level.

Continuing:

> While the Mercers have helped reshape the American political landscape, their work has all been done from the shadows. To talk more about the Mercers, we speak with Jane Mayer, staff writer at The New Yorker. Her latest piece is headlined "The Reclusive Hedge-Fund Tycoon Behind the Trump Presidency: How Robert Mercer exploited America's populist insurgency." She is also author of *Dark Money: The Hidden History of the Billionaires Behind the Rise of the Radical Right*, which just came out in paperback. (Goodman & Shaikh, 2017).

Remember the names Mercer and Koch (pronounced "Coke"). There are others but they are ultra-rich and they hate people of color. That is what this whole "dark money" thing is about: as I said before its about funding people and movements that are going to serve as buffers between the shriveling white majority in this country and the world and the flood of people of color. It's about skin color and white people maintaining their pale domination of the world.

Bannon and Trump are like white boys on college campuses who want to join and then lead the campus versions of groups like The Young Republicans, The Business Club, any fraternity or specialty club they can come up with. They want attention and they want to push their pro-white programs. And the fewer people of color they have to come into contact with, the more insulated and comfortable they feel. They are cowards and cannot fight, but with power they can command the services of other white people who can amass power and fight as "sub-groups," mobs, or various other types of groups.

[Type text]

People like Bannon and Trump use their money to promote a white way of life and more importantly, they want America to "remain white" and therefore to hell with all people of color. In my view this is the real America although most don't have the guts to admit it. But then again, these are the same people (white and "negro") who lie to their kids about the existence of Santa Clause (and Jesus).But it is called "dark money" because it is allocated, donated or contributed behind closed doors and in a clandestine manner. Remember: anything negative, dirty, inferior or feared in a white-run culture is prefaced with "dark" or "black."

The Coward Trump's Views on "Waterboarding"

In case they don't know it already, the American armed forces have a sassy and a coward as a commander-in-chief.

An article titled, "Trump: CIA Director 'Ridiculous' on Waterboarding" (Donovan Stack, USA Today, April 11, 2016) lends validity to the callous disregard that Trump has for morality and the law. But don't get it twisted: when it comes to torturing people of color, Trump's views are the rule, not the exception.

According to the article,

> Donald Trump is taking on CIA Director John Brennan on torture,
> saying Brennan's pledge not to allow waterboarding is
> "ridiculous."Brennan said on NBC News Sunday that he would not
> allow enhanced interrogation tactics, including waterboarding,
> even if a future president ordered it.(Stack, 2016).

The people who are giving America a run for its money in terms of these global battle are people who are well prepared for that battle. They know how cowardly most Americans are, even with superior weaponry. And they also know the hatred that America has for people of color and are therefore prepared for any form of torture that America might have waiting for them.

The fact is that reliable studies show that torture against people like this does not work. All it does is get the victims to say anything in order to get the torture to stop. The information may or may not be reliable. Trump is very bitch-like in his attitude and demeanors and has never been in a physical confrontation in his spoiled, rich life. What does he know? These white men are good at ordering young white men and people of color into battle and then taking the credit.

And moving ahead a little bit, just look at Trump's first foray into battle. He sent in some Navy SEALS who got their asses kicked, one of them got killed, and they lost a multi-million dollar Osprey helicopter and had to come back and

[Type text]

destroy it so it wouldn't get into enemy hands. The fact is, they went in to kill a certain person, but their intelligence information was flawed. So after the Seals landed, a firefight ensured and they came back with the excuse that they "were able to get a lot of good information." Bullshit! They lied because their commander-in-chief is a pathological liar.

Moving on with the waterboarding:

> "I think his comments are ridiculous," Trump said on Fox News Monday. "I mean, they chop off heads and they drown people in cages with 50 in a cage, in big, steel heavy cages, drop them right into the water drown people, and we can't water board and we can't do anything," Trump said. "And you know we're playing on different fields,' he continued. "And we have a huge problem with ISIS, which we can't beat, and the reason we can't beat them is we won't use strong tactics, whether it's this or other things." (Stack, 2016).

Trump was to torture people to get information but when it comes to his own toughness he responds to insults like a little bitch. You say something bad about him and he whines and pouts and then makes up lies as a way to respond to your statement. It doesn't even have to be an insult; it can be a truth that he doesn't agree with or won't cop to. Like ripping off all those students with his scam called Trump University; refusing to pay Latino workers who put in work at all those hotels, or giving them bad checks; refusing to pay accountants, secretaries and other people who he had hired; or lying about former President Obama, first claiming that he had a team of people who could prove that Obama wasn't born in America and then when that was proven to be a lie, claiming that Obama "bugged" Trump Tower when no such evidence could be found anywhere. But this lying sassy wants to torture other people because they have the courage of their convictions and refuse to snitch.

Moving on:

> He and fellow Republican presidential hopeful Texas Sen. Ted Cruz have both signaled they would not rule out bringing back tough interrogation techniques in the war against terrorism. But Brennan said such measures would damage the CIA. "I will not agree to carry out some of these tactics and techniques I've heard bandied about because this institution needs to endure," he told NBC.(Stack, 2016).

The white man is perhaps the biggest liar and violator of treaties in the history of the world. Trump himself, who claims credit for writing The Art of the Deal (when he really didn't) is a liar and a cheater himself. But yet these are the men who throw the word "liar" around as if it was the only word they knew. In fact, during the Republican debates Trump labeled Ted Cruz, "lyin' Ted" when as we now know, Trump may well be the biggest liar in the history of the American presidency.

Finally, Stack concludes,

> Trump, however, suggested the United States needs to match the ruthlessness of its enemies. "Can you imagine these ISIS people sitting around eating, and talking about (how) this country won't allow waterboarding and they just chopped off 50 heads?" he asked. He and Cruz are heading into an important primary next Tuesday in New York, where 95 delegates are at stake. That's the biggest haul until June 7, when California will award 172 delegates. (Stack, 2016).

Trump is another one of his type – you know, trying to make the United States appear to be the victim that must "watch its back." The reason why the U.S. has to be vigilant is not because it is an innocent lamb that the wolves are out to attack; it is because of the dirt that this country has done in centuries past and has gotten away with. And these people who are now threatening them from all over the so-called "Third World" – these are the orphans and offspring of the men and women that this country murdered with bombs, bullets and beast-like men.

It's called "karma" – deal with it. And all the "waterboarding" in the world ain't gonna fix that.

Glenn Beck: Is Trump a "Real Christian"?

You can't talk about ideological views or philosophy without addressing some aspect of a person's moral code, spiritual beliefs or religion. In this section of the book I address Christianity because that is the religious basis that Trump claims to believe in. Of course he is a pathological liar and devil worship would probably be more likely than any tenet of Christianity. But in my view Christianity is flawed on its own face and as Marx said, it is the "opiate of the oppressed masses."

A March 25, 2016 article by Mark Hensch appeared in The Hill under the headline, "Glenn Beck: 'No Real Christian' Should Support Trump." This article provides insight not only on how Beck views Trump, but how silly Beck is and how shallow the religious views of sick men like both of these bastards can be. Therefore we can solve a plethora of problems by gaining a deeper understanding of how men who do what people like Glenn Beck (a conservative radio talk show host) and Donald Trump) tend to do nevertheless have the gall to claim to believe in a higher force. The following article includes Beck's words and I will analyze them based on his criticism of Donald Trump – akin to the pot calling the skillet black.

The article begins, thusly:

> Glenn Beck on Thursday suggested that GOP presidential front-runner Donald Trump is incompatible with Christians who take their faith seriously. No Christian, no real Christian I don t mean a judgmental Christian, I mean somebody who is living their faith no real Christian says, I want that guy, that guy is for me, he said during <u>a broadcast of his radio show</u>. "Nobody, nobody.(Hensch, 2016).

Let's get something straight off the bat: Christians, in general, are some of the most hypocritical and sick individuals there are in this country. It was the Christian mind that, to begin with, created a "Hell" in the first place. The myth of a "Heaven," which black people buy into, is equally as daffy. The Christian name and related symbols were emblazoned on the hulls of many a ship that sailed to Africa and came back loaded down with black bodies for enslavement. The Christian used that whip and raped black women with the quickness. The Christian, in my view, is a member of a large corrupt organization aimed at bullshitting the masses and keeping them passive. As Marx once said, "Religion is the opiate of the oppressed masses."

With that having been said, Glen Beck is a perfect example. He talks all that Christian shit but is a leading racist on America's radio airwaves. He is out to maintain the façade of Christianity with concepts such as those that follow:

> Beck also argued America is moving away from its Christian underpinnings, causing myriad moral and social problems nationwide. I honestly don t know what else to do, he said. "We have got to be a people of principles. We are a Christian nation.Are we really? Beck asked. "Then why are we in so much trouble? Why do we have the same kind of problems that non-Christian nations do with pornography and drugs and everything else? .(Hensch, 2016).

He is answering his own question. This nation is in trouble because it continues to believe that Christianity is some major religion that will solve all problems. Christianity is a scam represented by the cross and a myth about a guy being hung on it; Islam is a scam represented by a crescent and their mythology is equally ludicrous. Both are totally anti-female. And yet assholes like Beck continue to act as if Christianity is some kind of ideal that will solve all problems. No: Christianity is a key part of the problem, and as far as black people are concerned, it is going to prove to be the undoing of our race.

Continuing with Beck:

> We should be setting an example if we're actually living our
> Christian faith. The problem is we all say we re living our
> Christian faith [and] we re not living our Christian faith. Beck
> additionally vowed he would challenge any religion or
> denomination he believes is ignoring its own guiding principles.
> .(Hensch, 2016).

Who does this peckerwood think he is? In fact, the way he's acting – pontificating and bloviating about what he thinks is right and how he will take on anyone who deviates – that is what a dictator of any belief system believes. He fired a woman from his radio station who expressed anti-abortion views; so in other words the Christian belief is more important than the First Amendment. Not only that, but he was dating Nia Malika Henderson, a CNN host and she's black: what does he think about interracial marriage? He talks about black people like dogs but I guess he doesn't mind it when it's a black woman. This is vintage thinking of the slave master.

The dogmatic dickhead continues his rant:

> I'll take on the Jews, and I'll take on the Lutherans, and I ll take on
> the Catholics, and I ll take on the Mormons, he said. "I'll take them
> all on. You re damn right. Where are you? You're not living your
> principles. We ve got to shore these things up, added Beck, who
> backs Sen. Ted Cruz (R-Texas) and his GOP presidential
> campaign. "Somehow or the other, our side didn.t catch the memo.
> .(Hensch, 2016).

Ted Cruz? That crazy muthafucka is hated even by his own people in Congress! Beck has a cult following of Christian rednecks and these are the same ones that follow Cruz, a sellout Cuban (similar to Marco Rubio). Trump is a mentally sick individual who white people elected so that he could challenge black people and others who were constantly begging for the rights that they were supposed to have by birth. In Beck's world, Trump is not going far enough. Check it out for yourself:

> Beck has emerged as a vocal critic of Trump, arguing that the GOP front-runner does not represent conservative values. Cruz, meanwhile, has repeatedly asserted he is the only Republican contender who can keep Trump from securing their party s presidential nomination .(Hensch, 2016).

Beck has his hands full with a lawsuit where he castigated a female employee that he fired and now he's in the courts. In April of 2017 Beck went after Trump for "misdirecting" the American public and promising everything to everybody – points that most people, especially black people, already knew. Beck is as two-faced as Trump and is no religious scholar. He's an exploiter of American stupidity and there is a lot of it out there. Trump is not a Christian, but he has his own religion, one that is rooted in everything that makes Trump the center of the universe.

Donald Trump: The Art of The Deal

Donald Trump did not write *The Art of the Deal*. Some Jew named Tom Schwartz did, a Jew who turned on Trump in July of 2016 and had a lot to say about Trump after he "followed Trump around" for a year to write a major article/book on him. I read the book and got bored after the first 40 pages where all he does is boast about how many businessmen he "negotiated with." Most of those men, judging from their surnames, were Jews.

The white majority understands and lives on lies. Outright lies of various kinds: the lies within the vows of what they call "holy matrimony," the lies they commit every day in their interpersonal relationships, the lies inherent in their revisionist and "whitenized" versions of their history, the lies they tell about their "discoveries" which are really thefts from other peoples, and the lies they get caught in and then "apologize "for, and the lies that their leading businessmen and corporate leaders tell in order t bilk the American public out of trillions of dollars, examples well documented on the TV show, "American Greed." And the list goes on and on.

As it relates specifically to the book The Art of the Deal, I remember when I first made the decision to read it. I had to put it down after the first fifty or so pages

[Type text]

because all the writer was doing was dropping the names of the Jews who Trump associated with, borrowed money from or entered business with. After a while, it gets tedious.

But now in 2016, more than a decade after I read the book and came to my initial conclusion that this dumb fuck didn't write the book, here comes the Jew who did actually write it, and he was pissed. After making his money (Jews never "come clean" until after they've made money, as in the case of Bernie Madoff and many others), he decides to expose Trump in a July 19, 2016 article that appeared in the *Los Angeles Times* by Robin Abcarian under the headline, " 'I Put Lipstick on a Pig,' Says Trump's 'Art of the Deal' Ghostwriter, Breaking a Decades-Long Silence."

Following are excerpts from, and my analysis of, that article from *the Los Angeles Times* (which originally appeared in the *New York Times* on the same day, by Robin Abcarian:

> Days before Donald Trump accepts the Republican nomination for president, the New Yorker has published a regret-laden interview with the ghostwriter of his best-selling 1987 memoir, "The Art of the Deal."Tony Schwartz, writes Jane Mayer, was a respected magazine writer when he made a conscious decision to sell out (his phrase) and write a book that made him rich but robbed him of his integrity along the way. (Abcarian, 2016)

While no big fan of Donald Trump, this Jew who served as the ghostwriter of the *Art of the Deal* appears to have betrayed Trump's trust. If Trump is so good at cutting deals, then there must have been a contract somewhere. And if there was, then Schwartz, who claims he was robbed of his integrity as he wrote the book, is nevertheless of breach of contract.

According to one source,

> Schwartz spent 18 months with Trump, much of that time eavesdropping (with Trump's permission) on phone calls, both personal and professional. The resulting portrait, he now says, was skewed and dishonest. "I put lipstick on a pig," Schwartz told Mayer. "I feel a deep sense of remorse that I contributed to presenting Trump in a way that brought him wider attention and made him more appealing than he is." (Abcarian, 2016).

To eavesdrop on phone calls is already an ethical violation as far as I'm concerned. But having seen Trump in action many years after I read *The Art of the*

Deal, I realize that such actions are small potatoes when compared and contrasted with the travesties that this man has heaped upon black and white citizens. Even the ones who voted for him will, I predict, begin to feel like complete assholes as, each day, he gives them one more reason to feel betrayed. Good. Now white people know how these "negroes" who go around marching, protesting, sponsoring prayer vigils and otherwise kowtowing to the system, have grown to feel.

Back to the article on The *Art of the Deal*:

> Among the revelations:
> Trump asked Schwartz to ghostwrite "The Art of the Deal" after
> Schwartz published a negative profile of him in New York
> magazine in 1985. Trump loved the piece. (Abcarian, 2016).

Trump acts like a sassy who used to be a bully in the schoolyard. But then someone comes along who doesn't accept the bullying and he (the sassy) gets his ass kicked. Immediately following that humiliation, the sassy goes out of his way to become "pals" with the new kid who just stomped his ass. But never fear: in vintage bitch-like pique, Trump would end up insulting Schwartz during the Republican presidential run. Schwartz, in vintage Jew-like manner, backstabbed Trump and broke the confidentiality agreement and now all of America knows that Trump can't write worth a shit and basically took credit for someone else's work product.

But even before that, Trump was on the "payback" trail:

> Trump denies that Schwartz wrote the book, even though Schwartz
> received half the advance and has received half the royalties,
> millions of dollars. "Tony was very good. He was the co-author,"
> Trump told Mayer. "He didn't write the book. I wrote the book. I
> wrote the book. It was my book. And it was a No. 1 best-seller, and
> one of the best-selling business books of all time. Some say it was
> the best-selling business book ever." (Mayer said that was untrue.)
> (Abcarian, 2016).

More lies. So the white male prototype has not changed his spots. He takes credit for things he did not do and when things he tries to do don't work, he denies ever having done them. Read American history: it is replete with examples of white "leaders" doing this time and time again. Why then, are people so "shocked" or "appalled" when Donald Trump pulls one of his childish pranks, engages in rants and conniption fits, and, to put it bluntly, makes a complete ass out of himself in front of tens of millions of people?

[Type text]

How do you explain it? According to the article,

> Schwartz created a term that Trump loved — "truthful hyperbole" — to describe Trump's relationship to the truth. Schwartz now disavows the phrase. "'Truthful hyperbole' is a contradiction in terms," he told Mayer. "It's a way of saying, 'It's a lie but who cares?'" "I created a character more winning than Trump actually is," Schwartz said, telling the New Yorker he omitted a number of unflattering incidents and details because the book was aimed at making Trump "the hero of every chapter." (Abcarian, 2016).

Since that time the updated term, courtesy of Trump lackey Kellyanne Connolly, is "alternative facts." But it really doesn't matter what you call it. The psychologists have a more fitting term for people like Trump and how they continue to contort basic facts. It's called *reality denial.*

Trump's on-going megalomania can obviously be seen as a product of "the hero syndrome." He wasn't one in real life, spoiled by mama and daddy, probably got his ass kicked on more than a few occasions, so he uses his money to promote a façade of bravado, courage and machismo when, in reality, the opposite may well be the case. To reiterate my earlier comments on the REAL Donald Trump:

> Far from being a self-made man, Trump was supported by his father, who successfully lobbied New York City officials for a large tax abatement that they had denied the son, which allowed Trump to build the Grand Hyatt Hotel next to Grand Central. His father also co-signed many of the required contracts, which was not disclosed in "The Art of the Deal." (Abcarian, 2016).

As a black man, I am but one of hundreds of thousands who have known white boys like this. They're spoiled and their parents have convinced them that they (the children) are invincible. They grow up and attend private schools. But if they get into college and they want to "hang out," the first place they head is to find out more about "the negroes." The women end up getting screwed and the keys to their cars taken, and the young men – like Trump – end up getting into fist fights and learning "the art of the right cross."

So he's a daddy's boy who thinks he's something special. How is he different from most other white boys? Imagine their disappointment when forced busing introduced them to black boys who were their athletic superiors? The kid whose daddy financed the football team (which is why the kid was the starting quarterback or point guard) had to "understand" that the key was winning and these white teams couldn't win without the bruthas! This applies to high school reality and collegiate level situations.

There are two ways to lie: through "commission" (outright telling of a falsehood) and through "omission" (leaving out key points so that your description sounds more valid. As you can see, the "art of the deal," in the hands of Donald Trump, involves BOTH of these. And again, this is an American business and corporate tendency and method of operation. And again, Trump is no exception; he is the rule.

More background on the Trumpster:

> "The Art of the Deal" said that Trump's father was born in New Jersey to Swedish parents; he was born in the Bronx to German parents. (And this, notes Mayer, was long before Trump spread falsehoods about President Obama's origins.) (Abcarian, 2016).

It doesn't matter where he was born. He's white. It doesn't matter if Vladimir Putin is the leader of Russia and Trump now leads America. They are both white men and therefore suffer from the same fears of "colored men" that they all suffer from. They all have deep-seated feelings of inadequacy which they use political power to cover up. It's very simple. The white ethnics came over here and immediately knew that when they saw someone with dark skin, the key was to administer hatred and vitriol. That applies to all of them, from the Slavs, Italians and Irish, to the Jews. And their culture even programmed many of the Asian races to hate black people as well. It's not about "ethnicity"; it's about RACE.

Trump lied about the book like he lies about almost everything else. His wives know this to be true, which is why they never say anything. The two who divorced him are being paid really well and the one he has now is a glorified slut (read: model) who has to stand by while, each day, her husband makes an ass out of himself. Not only that, but his questionable "touchy-feely" relationship with his daughter Ivanka also brings to the fore another dimension of his questionable behavior (can you say "incest"?).

Continuing:

> Schwartz, who still received royalties from the book, said he plans to pledge all 2016 proceeds of the book to the National Immigration Law Center, Human Rights Watch, the Center for Victims of Torture, the National Immigration Forum and the Tahirih Justice Center. "I like the idea that the more copies that 'The Art of the Deal' sells, the more money I can donate to people whose rights Trump seeks to abridge." (Abcarian, 2016).

[Type text]

And "abridge" them he has. He's violated human rights, he's advocated for torture, he's banned immigrants and seeks to deport even more and "justice" is the last thing that Trump cares about.

He's no exception. When a grown-ass man has dyed hair that has to be combed by other people every morning, when he sports a sun tan and is grossly overweight while calling other people names, you know something is not quite right in his mind. These are all decisions that have to be made about one's physical appearance. And if looking like Donald Trump is the best you can come up with, and his posing and primping is the best he can do while totally making an ass out of himself on the dance floor – then something is frightfully wrong.

Finally, Abcarian (2016) offers the following:

> When Mayer called Trump for a comment, Trump dismissed
> Schwartz: "He's probably just doing it for the publicity. Wow.
> That's great disloyalty, because I made Tony rich."

And so it goes. The Art of the Deal is akin to the "deal" that these white people made with the Natives of this country just before they murdered and relocated them. It is akin to the "deal" that these white men made when they bartered for and kidnapped millions of Africans to enslave and work the Southern part of this country. It is a kin to what the natives call "the Trail of Broken Treaties," and have coined the phrase, "The white man speaks with forked tongue." The Latinos fared no better. Entire eugenics laws were proposed and passed by these white men, banning Chinese and castigating the Japanese. And in the latter case, don't forget the two atomic bombs dropped on Hiroshima and Nagasaki.

And so it goes. More evidence follows.

Donald Trump: Physical Appearance and Statements

Black people have a way of seeing through white people's fakery in many instances. Many of us can, for instance, look at someone and pick up "racist vibes" if that person is fronting. This is based on centuries of interacting with them, having to kowtow to them, having to take their orders, and seeing how low they can be behind closed doors and in public when the public is not watching. Just looking at how they acted in public around each other – manhunts, lynching bees, slave auctions and the like – is a further testimony to their doggishness.

Donald Trump is a white male prototype in many ways, and was and remains one of those types of white boys: he even smells of duplicity, graft and manipulative tendencies. And his looks are just the tip of the iceberg, but a tip that must be explored before we get into "the essence of the man," as it were.

In February of 2016, Marco Rubio, a GOP presidential hopeful, decided to turn the tables on Trump and began returning the insults that Trump has been leveling at all of his Republican opponents. Rubio, out of character, went below the belt and in doing so, brought out the racism of Trump's supporters after forgetting that he (Rubio) was not white but a Cuban-American, born of immigrants. He would soon learn the error of his ways.

At one point he made a comment about how small Trump's hands were. He told the audience, "You know what women say about men who have small hands," implying that Trump also had a small dick. Trump responded with a direct retort claiming, "Believe me, I have no problem in that area." This exchange reveals something about both Rubio and Trump: both men are dickless and both have a homoerotic obsession with one another.

Then, on February 27, 2016, the *New York Daily News* carried a story by Meg Wagner under the headline, Marco Rubio mocks Donald Trump's 'spray tan': 'He should sue whoever did that to his face.' Here is what the article said:

> Orange you glad Marco Rubio loosened up? The GOP presidential
> hopeful poked fun of rival Donald Trump and the boisterous
> billionaire's orange-y glow with some catty quips at a Saturday
> rally. "Donald Trump likes to sue people; he should sue whoever
> did that to his face," the Florida senator wisecracked, after saying
> Trump has the "worst spray tan in America. (Wagner, 2016)..

Although what Rubio said was somewhat accurate, this again shows that Trump is the white male prototype. These white men help to make the sun tan industry a multi-billion dollar business. They want color in their skin because they believe it to be a sign of health. This, coming from a group of people who refer to people with natural skin color by every negative name in the book: Chink, Jap, Spic, Towel head, Nigger, Red stick and so on. But again, he can get away with it with nary a criticism from other white people because many of them suffer from the same craving for "a tan." And all the white, they risk various forms of skin cancer in order to obtain one, either with a lamp or by natural sunlight.

Then there is the issue of makeup for the white male, which Rubio also pointed out but something that Dr. Frances Cress Welsing mentioned a long time ago in her original "Cress Theory of Color Confrontation and Racism" (May 1974, Black Scholar magazine). She wrote:

> Whites' desire to have colored skin can be observed at the very first signs of spring or summer when they begin to strip off their clothes (as many pieces as the law will allow), often permitting their skins to be burned severely in an attempt to add some color to their pale bodies and rendering themselves vulnerable to skin cancer in the process. Most cosmetics are also an attempt to add color to white skin. *Such coloring makeup is provided for the white male as well as female.* And finally, untold millions are spent annually on chemicals that are advertised as being able to increase the tanning potential of whites (Welsing, 1991: pp. 5-6 – emphasis added).

Again, Trump is a prototype and there are millions more like him. Observe the use of "makeup":

> "Rubio was speaking to a crowd in Kennesaw, Ga., when he pulled out a cellphone. "You guys wanna have a little fun today?" he asked as he pulled up Trump's Twitter account."So here's the one tweet he put out, he put out a picture of me having makeup put on me at the debate," Rubio said. "Which is amazing me to me, that the guy with the worst spray tan in America is attacking me for putting on makeup." (Wagner, 2016).

Spray tan for a white man with dyed bleach blonde hair. Sounds rather effeminate, doesn't it? And yet he bloviates and bombastically sells woof tickets all over the world as if it is HE who is going to fight and inflict damage. Only his fellow politicos and cowardly people of color fall prey to this facade.

> Sen. Marco Rubio on Friday unleashed a series of personal attacks against Republican front runner Donald Trump, ratcheting up the aggressive new approach to campaigning that he unveiled during Thursday night's debate.Speaking to an outdoor rally in Dallas, Texas, the Florida senator ridiculed Trump, suggesting he wet his pants during the debate. (Condon, 2016).

If this is true then Trump does have some serious physical problems. He's over 70 years of age and has a schedule that wears down most presidents. And yet he has enough energy to insult black people, immigrants, Mexicans and women.

His hate is the engine that drives his life – as is the case with most white men, whether they have power or not. Rubio continues:

> "Let me tell you something: Last night in the debate during one of the breaks... he went backstage, he was having a meltdown," Rubio said. "First, he had this little makeup thing applying, like makeup around his mustache, because he had one of those sweat mustaches. Then he asked for a full-length mirror. I don't know why... Maybe to make sure his pants weren't wet. I don't know." (Condon, 2016).

In my view there is no way that he and Melania sleep together. She has the look of a well-heeled prostitute and exudes confidence; he is an overweight white man with a plethora of hang-ups, some of them pointed out above by Sen. Marco Rubio – much to his chagrin. Rubio should also be remembered for other wise cracks me hade about Trump's physicality, jokes he later apologized for:

> By Wednesday, Rubio himself said publicly on MSNBC that he's "not entirely proud" of slinging personal insults about Trump's tan, his hair and the size of his hands — which set off Trump's racy comment about his anatomy. Rubio said his own children were "embarrassed" by his actions. In a town hall with MSNBC, Rubio says he knows the attacks are "not what we want from our next president." (Kellman, 2016).

And so it goes with these white men. They have to be taught how to dress, what to wear, what tie goes with what suit, which shoes match and so on. Trump, with all his money and the fact that he designs clothing, is no different than the typical white man who has power: he expects people to do everything for him and flatter him no matter what he wears or how he looks. And America is filled with chumps, male and female, who are more than willing to do it.

Trump Implies He Has a Large Penis

It is my contention that all of this craving for money and power that Donald Trump has displayed are actions to compensate for the fact that he has a small dick. I believe that when he talks about all the women he's bedded, he may not be lying, but he is omitting a key point: he's paying for it. And that money buys the silence of these women who know that Trump is a limp-dicked asshole who does more talking than he does performing.

[Type text]

He's been divorced from women who actually look like prostitutes.First there was Ivana, who he was married to for 15 years (1977-1992), then Marla Maples for six years (1993-1999) and most recently to the mannequin looking model Melania, who he married in 2005. More likely than not he and Melania do not get along, do not sleep together and appear very cold and distant to each other in public. In other words, he ain't getting' any. He's seventy years old and the only exercise you see him even remotely involved in his "golf." Only the white man would consider hitting a white ball into a little black hole an athletic competition. The fact is, the golf course is one place where whites can get away from blacks, where most of their plans are made and they can also rest in their lily-white "members only" club houses and golf properties can be found.

Only in white culture could these facts be overlooked. In a society that is so obsessed with sex and virility, when the topic of sex is avoided this way, that means that the media is keeping it "under wraps" on purpose. Every time Barack held Michelle's hand it was a news event; every slow dance or him crooning to his wife was something to write about. Their two daughters were the subject of a number of articles about "family." The media may be afraid to delve into these facts when they come to Trump and his sexuality, but the facts speak for themselves. More than that, some of his own defensive comments that were raised during the Republican Presidential debates during March of 2016 show someone who has a schoolboy-like deep-seated feeling on inadequacy when it comes to his dick.

Resnick (2016) pointed out the debate between Trump and Marco Rubio during the debates, when Rubio decided to take the low road and crack on the size of Trump's hands. Following is the March 3, 2016 story and my analysis of it

According to the article by Resnick,

> Donald Trump, an adult man running to lead the United States of
> America, bragged about the size of his genitalia on the debate stage
> on Thursday night. The trouble started when Marco Rubio joked
> about the size of Donald Trump's hands, an insult that—as any
> 6th-grade prepubescent boy could tell you—is a veiled reference to
> the supposed size of a man's penis. And it is an unwritten law of
> American politics that no man who can become the president of
> this country can have a small member. (Resnick, 2016).

That hands to penis connection, or rumors associated with it, are legion and they were started by the white man. During slavery he would measure the size of black men's hands and their genitals. This was not how he arrived at the conclusion because he already believed it: since the hands were different sizes and noses came in different sizes and cranial capacity differed, then the penis must be an indicator of something. In the white man's "biggest is best" culture, there is no way that he was going to be able to justify the teenie-weenie as a mark of machismo!

And it is clear that Trump believes it as well. Any man who spends that much time dying his hair and his skin is someone who is very self conscious. Have you ever seen him without a suit jacket or without his shirt tucked in? His ties extend far past his waist which could be another example of his trying to hide his penis, could it not. When you hear Donald Trump have the nerve to call someone else a liar, then it is clear that his gall has no limits. Therefore remarks about "little Marco" – which is how he referred to Rubio – could be a clear cut example of transference ("I have a little one so I'm going to say that my opponent has a little one").

Moving on:

> "He is really not that much of a lightweight," Trump said,
> retreating from his favorite adjective used to describe "Little
> Marco." "And as far as—and I have to say this, I have to say this.
> He hit my hands. Nobody has ever hit my hands. I have never
> heard of this. Look at those hands. Are they small hands?"
> (Resnick, 2016)

Can you see how childish Trump is? If you want to look at something in order to get an indicator of how great Trump is in the bed, simply look at the face of Melania Trump. She is always statue-like and looks like she hasn't had an orgasm in decades. They don't even sleep together most of the time. Trump uses his international travel and schedule to justify being away from her. And on the plane even if they do sleep in the same room, it doesn't mean that they're in the same bed. And even if they're in the same bed it doesn't mean that they're having sex. In fact, that may be an "arrangement" that the two of them have after Baron was born. Who knows? What we do now is that Trump has homoerotic tendencies and judges other men (except for Vladimir Putin) by their size – another reason why he is obsessively jealous and envious of former President Barack Obama.

But the dick discussion was a long way from being over. Again, Resnick:

> Trump then lifted his bronzed mitts for the whole world to see,
> hoping that men would be shocked and women would faint at their
> mere size. His hands are in fact stubby little monstrosities and the

[Type text]

truth is that he's quite sensitive about them. In 1988, *Spy Magazine* called him a "Short-Fingered Vulgarian," which Trump interpreted as a threat to his masculinity. As recently as 2015, the sallow spray-tanned plum would send letters to the original author of said amazing phrase, including an image of his circled hand with these words written in gold Sharpie: "See, not so short!" (Resnick, 2016).

What you just read is a clear-cut example of bitch-like pique. But it is also apparent that the writer of the insult may have issues as well – as did Marco Rubio. You have never heard a black man insult another black men's "stubby fingers" or "short fingers." We don't see things that way. It is assumed that we all have penises and what we do behind closed doors is our business. Not only that, but like heterosexual men should do, we stand back and let the women decide how we rate in size and in performance. That is why once we piss them off (women), the first thing they attack is out genitalia, both physically and verbally.

Keep in mind that the world is watching this man. The "size of the dick" ethic has already been circulated all over the globe, largely due to the white man's deep-seated feelings of inadequacy. At any rate, this didn't stop the President of the United States from playing kindergarten games with his commentary on dick size:

But on Thursday night, Trump took his defense a step further— because implying that one's penis is of adequate size is not enough to be president. You have to go out there and shout it loudly from the hilltops. "And he referred to my hands, if they are small, something else must be small." Then he overtly talked about his dick on national television. Stone-faced, Trump looked into the camera and let the world know the truth. (Resnick, 2016)/

Women have known this for centuries. A guy who goes around talking about his dick usually can't back it up. And that's how you can tell: by the response of the female, not by going around talking about it. The height of a man is no indicator – look at the pro athletes whose women screw around behind their backs: do you think that has anything to do with length or performance? It's how you make her feel before you get her into the bed that adds to the activity inside of the bed. If she trusts you with her body, that's half the battle right there.

Look at what Trump said in front of millions:

[Type text]

"I guarantee you there's no problem, I guarantee you," Trump cooed, smug and proud like a bully after a swirlie. His campaign has not responded to a request for comment about the size of his manhood. So it would seem that not only is Trump a liar, a bigot, a misogynist, and a greedy power-hungry manipulator. He also has a fragile masculinity as well. (Resnick, 2016)

Any time I've heard Trump say, "Trust me," "Believe me," "I promise" or in this case, "I guarantee," I know that the words he is about to say are lies. This guy is pathological and he doesn't care. When caught in a lie he simply ignores the fact that he told it. I deal with this fact in another section of the book. But the point here is that the size of man's penis was created and circulated by none other than the white man. His own hang-ups are his worst enemies. Trump suffers from this malady and in vintage homoerotic fashion, imposes it on those around him.

Donald Trump Mental Appearance and Statements

Over time, hundreds of people have asked me or wanted my views on the mental state of Donald Trump. I tell them that he is like any other white man with power. The only difference that may exist is that he is too involved with promoting himself to understand what other white men understand: cover up what you really are and pretend to be the kind of person that American citizens will view as just "another guy."

An article by Gersh Kuntzman of the *New York Daily News* was titled, "President Trump Exhibits Classic Signs of Mental Illness, Including 'Malignant Narcissism,' Shrinks Say. As black people we have been around white people so long that it has gotten to a point where we know them better than they know themselves. We can see right through their various facades, but pretend not to so that we can curry favor. But the fact still remains that black folks can oftentimes just look at a white person and tell what kind of character he or she has.

But in this case, let's take the word of the professionals. The article that I am quoting from is one that contains some important information for those reading this book and it is my duty, as a master teacher, to impart knowledge wherever possible. My views will filter in and out, but the main thing is to provide a record about Trump as a white male prototype, not as the "exception" that he and so many others are trying to make him out to be. View it like this: most men, black and white, who get power may have a cold; Trump, on the other hand, has pneumonia.

With that having been shared, let's get to the article that appeared in the January 29, 2017 edition of the *New York Daily News*.

[Type text]

> *The time has come to say it: there is something psychologically*
> *wrong with the President.* The fuzzy outlines of President Trump's
> likely mental illness came into sharper focus this week: in two
> interviews with major networks, he revealed paranoia and
> delusion; he quadruple-downed on his fabrication that millions of
> people voted illegally, which demonstrated he is disconnected
> from reality itself; his petulant trade war with Mexico reveals that
> he values self-image even over national interest; his fixation with
> inaugural crowd size reveals a childish need for attention.
> (Kuntzman, 2017 – emphasis added).

As of February of 2017, increasing numbers of psychiatrists and psychologists are coming forward, in fact teaming up, to make their views public. They are not violating doctor-patient privilege because first of all Trump is not a patient. But even if he were, such a "violation" would be justified in the name of the public good. This racist bastard Trump has access to the nuclear codes! He is not only thin-skinned but he's also paranoid; he thinks everybody is out to 'get him," and that is the kind of mindset that could easily send somebody off in a warlike snit.

Moving on:

> Partisans have been warning about Trump's craziness for months,
> but rhetoric from political opponents is easily dismissed; it's the
> water of the very swamp the President says he wants to drain.
> (Kuntzman, 2017).

White people and black people observe things and people differently. As black people we knew that Trump was a racist and to those of us who are scholars, it is clear that racism is a mental disease. But during those debates it became clear that Trump was in a world of his own. The answers to questions were not only avoided, but he was able to skirt the questions as well. He intimidated every one of the 16 other Republican presidential candidates and indeed, was able to get them to focus all the attention on him. It was as if the people around him were afraid to say what most people could see: Trump was a fuckin' nut.

> But frightened by the President's hubris, narcissism, defensiveness,
> belief in untrue things, conspiratorial reflexiveness and attacks on
> opponents, mental health professionals are finally speaking out.
> The goal is not merely to define the Madness of King Donald, but
> to warn the public where it will inevitably lead. (Kuntzman, 2017).

[Type text]

It is clear where such madness is going to lead if you just read history. There are two general tendencies: that which rises and comes into power and that which crumbles into dust. America is headed for the latter, and would have arrived there eventually even without the rise of Trump. But Trump, because of his mental problems, is going to make the end come all that quicker. He is going to piss off the wrong dictator, say the wrong thing at the wrong time, and the country is going to experience a major catastrophe that will make the attacks on the twin towers look like the Macy's Thanksgiving Parade.

Moving on:

> "Narcissism impairs his ability to see reality," said Dr. Julie Futrell, a clinical psychologist, who, of course, added a standard disclaimer because she has never actually treated Trump. "So you can't use logic to persuade someone like that. Three million women marching? Doesn't move him. Advisers point out that a policy choice didn't work? He won't care. The maintenance of self-identity is the organizing principle of life for those who fall toward the pathological end of the narcissistic spectrum." (Kuntzman, 2017).

I disagree with Dr. Futrell when she says that narcissism impairs Trumps ability to see reality. Narcissism is the love of self in spite of others and in that context, I think that he sees the only reality that he gives a shit about: his own! Based on that, all other things take shape. The reason why you can't use logic to persuade someone like that is because your reality doesn't jibe with his universe. This is somewhat different from the take that is offered above. It's not that he can't see reality: it's that he can't see any reality other than his own and therefore he CAN see other realities but they are inferior to his and therefore, in his mind, deficient.

Continuing:

> A little background: Shrinks don't typically analyze public figures. The reticence dates back to 1964, during Barry Goldwater's run for President. Then, like now, many shrinks believed that the candidate was psychologically damaged — but unlike now, many diagnosed him for a Fact magazine special issue titled, "The Unconscious of a Conservative: A Special Issue on the Mind of Barry Goldwater." (Kuntzman, 2017).

The only reason these white people suspected Goldwater was because he was making nuclear threats as they related to Russia. That is when these cowards

[Type text]

said that he must be a nut and began labeling him. This is nothing like Trump: Trump simply lies because the truth doesn't fit into his universe. He wants reality to fit into his model of reality so he can look like numero uno, the greatest, the top dog, the head honcho. He wants to be all things to his race members and doesn't care about any other people who are not white, In fact, he really doesn't give a shit about his wife Melania – she's just there so that there won't be suspicions about Trump's sexual preferences – and there well should be.

White folks protect one another – even people like Barry Goldwater. They provide them with rationale, reasoning, explanations and excuses and the media uses these kinds of people as fodder for their front page news stories. Kuntzman (2017) writes,

> The headline itself — "1,189 Psychiatrists say Goldwater is
> Psychologically Unfit to be President!" — prompted the American
> Psychiatric Association to issue the so-called "Goldwater Rule": "It
> is unethical for a psychiatrist to offer a professional opinion unless
> he or she has conducted an examination" of the patient in question.
> (Kuntzman, 2017).

One need not be a doctor to know that if someone is coughing or wheezing that this is one individual who is sick. Trump's "symptoms" are along these same lines: pathological lying, grandiosity, narcissism, taking credit for the work of others, on-going insults of people who challenge him. And he is only a small part of the problem that America is facing: the people who support this guy are the ones who need their asses kicked. But black people do the same thing with these so-called "ministers" and "preachers." So on both sides we see the Messiah Complex in full operation and the American people falling for it as they collectively fiendishly search for "leadership."

When white folks are pointing their fingers, then you know something is wrong because as a race they are the most duplicitous and scandalous group on earth, and that includes their psychologists and psychiatrists. Though this be the case, check out the following:

> As a result, shrinks are the only professionals who are not allowed
> to offer their expertise to journalists trying to explain complicated
> issues to the public. Indeed, scientists can tell us about global
> warming, engineers can tell us if a bridge is about to give way, and
> soldiers can tell us if an enemy is weak or strong. But the mental
> health of the President? The experts are handcuffed, even as we
> elected the most paranoid President since Nixon and, clearly, the

most self-deluded and dangerous American political figure since
Aaron Burr. (Kuntzman, 2017).

Kuntzman claims that when it comes to the mental health of the president, "the experts are handcuffed." No they're not. They're white, and as the saying teaches us, "white doesn't represent a color, it represents a mentality that is anti-black." These people may fight but brothers will still be brothers. They know a nut when they see one because Trump is not the first, as this book clearly shows. He is just more identifiable and visible and that is what is pissing off the white supremacists: they agree with him but they just don't like his tactics.

It's easy for people like Kuntzman to therefore conclude that Trump is, "the most self-deluded and dangerous American political figure since Aaron Burr." Not if you ask black people and then look at what has been done to black communities all over the nation by white leadership over the centuries. With legal approval and presidential knowledge, we have had black communities bombed and destroyed, black men lynched, murdered and arrested en masse, black women raped and black children mis-educated and harassed by the tens of thousands. When it comes to "self-delusion" and being "dangerous" the white man reigns without rival.

Continuing with the analysis of Trump's mental state by Kuntzman:

> Not anymore. For the past few weeks, psychologists have been speaking out, arguing that their professional integrity, and patriotism, can't be silenced. The latest? A top psychotherapist affiliated with the esteemed Johns Hopkins University Medical School said Trump "is dangerously mentally ill and temperamentally incapable of being president." (Kuntzman, 2017).

Where were these psychologists been all this time? White men, in general, have issues. And as this book shows, anyone who strives to run for the top job in the world has some kind of "god complex," and that includes Lenora Fulani and other women, from Hillary Clinton to Jill Stein, as well. This "special kind of person" who would strive to have a job with the world at their fingers is someone who has to be assessed and evaluated. The only difference between the other presidents and Trump is that he just doesn't give a damn what people think. The others adapted to protocols, procedures and practices where their actions and words gave them a "pass" to get past the watchful eyes of the pundits and the public.

Continuing:

[Type text]

The expert, John D. Gartner, went on to diagnose Trump with "malignant narcissism." Gartner has joined a growing chorus of experts who are so concerned about the president that they are willing to face the wrath of their professional organizations' gag rules. (Kuntzman, 2017).

These white men like Gartner are Johnny-come-latelys. Why don't they diagnose white people and assess that apparently global phenomenon that is known as white supremacy? Why wait until a man is vying for the top job in the land and in doing so, makes his racism known, when it is clear that ALL white people share this affliction? Remember the quote that I shared earlier? I wrote, "White doesn't represent a color, it represents a mentality that is anti-black." I liken it to police officers who claim that there are "good cops and bad cops." I have to say that they are all bad until the ones who are good snitch on and expose the ones who are supposedly "bad." If they don't then as far as I'm concerned they're all in it together.

This philosophy extends to white people in general. These psychologists who are concerned about Trump and his "malignant narcissism" should take a look at the genera behaviors and attitudes of their race. Look at the movies being made and the news articles being written. The underlying assumption is that the only people who count as human beings are white folks. They can't just come out and say it the way they used to day in the old days, but it is definitely an implied image.

Trump's mental appearance had a lot of people worried:

In an earlier effort just after the election, thousands of shrinks joined a new group called "Citizen Therapists Against Trumpism," which quickly released a "Public Manifesto" to warn America about its leader's apparent psychosis. "We cannot remain silent as we witness the rise of an American form of fascism," the manifesto states. (Kuntzman, 2017).

Where were these assholes a century ago when white men were running amok lynching black people? Where were they when the laws of the country that they live in justified racial and residential segregation? Where were they when the laws of Virginia said a black man and a white woman could not be married? Nowhere to be found. But now that a white man, who has done the same things that other white men have done (as proven in this book) has become more visible and refused to hide behind the veil of "political sophistication" and "protocol," here come these therapists pointing their pink fingers at Trump when, in fact,

[Type text]

fascism has been creeping up and engulfing American politics for the past century and a half!

Their evidence of Trump's "issues" are behaviors that affect every single white person who has any semblance of power in this country. As black people we have all worked for them, sat in meetings with them, and watched them fire our fellow bruthas and sistahs on a whim. At any rate, check it out:

> The psychological warning signs? "Scapegoating ..., degrading, ridiculing, and demeaning rivals and critics, fostering a cult of the Strong Man who appeals to fear and anger, promises to solve our problems if we just trust in him, reinvents history and has little concern for truth (and) sees no need for rational persuasion." (Kuntzman, 2017).

I just finished an essay called, "Blame It on the Niggers" where I document case after case of white men and women pointing their fingers are black people, both real and imagined, as "culprits" in crimes that they, the whites actually committed. Therefore scapegoating is not unique to trump, and these white therapists know it – that's how the concept got coined! It came from Jews in Israel casting blame on an innocent goat and then sending it into the forest to relieve them (the Jews) of their guilt.

Degrading, ridiculing and demeaning rivals? What' s unique about that? That's why I titled this book the way I did: Trump is a "white male prototype," not an exception! Even the sick individuals he ran against during the Republican campaign were doing it: Marco Rubio talking about Trump's little dick, Ted Cruz talking about Trump being a "pathological liar," and it went on down the line. This is what these white boys do: they insult each other and then turn around and, as in the case of Congress, refer to their colleague that they just demeaned as "my good friend." So you can add "hypocrisy" to the list.

As for promising to "solve our problems if we just trust in him," how can that be unique to Trump. These lying as white people have, on their currency, the phrase, "In God We Trust." Who do you think they're talking about? Not some entity in the skies. The white man has always viewed his religion as an extension of his own power. So when he says, "In God we trust," what he means is "we trust our fellow whites."

Reinvents history? This is the white man's greatest salvation. He takes what black people did and takes credit for it. He claims to have created things that he was taught by other people. He continues to lie and take the henchman from his history and turn them into hagiographical heroes. His movies continue to "re-do" the images of the worst among his people. Again, this is vintage Anglo behavior, so how is Trump any different?

And finally, the allegation that Trump "has little concern for truth (and) sees no need for rational persuasion." That is how this country was built! Look at the words of their own pledge of allegiance. Here, I'll show it to you:

"I pledge allegiance to the Flag of the United States of America, and to the Republic for which it stands, one Nation under God, indivisible, with liberty and justice for all."

Now what was that about showing no concern for the truth? How can you show allegiance to a flag and then claim that it stands for one nation under God when the very nature and essence of America is about gender, racial, ethnic and various other forms of "division." How can you pledge allegiance to a flag that supposedly represents liberty and justice for all when, up until 1954, the law of the land was "separate but equal" and when at one time there were laws like the "Fugitive Slave Codes" and "The Dred Scott Decision (of 1857)?

And these are just a few examples not only of little concern for the truth, but also the fact that since these lies have persisted for centuries it is clear that the people in power (whites) have "seen no need for rational persuasion." These bullshit beliefs are IMPOSED through their religion, educational system and cultural ethos!

Trump's mental appearance is as deceptive as the words of the Pledge of Allegiance. He has fake skin color based on an orange sun tan, bleached blonde hair, and those are not only physical statements – they are mental as well. These kinds of actions emphasize an "Aryan" aesthetic and that goes directly to one's ideological viewpoint. What grown man would bleach his hair unless he was making a statement about his politics? What grown man would continue to wear a tan but show an obvious hatred for people of color unless he had some kind of mental mission that he wanted to manifest behaviorally and physically?

As the Last Poets said in their 1973 poem, "Hands Off":

What manner of man is this, I ask? Who roams the seven seas
Who graces the skies of birds of iron and wanders where he please
Who walks into another's home and takes his properly
Then slays the man, his wife and child in the name of liberty
What manner of beast is this I ask who drops a napalm from the skies
Then send my sons away to war to maim and kill and die
What manner of man is this I ask, who arrogantly displays his might
What manner of man is this, my friend, needless to say he's white

[Type text]

Or in this case, "orange." And the mentality behind the appearance is in perfect harmony with the warped physicality.

Donald Trump: Liar Personified

Earlier I briefly mentioned Trump's chronic lying and the fact that when caught in a lie, he simply ignores it as if it never happened. According to the New York Times Fact Checker of September 3, 2017, "In 227 days, President Trump has 1,114false and misleading claims" (New York Times, 2017). And by October 10, 2017, that number had increased. According to Ari Melber of MSNBC's "The Beat," Trump had made 1,318 false or misleading claims over 263 days in office, about five lies per day.

Only a white man could get away with such a spate of prevarications and outright mendacity. Again, Trump is not alone – he is a prototype because all Presidents' have told lies. But Trump's border on the incredulous, akin to a dream that some child would have. Following are but a few examples.

Again, there is no doubt in my mind that most politicians are liars. As someone with a Master's degree in Political Science, I intentionally focused on the Presidency and in fact, wrote a 200-plus page paper analyzing the inaugural speeches of every President. In retrospect it was clear that all of them were lying through their teeth.

It sickens me to continually hear people talk about how much Donald Trump lies, as if he is the exception to the rule. He is the rule. It's just that his lies are so outlandish they border on pathology. Carl Bernstein, who helped expose the Watergate scandal and Richard Nixon would agree:

> Carl Bernstein, whose reporting broke open the Watergate scandal that led to former President Nixon's resignation, said Sunday that Nixon's lies were nothing compared to Trump …"Trump lives and thrives in a fact-free environment. No president, including Richard Nixon, has been so ignorant of fact and disdains fact in the way this president-elect does," (Hellman, 2016).

This then, sets the stage for what you are about to read. Ever since his election, the major media has been very cautious about and careful not to call Trump an outright "liar." They would use statements like "discarded the facts," or "false facts" and the like. Trump aide Kellyanne Conway even coined the statement "alternative facts" and then went on to explain how logical such facts really were. She continue to lie almost as much as Trump, so it was clear that dismissing the truth was an ideology or philosophy that Trump not only used but also endorsed.

On June 26, 2017, "Hardball With Chris Matthews" documented the lies that Trump has told since taking office. According to their news report, courtesy of the New York Times, said there were one hundred "demonstrably false claims" made by President Trump. Every day for he first forty days since his presidency he has said something untrue, the report said. Singer said that lies were a part of Trump's style and doesn't care if what he says is true or not.

Lies about the murder rate, the number of people at the inauguration, the Times said that Trump was trying to create a climate where reality is irrelevant. Paul Singer of USA Today said that his followers voted for the person with the right MOOD, not the right FACTS.

And Sargent explains,

> New York Times Executive Editor Dean Baquet has come closer
> to getting this right, pointing out that we must label Trump's lies as
> such because he has shown a willingness to go beyond the "normal
> sort of obfuscation that politicians traffic in." Writer Masha Gessen
> has gone even further, suggesting that Trump's approach to
> information — or disinformation — looks like a hallmark of
> Putinesque autocratic rule, in which the autocrat is trying to "assert
> power over truth itself," and convey the message that his "power
> lies in being able to say what he wants." (Sargent, 2017).

The lies that Trump tells are only a small part of the problem. The larger part, as I see it, is that the voice of the white supremacist system that we all live in and under is too spineless to call him the "liar" that he is. They pussyfoot around the on-going prevarications and perversions of reality and then use those lies as the basis of the next day's news reports so that they can sell newspapers or gain ratings points. As the saying teaches us, "Dress a liar as you will; a liar is a liar, still.'"

Continuing with the authoritarian allegation of Trump's lying mentality, the article adds,

> We don't yet know if this will prove an accurate description of
> Trump's approach as President. But given the authoritarian
> tendencies we've already seen from Trump, it seems like we
> should at least be on guard for this possibility. Baker's

nonchalance suggests a lack of preparedness for what we may be facing. (Sargent, 2017).

This is just the way it is. A white man, spoiled as a youth, grows up discrimination against black people as he builds hotels on other people's sweat, plasters his name (his "brand") all over them, has a Jew named Schwartz write a book called *The Art of the Deal* which he (Trump) claims that HE wrote, and the stage is set for a megalomaniac with a God complex becoming president of the gullible United States.

We all know that Trump is a pathological liar and it is clear that he doesn't care who knows it. There have been several news accounts from people who said that he has bragged about being able to lie. But according to Sargent (2017), there is another take on Trump's lying ways:

> This gets at why Baker's response is so worrying: It suggests an unwillingness or an inability to entertain the possibility that we may be looking at something new and different here. Take the example that Baker himself chose: Trump's claim that "thousands and thousands" of American Muslims celebrated 9/11. This was not some casual falsehood — this lie was key to a months-long campaign of vilification and scapegoating of Muslims that in turn was central to his broader appeal. (Sargent, 2017).

To begin with, we have to look at the origins. Trump was a spoiled white boy from a rich white family that lived in a sterile environment devoid of any people of color other than perhaps an occasional yard worker or a domestic. This kind of spoiled child approach paves the way for a mentality where a child grows up getting away with every and anything. Within this kind of psychologically distorted situation, lying is not really lying: it's just that your truth is the only reality that counts and everything else be damned

In light of this Trump, as an adult, isn't "scapegoating" Muslims because that would imply that he knew that his lies were deliberate. No, he truly believes what he said and his racism and hate runs so deep that he actually believed that Muslims were celebrating. Remember the poem, "The Night Before Christmas" where "visions of sugarplums danced" in the heads of little kids? That is Donald Trump. Even the Bible says something about, "as a man thinketh, so is he." Put another way, racist is as racist does.

If we can accept what I've just written, then the following passage makes sense in a different (and more realistic) way:

> In this and many other instances, Trump barely even tried to make
> a fact-based case for his version of reality. Rather, he seemed to be
> trying to obliterate any possibility of shared agreement on what
> constitutes an authoritative source, and even on reality itself.
> (Sargent, 2017).

And this is the man who ran through sixteen other Republican candidates who were far more trained in lying than he was, although on a more sophisticated level. Trump simply doesn't give a damn about the world of reality because he has his own reality. And this is what is going to make his Presidency the most deadly in the history of this country. Oh, not because of his decision making or incessant denials of reality; but because there are millions of people in this country who believe everything this sick man has to say. And therein lies the real danger.

Moving on:

> Take Trump's biggest lie of all — his racist birther claim. Trump
> himself originally conceived of it as a means of entree into the
> political consciousness of GOP primary voters. It was debunked
> countless times over many years. Yet Trump kept his birther
> campaign going all throughout anyway. (Sargent, 2017).

For those of you who don't know or can't remember, the "birther" claim was where Trump said that Barack Obama was not born in America, but was born in Kenya. He then sent claims to have sent private eyes to search out the truth and then claims that he found the evidence. But there was no evidence – just more Trump-sized lies. He never apologized for it but just went on about his business as if nothing ever took place. Then after being sworn in and he was seated next to Barack Obama, he shook hands and then told the media that Obama "was a good man" and that's how it all ended.

The article by Sargent ends with as dubious a conclusion which jibes with its rather shaky contents:

> If we don't call that "lying," or if we don't squarely and
> prominently label these claims as "false," don't we risk enabling
> Trump's apparent efforts to obliterate the possibility of agreement
> on shared reality? We're already seeing a preview of how this will
> work in practice when Trump is president ... (Sargent, 2017)

And now the lies are at work and the news media is falling right into Trump's trap by making the lie-telling the story instead of going directly to the source and airing television specials and mini-documentaries on "The Lying Ways

[Type text]

of Donald Trump." Former president Thomas Jefferson, a liar himself, once said in a letter to Peter Carr on August 19, 1785, that, "He who permits himself to tell a lie once, finds it much easier to do it a second and third time, till at length it becomes habitual; *he tells lies without attending to it, and truths without the world's believing him.* This falsehood of the tongue leads to that of the heart, and in time depraves all its good dispositions." (Notable Quotes, 2017 – emphasis added).

Sargent concludes with examples of Trumps prevarications:

> On multiple occasions, Trump has dubiously claimed credit for jobs he has supposedly "saved," and the headlines have tended to reflect his claims without also informing readers that those claims are unverified or open to doubt. People don't always take the time to learn the details. Even when they do, if news orgs don't take a clear stand on what is true and what isn't, confusion can often follow. (Sargent, 2017).

Here's what I think: Trump is a white man and like any white man who has to succeed a black man in any capacity, comparisons are going to be made. There are the general comparisons of who has the biggest dick, who can talk to women and get them in bed the fastest, who has the greatest leaping ability or who is the fastest. The white man loses all of these.

But then there are the Trump types who come into a position where his predecessor, Barack Obama, was beloved by so many people. A man who was articulate, well read, and had a wife that looked like a model and has a law degree. Obama, who also had a law degree, also saved the country during its economic decline. Trump comes in because when all is said and done, Obama was a black man in a racist country and white folks could never forget that. So they turned on Obama and his doctrine and then tried to undo it through the introduction and establishment of its opposite: "Make America great again," implying that Obama took away from previous greatness. More lies.

Being insecure, spoiled and jealous, what you see and hear from Trump is a defense mechanism. He had lied and claimed that Obama was not born in America and after becoming president, he continued the lie and then also falsely claimed that Obama had Trump Tower "wiretapped." This is the behavior of jealous, bitch-like men; akin to the woman who fears her man is seeing someone else so she cuts up his clothes or puts bleach all over his shoes. White women do worse things: they take their men to court and take half his shit.

Be that as it may, Trump lies because he wants to be seen as a "big man." He is not a big man except in girth. He doesn't even sleep with Melania and, in fact, I believe he has slept with (read: fucked) his daughter Ivanka. This is a man with serious issues and the lies will continue to fly at the American public for as long as he remains dickless.

And that means *forever*....

With that having been said, let's check out a few lies that Trump has told in the following areas: Lies about charity, Falsified identity (pretending to be a public relations agent calling the media to talk about Trump's incredible sex life), The "Loyalty Pledge" to the Republican Party, Campaign promises reneged upon with emphasis on two examples, and the lies he's told before Congress.

<u>Lies About Donations to Charity</u>

In March of 2017, Trump got caught in yet another lie. He claimed that his $400,000 a year salary would not be "donated to charity." Without naming the charity, this declaration is a contradiction to his "I will not accept a salary" pledge that he made while running for the office. But not accepting a salary, that implied that the $400,000 would go into the Federal budget and cut into the deficit. But by claiming now that he is going to donate it to charity, he is going to cost the people more money. How? Because he gets the salary and then by donating it to charity, he will take a tax write off of some $150,000. So now not only does he collect the check for the $400,000 but he also gets paid for the tax write-off. T he total: a whopping $550,000 per year.

Going back a few months, another lie was told and documented in an article that appeared in the June 28, 2016 issue of the *Chicago Tribune* documented some of the lies that Trump has told, how he claimed to be donating money to charity. But according to the article, these were all outright lies. Following is the documented trail of those lies and my views and retrospective analysis of those lies. It begins:

> In May, under pressure from the news media, Donald Trump made
> good on a pledge he made four months earlier: He gave $1 million
> to a nonprofit group helping veterans' families. Before that,
> however, when was the last time that Trump gave any of his own
> money to a charity? (Fahrenthold, 2016).

This donation was very late and came only after the media hounded him about his exploitation of his veterans pledges. In other words, he was forced to make the donation. This then prompted the writer of the article to assume the following:

> If Trump stands by his promises, such donations should be occurring all the time. In the past 15 years, Trump has promised to donate earnings from a wide variety of his money-making enterprises: "The Apprentice." Trump Vodka. Trump University. A book. Another book. If he honored all those pledges, Trump's gifts to charity would have topped $8.5 million. (Fahrenthold, 2016).

Trump's lies have no end and he has no bottom when it comes to telling them. He's not giving anything to charity and he knows it. Just like when he said he wasn't going to take a salary but instead was going to donate his $400,000 a year pay for being President to charity. Not taking a salary and donating it are two different things. He can write off the tax donation and still end up making money. If he refused the salary the government would benefit by having $400,000 extra dollars in the kitty to help cut the deficit.

Moving on:

> But in that time, public records show, Trump donated about $2.8 million -- less than a third of the pledged figure -- through a foundation set up to give his money away. And there is no evidence that Trump has given to his foundation lately: The last record of any gift from him to his foundation was in 2008. (Fahrenthold, 2016).

How are you going to donate to your own foundation? This sounds like the same scam that Warren Buffett and his sister Doris Buffett are running: fake as if you are a philanthropy while all you are really doing is "investing" and taking a tax write off.

And the bare-faced lies continue:

> Trump and his staff are adamant that he has given away millions privately, off the foundation's books. Trump won't release his tax returns, which would confirm such gifts, and his staff won't supply details. "There's no way for you to know or understand," Trump spokeswoman Hope Hicks told BuzzFeed recently. Hicks did not respond to repeated questions about Trump's charity from The Washington Post, which has had its press credentials banned from Trump's public events. (Fahrenthold, 2016).

Trump's staff, wherever he goes, are trained liars in the same way he is. They will say whatever needs to be said to protect their master … oops! I mean "their boss." Hope Hicks and then later Kellyanne Connolly and Sean Spicer – all flunkies who will stare directly into the camera and lie their asses off – just to explain or rationalize yet another lie by Trump. When you are a multi-millionaire and you lie about how much you contribute to charity, this may well be considered to be an all-time low.

Donald Trump has always been a leech and a liar. He shares similar traits with Warren Buffett and Bill Gates. They talk about how much they "give" but as Buffett has said publicly, he doesn't "make contributions" he "makes investments." Moving on;

> One of the clearest cases of Trump not making good on a promise to give to charity is Trump University, the real estate seminar business that has spawned lawsuits in New York and California alleging widespread fraud. Trump made at least $5 million from Trump University, according to the New York state attorney general. But Trump's lawyers say that none of it went to charity because it was used for legal fees. (Fahrenthold, 2016).

Trump settled the lawsuit and the white media has been relatively quiet about the scam that he ran on people. But he is the rule, not the exceptions. Just pay close attention to all of those "proprietary schools" (also known as "for profit schools") that pop up: DeVry, Vatterott, ITT Tech, Kaplan College and so on. You see their commercials, most of them aimed at laying a serious guilty trip on people who dropped out of or never attended college and giving off the image that they represent "that second chance."

Many have closed down in recent times. In addition to Omaha's own Wright Career College, there was also Trump University, Briarcliff College, Le Cordon Bleu, ITT Tech, the Technology Institute of Milwaukee (which I personally closed down in 1990) and Everett College, to name but a few. Taking people's money, most of whom borrow student loans, is what people like Trump do. As you can see, he was not the first and in all likelihood, will not be the last.

Giving to charities is a façade. According to Fahrenthold (2016),

> Of the 167 charities reviewed by The Post, 39 declined to comment. Another 40 -- including the Eric Trump Foundation -- did not respond to The Post's inquiries. Another 77 charities had no record of receiving a personal donation from Trump.That left just 11 which acknowledged receiving the kind of personal donation

that the Trump claims to be giving all the time. The most recent of those was the gift to the Police Athletic League in 2009. (Fahrenthold, 2016).

Donald Trump is what white America wants to be represented by. He is what they are. And this is one more example of him being no "exception," but indeed, a "prototype."

Falsified Identity

To show how devilishly sick Trump is and the trails of "super-lies" that he has left behind, he even has a fake identity – or at least he did before he became President and now has people like Sean Spicer, White House Press Secretary and Communications Director and Kellyanne Connelly, Counselor to the President, to do his lying for him.

In May of 2016 an interesting story about another "personality" was printed in the Washington Post. The title of the article was, "The Daily Trail: Donald Trump finds out his past isn't over. It isn't even past." Check out what the writer, Rebecca Sinderbrand, shared with the public and about how cowardly and silly Trump is as his lies and deceptions continue to pile up.

Trump's sick lies and schizophrenia were discussed in an article, "The Daily Trail: Donald Trump Finds Out His Past Isn't Over. It isn't Even Past." Check it out:

> **MILLER TIME:** Donald Trump has said that as president, he would surround himself with the very best people. In prior positions, his leadership approach seems to have been a bit more...hands-on. "The voice is instantly familiar; the tone, confident, even cocky; the cadence, distinctly Trumpian," report Marc Fisher and Will Hobson. "The man on the phone vigorously defending Donald Trump says he's a media spokesman named John Miller, but then he says, 'I'm sort of new here,' and 'I'm somebody that he knows and I think somebody that he trusts and likes' and even 'I'm going to do this a little, part-time, and then, yeah, go on with my life.' (Sinderbrand, 2016).

So this sick bastard plays games to support himself. How is this any different from a system where every institution kisses the ass of a race and a culture that has the kind of track record that white folks have? It's not just fake phone calls; it's fake social media, fake newspapers filled with lies about how great they are, films that depict them as infallible and invincible and so on. But the story about this "Miller" impersonation by Trump goes much deeper:

> "A recording obtained by The Washington Post captures what New York reporters and editors who covered Trump's early career experienced in the 1970s, '80s and '90s: calls from Trump's Manhattan office that resulted in conversations with 'John Miller' or 'John Barron' — public-relations men who sound precisely like Trump himself — who indeed are Trump, masquerading as an unusually helpful and boastful advocate for himself, according to the journalists and several of Trump's top aides." (Sinderbrand, 2016).

What a strange coincidence that one of the people is named "John Barron" and Trump has a young son with Melania who is named "Barron." At any rate,

> "Some reporters found the calls from Miller or Barron disturbing or even creepy; others thought they were just examples of Trump being playful. Today, as the presumptive Republican nominee for president faces questions about his attitudes toward women, what stands out to some who received those calls is Trump's characterization of women who he portrayed as drawn to him sexually. (Sinderbrand, 2016).

Being playful? This is the sign of a sick asshole. And yet this is what these white people voted into office and that's why to this day he can make comments about anything he wants and quite literally get away with them. And since most white men are cowards, they like to "throw the rock and hide the hand," as the saying goes. Check it out:

> Then, **Friday afternoon, Washington Post reporters who were 44 minutes into a phone interview with Trump about his finances asked him a question about Miller: "Did you ever employ someone named John Miller as a spokesperson? The phone went silent, then dead.** When the reporters called back and reached Trump's secretary, she said, "I heard you got disconnected. He can't take the call now. I don't know what happened." (Sinderbrand, 2016: emphasis original).

A game player and a coward. A child. That's what Donald Trump was before he even ran for President and as you can see almost every night on the news, he continues his reckless ways. In my view he IS America – he is no exception to the rule. He IS the rule. The sooner these white people and these house negroes stop acting as if he is "hurting the nation," the better off things will be. He is doing what others have talked about and also done, but only they had the brains to do it undercover or behind closed doors.

The Loyalty Pledge to Republicans

This is the same man who claims that standing for the Pledge of Allegiance and the National Anthem should be mandatory. But what about the "pledges" he's made? How can you expect a pathological liar to take a pledge that he would keep and honor? The Republicans knew how duplicitous and perfidious Donald Trump was. In vintage psychologically damaged manner, he "projected" his lying ways off on Ted Cruz by nicknaming him "Lyin' Ted."

Although Trump eventually took it (long after the fact) and signed it in September of 2015, joining the other 16 Republican candidates who had already signed it. Trump's hesitancy should have been a warning for the voters of America, but millions gave him their vote despite his plethora of screw-ups. But remember: he took the pledge and signed it – that doesn't mean that he would keep it. As the old saying teaches us, "Dress a liar as you will, a liar is a liar, still."

An article in the April 3, 2016 edition of Time magazine by Zeke Miller pretty much spells out what happened:

> Donald Trump's reversal on a pledge to support the eventual Republican nominee could have consequences, Republican National Committee chairman Reince Priebus said Sunday. In appearances on all five Sunday news shows, Priebus sought to reassure Republicans that the party is preparing for the likelihood of a contested convention, while rebutting criticism of the arcane delegate selection rules leveled by the front-runner. (Miller, 2016).

Trump is not only bitch-like but also very much like a spoiled child. If he cannot get his way, then he takes his ball or his marbles, packs up and then goes home. This is the kind of behavior that you read about being displayed above. Here is a man refusing to take the loyalty oath because at that time, he was afraid he was going to lose. When it later became clear he might win, then he took the oath. This is the kind of man who makes racist remarks and allegations, gets lambasted for doing so, gets caught in lie after lie and then just turns around and walks away without nary an apology.

Another childish tactic is the attempt to change the rules of the game if things aren't going your way. As one article documented it,

> Trump has called the system "unfair" and has said he should be
> awarded the nomination even if he falls short of the 1,237
> delegates—a majority—required to win the nomination at the
> party's convention in Cleveland in July. (Miller, 2016).

This is the man who won the Presidency of the United States, and then people have the nerve to act shocked when he immediately began nominating the caliber of people that he nominated – fellow wealthy individuals who, like Trump, also acted like spoiled bitches in their management of corporations and as a result, had no regard whatsoever for the conditions of the masses of people.

Trump as White Male Prototype: Race

One of the reasons for the Russian sabotage of the 2016 election was, according to pundits, was to exaggerate and exploit and then take advantage of the racial and class divides with American society. There is no doubt in the mind of this writer that this is one mission that was surely accomplished.

Most recently Trump got involved in the issue of police shootings of blacks. A protest was launched by Colin Kaepernick and he kneeled rather than stood, when the National Anthem was played. This set off a major protest with white people, mainly Jews who own the stadiums, running scared. Trump got involved and here is what he said:

> Donald Trump launched a sensational attack on NFL players who
> have kneeled in protest of the national anthem during a speech in
> Alabama on Friday night, challenging the league's owners to
> release anyone who engages in the movement started last year by
> former San Francisco 49ers quarterback Colin Kaepernick.
> "Wouldn't you love to see one of these NFL owners, when
> somebody disrespects our flag, to say, 'Get that son of a bitch off
> the field right now. Out! He's fired. He's fired!'" the president said
> at a rally for Republican senator Luther Strange, who is running in
> a special election next week to remain in the seat vacated by
> attorney general Jeff Sessions (Graham, 2017).

And he repeated the slur after that, referring to those protesting (99% of them were) black as "those sons of bitches." Now these black men allowed this white asshole to call their mothers "bitches" in front of the entire world. Trump's hatred of black people is well known, but it is especially clear that he hates black women.

Other than his concubine Omarosa Manigault, he has no concerns about black women or black families. That may be why when four soldiers were killed in Niger while on a mission, the issue of race came up with the media and others totally avoided. But it was clear to me what the issue was.

Three of the soldiers were white boys. Their bodies were found and there was no problem. But the media wants us to believe that the fourth soldier, a black man by the name of La David Johnson (a fucked up name in and of itself) wasn't with the group and wasn't found until two days later. And when he was found his monitoring system was on so there was no reason why he could not have been located.

Here's what I think happened.

These four men had been out there in the jungles of Niger for weeks with no problem. But Trump decided with withdraw the Americans from the area and when he did, Isis got the word and went in, guns blazing. The soldiers got caught in a firefight and got their asses kicked. But how did the lone black soldier get left behind? Why did they find the white boys but the black soldier wasn't found until two days later? Now here is where Trump and his hatred of black women comes to the fore.

Now we find out that the black man's body was found nearly a mile from the Niger ambush, according to Barbara Starr of CNN. On a strictly racial basis, how is it that the white boys were together but the lone black man was found a mile away and was so mutilated that he had to have a closed casket funeral?

During a press conference Trump was in the middle of telling a lie about president's who contacted the families of slain soldiers. Because he's a borderline fag he had to bring up Obama and claim that Obama never did it. After he got caught in the lie he then was confronted with why he hadn't contacted the families of the four slain soldiers. And being the asshole that he is, he managed to mess that up as well. Check it out:

> President Trump showed obvious "disrespect" during a condolence call to the family of an Army sergeant killed during an ambush, the soldier's mother said Wednesday. Trump defiantly denied accounts that he told the family of Sgt. La David Johnson, <u>one of four Americans killed</u> nearly two weeks ago in Niger, that "he knew what he signed up for... but when it happens it hurts anyway."
> (Cullen & Slattery, 2017)

[Type text]

Trump wouldn't say that to a white woman, but then why expect him to? His own wife hates his damn guts and you can tell by the way she looks at him that she'd cut off his scrotum if she ever got half the chance. Be that as it may, the wife of Johnson was not the only sistah he insulted. He also insulted Johnson's mother, who overheard the comments and a member of Congress who was Johnson's mentor and had been a long-time friend of the family:

> Despite the protestations of the President, Johnson's mother,
> Cowanda Jones-Johnson, said Wednesday that Trump called as she
> and her son's widow, Myeshia, drove to Miami International
> Airport to meet her son's body. "I was in the car and I heard the
> full conversation," Jones-Johnson told The Associated Press.
> "Not only did he disrespect my son," but he disrespected his wife
> and me and my husband, she said. (Cullen & Slattery, 2017)

To add insult to racist injury, on October 21, 2017 – the day of the funeral for La David Johnson – Trump was tweeting on that very morning more insults aimed at Congresswoman Wilson, referring to her as "wacky." This makes three direct racial insults aimed at black women – calling black athletes "sons of bitches," insulting the wife of La David Johnson and then hurling insults at a black Congresswoman.

This is all about race, but it's been going on for centuries. The only difference is that Trump is too dumb to care about any future repercussions of his actions. He's surrounded by negroes like Dr. Ben Carson and Paris Dennard who are as spineless as they come and he doesn't fight his own battles anyway. The controversy continued as a diversion to get the public's attention off of Trump's ties to Russia and Vladimir Putin.

> The back and forth came amid new revelations of how Trump has
> and hasn't dealt with families of the fallen — in one instance
> promising a grieving father a $25,000 personal check and in other
> instances having no contact at all. It was also reported that Trump
> had surprised his chief of staff John Kelly when he defended his
> actions by referring to Kelly's dead son. Jones-Johnson's account
> backs up what Rep. Frederica Wilson (D- Fla.) said a day earlier of
> Trump's insensitive comments. The President stayed on the
> defensive, **calling Wilson a liar and later insisting that she
> should recant her claim.**(Cullen & Slattery, 2017 – emphasis
> added)

He literally calls black women bitches and he's calling three more liars. The powerlessness of black people should be clearly seen since not one muthafucka who claims to be a "leader" has had the guts to walk up to Trump and hit him in his god damn jaw.

But don't get it twisted: Donald Trump is the typical "American" meaning that he is racist. In America, to be racist has been elevated to the level of a sacred norm using several dupes that the public continues to fall for. One of those lies is being a hypocrite.

In regard to the most powerful man in the land, Trump once had different views of Barack Obama:

> In February 2009, he praised President Obama's efforts to cap the bonuses of Wall Street executives from companies that were being bailed out by the government, in a post titled "Obama is Absolutely Right." (Singer, 2016).

So he was praising Obama in 2009 and then again in 2016 when he (Trump) was elected, telling the media that Obama was "a good man." But this two-faced bastard turned around and in March of 2017 was claiming that Obama had wiretapped Trump tower during the election between him and Hillary! That's a felony charge! When asked for proof, Trump dogged the media and ran like a little bitch.

But it's much deeper than just a spoiled white man like Donald Trump, which is what I am trying to teach in this book.

In addition to being two-faced and dodging responsibility for what one says is does another white supremacist trick. *It is the use of the term "white supremacist" itself.* White men, all of whom are racists, use this term to define their fellow whites who subscribe to the more visible and overt manifestations of racism or who belong to organizations that do. These white men point to the Ku Klux Klan, the White Citizens Councils, the Aryan Brotherhood, the Nazi Party as "white supremacist organizations." This is aimed at duping the public into thinking that the majority of whites, who do not belong to these groups, could not possibly be white supremacists.

But they are wrong.

Karenga (1967) once wrote that, "White doesn't represent a color, it represents a mentality that is anti-black." I say that whites in America are racist because not only to they hate and fear black people, but they also have an unjustified feeling of superiority. Furthermore, the ones who claim not to be racist stand by and watch those who do discriminate to go about their business. So, like the cop who knows his colleague brutalizes black people but says nothing (and is therefore just as bad as the perpetrator), white people stand as a unit as racists, pure and simple.

Trump is of this ilk, and there are an abundance of examples. Racial tensions exploding, or so said the white media. I will present the news story from the Washington Post (with m y commentary filtering throughout) and you can be the judge. Sometimes the tension was because of what Trump stood for or said. Some of the tension was not directly about race, but when you have large groups of white people together and you hear the terms "conservative" and "Republican," then you know that race-hatred is right around the corner.

For example, the headline of the March 12, 2016 article on the *Washington Post* website was, " 'Get 'em Out!': Racial Tensions Explode at Donald Trump's Rallies." It begins, thusly:

> Violence at Trump rallies is nothing new
> ST. LOUIS — Protesters and supporters of Donald Trump clashed in sometimes-violent fashion here and in Chicago on Friday, the latest in an escalating series of confrontations that have come to define the front-runner's rowdy campaign rallies even as he gets closer to securing the Republican nomination. In the evening in Chicago, Trump canceled a rally at the University of Illinois at Chicago after brawls broke out at the event site. (DelReal, 2016).

Trump, like most wealthy white men, is afraid of black people. Like most wealthy white men they will parade around for photo opportunities with black celebrities and athletes, but they fear the black masses. Trump is not alone in this fear. White people know the dirt they've done and they anticipate that black people will be seeking payback. Unfortunately, they over-estimate the courage and vengeance factor of the black masses, most of whom have been pacified by negro ministers, interracial advertising featuring half-naked white women, and the threats of losing their menial jobs if they dare to attack,

As Trump's crowds got bigger, he became brasher because those crowds were white. Chicago, on the other hand, had a lot of black people who were holdovers from the black nationalist thinking of the 1960s, and Trump knew it. He saw all the hell and heartache that black people were giving to Mayor Rahm Emanuel, and he read the stats about all the shootings that were taking place all over the city, shootings that would become a part of his "inner cities" speeches in the days ahead.

[Type text]

As a result and combination of what I have just described, DelReal (2016) writes that, "Trump's camp issued a statement saying that "for the safety of all the tens of thousands of people that have gathered in and around the arena, tonight's rally will be postponed to another date. Thank you very much for your attendance and please go in peace." Trump could have cared less about the safety of the people in the crowds. When the name "Chicago" came up, all that flashed in this racist's mind was black people. And he knew that like the black people in New York, Philadelphia, Detroit and Los Angeles, Chicago bruthas and sistahs do not play around. So he cut and ran under the umbrella of false bravado

Another city known for resistance is St. Louis. Check out what happened there:

> Inside the Peabody Opera House in St. Louis earlier in the day, protesters interrupted Trump eight times, prompting catcalls and chants from the crowd as security officers removed them. Scores were injured or arrested in clashes between Trump supporters and critics outside the venue, where thousands had gathered in an overflow area to listen to the event over loudspeakers. (DelReal, 2016).

In vintage racist fashion, throw the rock – and hide the hand. People like Trump never learned how to engage in hand to hand combat. If he had any rights at school they were with fellow white boys who were as unskilled as he was. He's all talk and comes off that way. When the subject is race, he has to read his views from a teleprompter screen. Like most white people, he is clueless when it comes to issues involving Blacks or Latinos. And the reason for that is because we don't matter to them unless the subject is sports or music. They continue to play the role of victim in the real world and their movies reflect that mentality. Everybody wants to attack "Earth", meaning white folks. Everybody wants to rape the white woman – meaning black and Latino men. Everybody wants to steal from the white man, meaning everybody in the world.

Trump managed to convince his followers that they, white folks, were the victims. That is why he immediately hired Steve Bannon when he won the presidency. Bannon is a white nationalist and isn't afraid to admit it. All white people are white nationalists but don't want to come clean. But just wait until the Fourth of July – those flag-wavers are promoting and celebrating white supremacy, plain and simple.

On issues of race Trump is clueless and spineless. One of the books that Bannon makes references to in some of his speeches is by Jean Raspail and it titled, The Camp of the Saints. Basically it's a book about people of color invading a white country and taking it over. That is the white man's biggest fear. So in promoting the book they use sugary language. For instance, note the description on the Goodreads website:

> The Camp of the Saints is a 1973 French novel by Jean Raspail. The novel depicts a setting wherein Third World mass immigration to France and the West leads to the destruction of Western civilization. Almost forty years after its initial publication, the novel returned to the bestseller list in 2011.

It's a book about a black takeover, and it is used to provide justification for people like Steve Bannon to "warn" white folks about the impending takeover of America. And remember that Trump placed Bannon on his executive council and listens to Bannon's every word. The fear of black people and the hatred of people of color in general, is at the core of Trump's thinking and actions. With that in mind, let us now continue:

> Trump is known for his massive, raucous rallies — part campaign events, part media spectacles, part populist exaltations for his most loyal supporters. But the events have also become suffused with the kind of hostility and even violence that are unknown to modern presidential campaigns. The candidate himself often seems to wink at, or even encourage, rough treatment of protesters. "Come on, get 'em out, police, please. Let's go!" Trump shouted here on Friday, complaining that protesters could not be removed more quickly because "nobody wants to hurt each other anymore." (DelReal, 2016).

Black men were arrested for such rallies and meetings during the 1960s and 1970s. Among them were Huey P. Newton, H. Rap Brown and James Forman, to name but a few. White boys like Bernie Sanders can stand in front of thousands and shout about "revolution" and talk a lot of what they stole from black radicals, and get away with it. Trump takes advantage of white privilege politically in the same way that he did financially. And since white privilege is a norm, and since the people reporting the news are members of the same race, no serious racial analysis is ever a part of what is taking place. But these Trump rallies, in my book, were nothing short of a prelude to race war.

The Lambasting of Chicago

[Type text]

Let me paraphrase a passage from a poem by the Last Poets:

No, those were not mere verbal slights/
aimed at the Chicago slums/
They were only dress rehearsals/
For insults that are yet to come …

Trump's lack of cultural competency – some would say outright "competency" period, is most evident in his castigating of the city of Chicago and his feigned concern about all the murders that take place in that city. Headlines like, "Trump Threatens to 'Send in the Feds' Because of Chicago 'Carnage'" (ABC News) and "Trump Threatens Federal Intervention in Chicago, Citing 'Carnage'" in the New York Times" were prominent and dominant throughout the media. Evidently hoping to stir up contagion, he compared what was taking place in Chicago with Afghanistan. But this wasn't his first attack on the Windy City.

Recall back in March of 2016 when he was supposed to be having a rally in Chicago as the frontrunner in the Republican race. What happened? He blamed "thugs" for the reason why he canceled it. Following are my views on an article that appeared in USA Today regarding the cancellation.

> Donald Trump, the GOP presidential front-runner, on Saturday blamed "thugs" for his decision to cancel a rally in Chicago over alleged security concerns and said the activists had "totally energized America." (Stanglin & Madhani, 2016).

People like Trump are afraid of black people, in general. The main reason is of course that people like Trump are racists. But as importantly is the fact that these are people who have never had black people in their lives except as servants, employees or flunkies on some level. So because of that "alienated arrangement," there is no need to have respect for black people. And it is out of this racism and blatant lack of respect that statements like the ones Trump has made about Chicago, and the lies that he has told about "walking to the store and getting shot in Chicago", hail from.

In reference to this specific situation where Trump cancelled his rally in the Windy City, the news report noted the following:

> The Chicago Police Department said late Friday that four men and a woman were arrested at the rally after brief scuffles broke out at the event at the University of Illinois at Chicago Pavilion.Police

[Type text]

officials did not detail charges or release names of the individuals
taken into custody. However, CBS News said its reporter, Sopan
Deb, was detained by law enforcement while covering the scene.
(Stanglin & Madhani, 2016).

In Chicago, where I lived for two years (and even attended the University of
Illinois Circle Campus for a course in Public Administration), I know how these
cops think. I've also written a book on cops based on interviews provided by
Loyola professor Connie Fletcher. When my experience and research are combined
there is no doubt in my mind that these cops were in "detain and arrest first" mode
when they approached the protesters and the CBS News reporter. They figure that
once they get down to the station, that is when they will hash everything out.

But the cowardly Trump didn't know this: all he knew is that Chicago was a
big city and that meant that black people would be present. And he was aware of
some of the shots he had taken about the city and its violence. According to
Stanglin & Madhani (2016),

Anthony Guglielmi, a police department spokesman, said the
Trump campaign did not consult the police department before
canceling. "The decision was made by the campaign on its own,"
Guglielmi said. Trump was scheduled to hold rallies Saturday in
Dayton and Cleveland ahead of primary voting in Ohio on
Tuesday.

What we find is that Trump hates black people just like his father did. In
fact, he hates all men of color. The one group that he despises even more than
black men are black women. At any rate Chicago is viewed by many as a black
city and when that is combined with the violence, then Trump can point a finger at
the city, refer to the people at his rallies as "thugs" and then vent on stepping up
the police presence.

For instance, in 2016:

On Twitter, Trump blamed the protesters for Friday's canceled
rally. "The organized group of people, many of them thugs, who
shut down our First Amendment rights in Chicago, have totally
energized America!" he said on Twitter. (Stanglin & Madhani,
2016).

Trump was fanning the flames of racism that were already most evident to
the people who had to deal with discrimination every day. He felt the same way as
the average white man, but was too stupid to keep his feelings locked up the way

[Type text]

most of them do. And once busted for discrimination and paying out millions of dollars, Trump simply dropped the façade and used the "new and improved white nationalist" as his persona and mantra.

What did he have to say to stir things up and in doing so, perpetuate the fear of black people and big city crime in the minds of his fellow rednecks?

This white man has lambasted Chicago time and time again. He talks about all the murders that have taken place – as if he gives a damn about black people. What he wants to do is stereotype and stigmatize that city so that he can scare white people into standing back while he attacks black communities. He wants to "send in the Feds" under the guise of arresting and deporting gang members who are in this country illegally. But that's not the whole story.

Trump's descriptions of "inner cities" are rooted in promoting the fear of black people. He talks about the "carnage" in Chicago and exaggerates that you can't walk down the street without getting shot. The insults are continuing because Trump is an avowed racist of the new order: don't talk about black people in a degrading manner – simply degrade them with your policies and procedures!

An article that appeared in *The Atlantic* (October 12, 2016) under the headline, "No, Most Black People Don't Live in Poverty – or in Inner Cities" offers up some interesting insights that I will use to further make my case against Donald Trump's racist ignorance regarding black people. The article, by Alana Semuels begins:

> In his debates and speeches, Trump implies that African Americans are concentrated in urban cores. They're not.

More lies. And he doesn't care because he has no respect for the American people. Furthermore, he has a grandiose view of his own worth and it borders on the same type of mentality that so many other candidates for president have. Imagine: having all these people believing in something that I stand for! And they're contributing all that money!

But Trump concentrated on Chicago for another reason other than the multitude of murders in the city. Chicago was also President Barack Obama's "adopted home." What better way to take shots at a man who I believe Trump secretly envied, who was black but did so much better in terms of foreign policy, the economy, and health care, and who was beloved when he let office, than to insult the home town of that man? Trump, like most white people (as quiet as it's kept) had a low regard for black people, a low regard for the black communities where black people lived and a racist view of anyone who was not white

Chicago was not spared from Trump's insults:

> During the second presidential debate, Donald Trump was asked
> whether he could be a president to "all the people in the United
> States." He had a very specific answer: "I would be a president for
> all of the people, African Americans, the inner cities," he replied.
> Later in the debate, he spoke again of how he was going to help
> "the African Americans," who lived in "inner cities," suffering
> from high poverty rates, bad educational systems, and no
> jobs.(Semuels, 2016).

The very fact that this white man continues to differentiate between "all of the people" and then "African-Americans" shows that he doesn't see black people as Americans. He doesn't even see black people as human beings because when he talks about "inner cities" he is talking about them as if these areas represent a totally different planet. The "cities" are one thing, but the term "inner cities" implies something different, something separate – something *deficient.*

Trump Derides Mexicans, Native Americans

Donald Trump, in my view, is an avowed racist. Of course I believe that all white people are racist. I've learned that, "no man is more than the context to which he owes his existence. Therefore it is impossible to be born in a racist society and not be racist, either consciously or unconsciously" (Karenga, 1967). It's not even the racism that bugs me: it's the hypocrisy that these cowards display as they live in gated communities, benefit from white privilege and suburban locations, and then talk all that "brotherhood" bullshit.

In this section of the book we look at how Trump displayed his disdain toward two groups of people of color: Mexican-Americans and Native Americans.

<u>Mexican-American Judge, Gonzalo Curiel</u>

Because he's Mexican Donald Trump came to the conclusion that Judge Curiel was somehow not qualified to make a ruling in a case involving fraud lawsuits against Trump for his scam-riddled Trump University. But first came an attack on Susana Martinez:

> Another day, another Donald Trump attack on a Republican: Speaking at a rally in Albuquerque on Tuesday night, Mr. Trump lashed out at New Mexico Gov. Susana Martinez, the chairwoman of the Republican Governors Association who has criticized Mr. Trump's rhetoric about Mexicans … "We have got to get your governor to get going. She's got to do a better job, OK? Your governor has got to do a better job," Mr. Trump said, faulting the state's economy. "She's not doing the job. Hey—maybe I'll run for governor of New Mexico, I'll get this place going." (Heye, 2016).

This is a classic example of paternalistic racism. No one with skin color is ever good enough to do anything, if you are to believe Donald Trump. Because of his deep-seated feelings of inadequacy (just look at the dissatisfied look on the face of his wife Melania) and his color hangups (tanning his skin orange because the natural color is Casper-the-friendly-ghost-colored pale white), he is both jealous and envious of people of color, hence is obsession with former President Barack Obama. At any rate, he continued to lambaste the Latina judge as follows:

> Mrs. Martinez, who supported Marco Rubio in the primaries, was not present. By mid-afternoon Wednesday, much coverage had turned from Mr. Trump's criticism of the GOP governor to his targeting of Democratic Sen. Elizabeth Warren. But there's a message here not just for the anti-Trump crowd: This attack hurts Mr. Trump's efforts to unite the Republican Party and to expand his support outside a core share of Republican primary voters. (Heye, 2016)

Trump wasn't finished. Having already pissed off millions with his allegations of Mexicans being criminals, drug dealers and rapists, on June 1st Trump took off after a Mexican judge. On June 6 when another racist, Newt Gingrich attempted to criticize Trump's attacks, an article appeared in the Washington Post under the headline, "Trump says it's 'inappropriate' for ally Newt Gingrich to criticize his attacks on the 'Mexican' judge."

> Donald Trump lashed out Monday at former House speaker Newt Gingrich — one of his close allies who has been mentioned as a possible running mate — saying that it was "inappropriate" for Gingrich to criticize Republican presidential nominee's recent comments about the ethnicity of a federal judge. (Johnson, 2016).

One racist charging another with being racist. But Trump's on-going tirade was justbeginning. Check it out:

[Type text]

For more than a week, Trump has repeatedly said that U.S. District
Judge Gonzalo Curiel, who is presiding over fraud lawsuits against
his Trump University education business, should recuse himself
because "he's a Mexican." Curiel was born in Indiana to Mexican
immigrant parents, and Trump says his desire to build a wall on the
border with Mexico was in conflict with the judge's ethnic
background. Trump did not back down from that position during
an interview on Fox News early Monday morning, at one point
saying: "All I'm trying to do is figure out why I'm being treated so
unfairly by a judge." (Johnson, 2016).

Trump knew that his university was a piece of shit. He knew it was a scam
from the get-go. He lost his suit and had to pay out more than $25 million.

Gingrich strongly rebuked Trump's comments during an interview
"This is one of the worst mistakes Trump has made, and I think it's
inexcusable," Gingrich said in the interview Sunday. "This judge
was born in Indiana. He is an American, period. When you come
to America, you get to become an American." Gingrich compared
Trump's attack to a liberal attacking Supreme Court Justice
Clarence Thomas on the grounds that he's black. (Johnson, 2016).

There is no comparison because Clarence Thomas is black in skin color
only. He has about as much black consciousness and knowledge of black culture as
a wino has of building a laser gun. Trump's comments were racist because of the
color, culture and consciousness of that judge. Trump – and his pal Newt Gingrich
– are both assholes when all is said and done.

Forcing the Mexicans to Build the Border Wall

To show both his arrogance and his racist perceptions of the Mexican people
on the other side of the border, Donald Trump decided that he was going to build a
wall separating the two countries. He also had the audacity to tell the American
people that he was going to "make Mexico pay for it." He made this statement in
April of 2016 and continued to repeat it. At rallies he'd have thousands of
onlookers changing, "build that wall, build that wall." The anti-immigrant fervor
was in full swing and America's racist was rarely ever more evident.

An article titled, "Trump Would Seek to Block Money Transfers to Force
Mexico to Fund Border Wall," which appeared in the April 5, 2016 edition of The
Washington Post, documents this "plan" along with the goal of ending money
transfers sent from the workers here back to their families in their native Mexico.

Following is that article with my viewers interspersed.

The slave master mentality is alive and well in far too many white Americans. That's why huge numbers immediately bought into the concept of "we're going to build a wall and the Mexicans are going to pay for it." Trump knew what he was catering to: white people who want to use people of color to finance their own oppression. This is a legacy that has been financially lucrative to white folks for centuries. Trump knew full well that the Mexicans weren't going to pay for a wall that would prevent them from coming to a land that was at one time theirs. But white people, being both racist and ignorant of history, bought into it hook-line-and-sinker

As Woodward & Costa (2016) reported it,

> Donald Trump says he will force Mexico to pay for a border wall as president by threatening to cut off the flow of billions of dollars in payments that immigrants send home to the country, an idea that could decimate the Mexican economy and set up an unprecedented showdown between the United States and a key diplomatic ally.(Woodward & Costa, 2016).

The key words are "force Mexico to pay for a border wall." The question should have been, what type of force did he plan on using? This is a white man who is a coward and a milquetoast and is all talk and no action. He is afraid of his own shadow but talks a good game to his "base," which consists of white people who are the descendants of the ones who got their asses kicked when they tried to stop black kids from entering their schools and getting off the buses. Trump has never had a fight in his life, but when he opens his big mouth he's talking about, and convincing the equally cowardly media, that he's "a counter-puncher."

Back to the wall:

> In a two-page memo to The Washington Post, Trump outlined for the first time how he would seek to force Mexico to pay for his 1,000-mile border fence, which Trump has made a cornerstone of his presidential campaign and which has been repeatedly scoffed at by current and former Mexican leaders. (Woodward & Costa, 2016).

If Mexicans scoffed at it, then Trump's continuing claims both then and now means that he doesn't give a damn about what people of color have to say. This is the same approach he used when he referred to protesting black athletes as "sons of bitches." The Trump plan is briefly outlined:

[Type text]

> In the memo, Trump said he would threaten to change a rule under
> the USA Patriot Act antiterrorism law to cut off a portion of the
> funds sent to Mexico through money transfers, commonly known
> as remittances. The threat would be withdrawn if Mexico made "a
> one-time payment of $5-10 billion" to pay for the border wall, he
> wrote. "It's an easy decision for Mexico," Trump said in the
> memo, which was written on campaign stationery emblazoned
> with "TRUMP Make America Great Again." (Woodward & Costa,
> 2016).

As we now know, Trump was all talk. To date (as of October 2017), he has some "sample walls" set up to see which one he prefers. And six months before that date he came clean with the American people and told them that THEY would pay for the wall and then "be reimbursed." When the Mexican president was on the phone reading Trump the riot act, Trump sheepishly begged him not to mention the wall. These are the acts of a hypocrite and a coward.

The Mexican people, like Jews, send the money they earn here in America directly home. And the work they do is work that Americans think they are too good to do, and that is why Mexican labor is so sorely needed. As long as there are crops to be harvested and construction jobs to get done, Mexicans will always find jobs here in the States. But right now, *la familia* comes first:

> Nearly $25 billion was sent home by Mexicans living abroad in
> 2015, mostly in the form of money transfers, according to the
> Mexican central bank. In his memo, Trump said that "the majority
> of that amount comes from illegal aliens."But that figure includes
> cash from around the world, not just the United States. In addition,
> a Government Accountability Office report in January said that it
> is difficult to track how much money illegal Mexican immigrants
> are sending versus those working legally in the United States.
> (Woodward & Costa, 2016).

American greed is going to be this country's undoing. Mexicans know it, the Japanese know it, the Chinese know it, the Indians (in India) know it and the Russians know it. But America refuses to admit it; say the word "revenue stream" and there is some greedy asshole with access to power right here in the States wiling to "make a deal" (as in "the art of the deal").

Disdain for (Colored) Immigrants

Trump cut loose on immigrants as the year 2017 came to an end. Fredericka Whitfield of "CNN Newsroom With Fredericka Whitfield" revealed it on December 23, 2017.

Trump was quoted as saying, in regard to Nigerians: "Once Nigerians come to America, they never want to go back to their huts in Africa." One woman made it clear that Nigerians who come to America are among the most highly educated immigrants with disproportionate numbers having master's degrees or doctorates. The news report made it clear that Trump's travel ban rhetoric was a clear-cut case "where an enraged president fumes about immigrants flooding into the nation." Trump's views were aired at an immigration meeting in June of this year.

But he didn't stop with Nigerians. Trump also made derogatory comments about Haitian immigrants, saying that most of the 15,000 who come to America "arrive here with AIDS."

The article being referenced to on the previously cited CNN broadcast appeared in the New York Times. As reported on by Esquire magazine's Gabrielle Bruney on December 23, 2017, here is what stated:

> Just in time for the holidays, *The New York Times* is reporting that Donald Trump made some horrifically racist statements. The newspaper describes an Oval Office meeting in June which found President Trump infuriated at the number of foreigners who had been allowed into the US since his inauguration … (Bruney, 2017)

Not European immigrants – only immigrants of color. The proof is in the historical pudding. Check out the following

> More than 2,500 were from Afghanistan, a terrorist haven, the president complained. Haiti had sent 15,000 people. They "all have AIDS," he grumbled, according to one person who attended the meeting and another person who was briefed about it by a different person who was there. (Bruney, 2017)

And a more specific reference to the introduction of this section of the book is clear in the following account:

> Forty thousand had come from Nigeria, Mr. Trump added. Once they had seen the United States, they would never "go back to their huts" in Africa, recalled the two officials, who asked for anonymity to discuss a sensitive conversation in the Oval Office. (Bruney, 2017)

[Type text]

Why are racist statements made by Trump somehow "sensitive"? Was he acting in a sensitive way when he made the comments, comments that, by the way, were false?

Instead, the professional liars are brought in to sweep things that Trump says under the proverbial rung:

> White House Press Secretary Sarah Huckabee Sanders of course denied that Trump made the statements, and the president's supporters will likely dismiss them as lies from anonymous sources at the fake-news *New York Times.* But the fact that this *totally* sounds like something Trump <u>would</u> <u>say</u> is horrific enough. Merry Christmas everybody, this is the world we live in. (Bruney, 2017)

Dismissal and denial. That's what liars and cowards do. And that is why Trump's racist statements and his even more racist policies continue on, unabated.

The reason why I make it clear that these are immigrants of color is because I don't hear this peckerwood talking about Canadian, German, English, Scottish, Jewish or any other kind of immigrants who have white skin. When you say the word "immigrant" in America you think of brown skin: Latinos or Middle Easterners. The latter group tries to claim that they are "Indo-Europeans" and try to assimilate, but that dark skin gives them away every time – which is why Trump and his constituents hate their guts.

Trump has a lot of support in the state of Arizona, where racist rednecks treat Latinos and First Nation people like shit. Trump's "Make America Great Again" campaign in the state of Arizona caught fire when Trump included the support for Maricopa County Sheriff Joe Arpaio, who was going around claiming to be "America's Toughest Sheriff." Arpaio and Trump had something in common: hard line stances against immigration.

But this hatred went far beyond the boundaries of Arizona and the quest to lock up and deport Latinos.

For instance, on July 30, 2016, the Washington Post carried an article that addressed the negative comments that Trump once again waged at immigrants of color. The article, titled, "Backlash For Trump After He Lashes Out at the Muslim Parents of a Dead US Soldier," appears below with my commentary:

> Republican Donald Trump lashed out Saturday at two Muslim American parents who lost their son while he served in the U.S. military in Iraq and who appeared at the Democratic National

> Convention last week, stirring outrage among critics who said the episode proves that Trump lacks the compassion and temperament to be president. (DelReal & Gearen, 2016).

When Khan appeared at the Democratic Convention, he pimped the spirit of his dead kid for all he could get. These white people love it when somebody dies for the "red-white-and blue" and even give it a name: "Gold star." These middle easterners were no exception, and Khan showed that he also brought into linguistic racism when he later claimed that Trump has a "black soul." What? So even in the land of the camel jockey they too consider all that is negative or bad as being associated with blackness.

Continuing:

> Asked to comment on the convention speech of Khizr Khan, a Pakistani immigrant whose son, Army Capt. Humayun Khan, died in Iraq in 2004, Trump described Khan as "very emotional" and said he "probably looked like a nice guy to me" - then accused him of being controlled by the Clinton campaign. (DelReal & Gearen, 2016).

Trump, a coward who avoided the draft four times using student deferments, should never comment on someone who actually went into any kind of war-type situation. And yet he did it, and since Khan is a man of color, Trump pulled no punches. In case you haven't noticed, the only skin color that Trump can tolerate is that produced by a sun tan lamp which he sorely abuses on a daily basis. He may hate women even worse. Check out the following:

> "Who wrote that? Did Hillary's scriptwriters write it?" he asked in an interview with ABC. Trump also questioned why Khan's wife, Ghazala, did not speak on stage, despite the fact that she sat for an interview with MSNBC the following day. (DelReal & Gearen, 2016). "His wife, if you look at his wife, she was standing there. She had nothing to say. She probably, maybe she wasn't allowed to have anything to say," he said. "You tell me, but plenty of people have written that. She was extremely quiet and it looked like she had nothing to say." (DelReal & Gearen, 2016).

Trump's got the nerve to talk about a woman who stands next to a man and says nothing? What about that mannequin-looking bitch of his? She stands there, straight-faced, staring straight ahead as if she's under hypnosis. He should never

[Type text]

criticize anybody else's wife, and yet he did it with Ted Cruz when he went after Heidi and he did it to Mika Brzenski of "Morning Joe".

Continuing:

> "Trump's slur against Captain Khan's mother is, even for him, beyond the pale," tweeted John Weaver, a Republican strategist for Ohio Gov. John Kasich. "He has NO redeeming qualities." Matt Mackowiak, another GOP strategist, tweeted: "There is only one response for Trump to the criticism: 'As an American, I deeply appreciate the patriotic sacrifice of the Khan family.'"(DelReal & Gearen, 2016).

"Patriotic sacrifice." These white people put people of color in a damned-if-you-do-damned-if-you-don't situation every time they get the chance. If you use your brain and keep your kid from fighting in a war that white folks started, you catch hell. But when you kid goes over there and fights and comes back, they rip off his benefits. And if the kid goes over there and dies, he's given all kinds of kudos and compliments because he's dead.

The problem with Khan is that he's a middle eastern Uncle Tom. He thinks he's an American just because he was born here. He acts more white than white folks do. For instance,

> With Ghazala by his side on the convention stage last week, Khizr Khan blasted Trump's rhetoric on Muslims and immigrants. Pulling his pocket version of the Constitution from his jacket, he questioned whether Trump has read the document. (DelReal & Gearen, 2016).

The Constitution? Nigga, please! When the Constitution was written people with skin color like Khan were in various stages of servitude! The Constitution didn't apply to black people because the assholes who wrote it owned slaves themselves, and that enslavement was based on race! Reading the Constitution doesn't g
does not give a person any ingenious or incisive understanding of the system and how it works for people of color. It is a list of ideals that white people don't even fairly apply to each other, let alone people of color. In other words, Khan believes more in America than America believes in itself.

At one point, he said of Trump, ""You have sacrificed nothing and no one," Khan said in a halting and forceful voice. (DelReal & Gearen, 2016). That's because he's got brown lackeys like you and those of my race who do the sacrificing for him, butthead! But when Khan made that allegation it must have gotten under Trump's pale skin because he had a response —and that response made an even bigger ass out of him. Check it out:

> In the ABC interview, Trump pointed to the sacrifices he has made as a businessman: "I think I've made a lot of sacrifices. I work very, very hard. I've created thousands and thousands of jobs, tens of thousands of jobs," Trump said. "I think my popularity with the vets is through the roof," he added later. (DelReal & Gearen, 2016).

All lies. How are you sacrificing when all you do is put your name on a building that someone else already built? How are you sacrificing when you have to be sued because you refuse to pay your employees? This guy has never sacrificed in his life and that is part of his problem: born with a silver spoon in his ass … oops! I mean "mouth," and he's never had to really work for anything. He even takes liberties with his own daughter that border on incestuous. If a man can stoop that low in the belief that he's above the law, then on what grounds should be worry about "sacrificing" anything?

After Trump made that statement comparing his bullshit self-described "sacrifices" with those of veterans, all hell broke loose:

> Paul Rieckoff, the founder and chief executive of Iraq and Afghanistan Veterans of America, told ABC that Trump's comparison of his own sacrifice to that of war veterans is an insult. "For anyone to compare their 'sacrifice' to a Gold Star family member is insulting, foolish and ignorant. Especially someone who has never served himself and has no children serving," he said. "Our country has been at war for a decade and a half, and the truth is most Americans have sacrificed nothing. Most of them are smart and grounded enough to admit it." (DelReal & Gearen, 2016).

Donald Trump is protected which is where is audacity comes from. He talked a lot of shit about China when he was running for office, claiming that China was "raping" the American economy and ripping the United States off. But in November of 2017, this asshole made an Asian tour and was kissing more ass than a well-trained prostitute. In fact, he made the statement that China was not responsible at all! So he talks big when he's on American turf, but once he goes to the locale of the people he had talked shit about, he's as quiet as a church mouse.

But don't get it twisted: if you have money, whether you're Muslim or not, you can get into this country. On April 1, 2016 an article by USA Today reporter

[Type text]

Josh Hafner appeared under the heading, "Trump Says He'd Allow 'Rich Muslims' To Enter U.S." Following are the facts any my views:

> During Donald Trump's Wisconsin town hall Wednesday — where he said women should face 'punishment' for illegal abortions — the Republican front-runner revealed another interesting tidbit: His proposed temporary ban on Muslims entering the country, the cause of much controversy, would not apply to Trump's wealthy Muslim friends. "I have a lot of friends that are Muslim and they call me," Trump told MSNBC during the event. "In most cases, they're very rich Muslims, OK?" (Hafner, 2016).

Just because you say a person is a friend doesn't mean that they are. They might just be "associates," and that is what these people are to Trump. If they know him at all then they have to recognize that he is someone that no one in their right mind would want to "befriend." He uses them and makes these claims in their absence and knows that when he makes the claim he is telling an outright lie.

He's got Muslim friends who have money, right? Now, check out the following:

> OK, Donald. MSNBC's Chris Matthews then asked Trump whether his very rich Muslim friends would be allowed to enter the U.S. during President Trump's Muslim ban. "They'll come in," Trump said. "And you'll have exceptions." So a rich guy, should he become president, would make exceptions to the law for other rich folks who are his friends. All right, then (Hafner, 2016).

And Trump is a white male prototype once again. He is a model for those white men who think the way he does – which is most of them. But he is hardly an exception. That is why white racism and white nationalism continue to permeate the American landscape. That is what they are talking about when they talk about "patriotism," a belief that you accept America's on-going abuse of the rest of the "colored" world. To be "patriotic" is to be racist, plain and simple.

Vintage white thinking is that if a person of color wants to be "in," then they have to do the bidding of the white man. That is what these white boys did when they vanquished the First Nation people and forced their children to assimilate, that is what they did when they forced the Latinos out of America and down into Mexico, that is what they did during the enslavement of more than 100 million Africans and that is what they are doing now. In simple terms, when it comes to people of color, you literally have to "earn your stripes," and when they say stripes they're not talking about stripes on your uniform in the armed services; they're talking about the stripes that are left after being flogged with the nearest bullwhip.

In case you need proof of such a mentality existing, pay close attention to the following:

> Trump also suggested that America, once Made Great Again, would be so alluring that Muslims would fight ISIS just to get Trump to lift the ban again. "Maybe they'll be *more* disposed to fight ISIS," Trump said of the banned, presumably not-rich Muslims. He continued: "Maybe they'll say, 'We want to come back into America, we've got to solve this problem.'" Hillary Clinton, for her part, disagreed:

There you have it. If you are an immigrant then you have to be willing to fight for the very country that Trump turned his back on when it was HIS turn to go into the military.

Elizabeth Warren, part Native American, called "Pocahontas"

Not only did the spineless Trump call Warren a name that was a knock against her alleged ethnicity or racial background, but then he tried to throw stones at her business practices, as if he was some kind of model entrepreneur. But first, some background.

Before moving on, let us clarify that Trump calling Elizabeth Warren "Pocahontas" was a racist slam, especially to those of us who know the true story of what happened, and not the racist myth that people like Trump were probably force-fed in grade school.

The myth in America is that this lovely First Nation woman saw a blonde white man, Captain John Smith, fell in love with him, and time and time again risked her life and betrayed her people to defend him. A website called Indian Country Today offers some insights about Pocahontas and Smith that I would like to share before moving on to address Trump's cacophony of emotive labelling.

For instance, "Pocahontas' Mother, Also Named Pocahontas, Died While Giving Birth to Her John Smith Came to the Powhatan When Pocahontas Was about 9 or 10," Pocahontas Never Saved the Life of John Smith" and "Pocahontas Never Defied Her Father to Bring Food to John Smith or Jamestown." What these facts tell us about the white man and his storytelling is that he is always going to put down women of color and make them appear as if they are nothing more than pawns who cannot resist his whiteness. This brings to mind the Aesop fable about the lion and the hunter.

In a nutshell, the young boy asks his father, "Father every day I sit on your lap and you tell me the story of the lion and hunter. You say that the lion is the king of the jungle, but in each of your stories, the hunter is the winner. Why is that? The father looks down at his young son and says, "My son, that is the way it will always be – until the lion learns how to write."

In this day and age of late 2017, white women are having their revenge. They have been the whores of the world in both myth and reality and in America this group is getting payback through lawsuits and exposes where they point out the "sexual harassment" and "sexual assault" of the men they have encountered, men who had power over them and used that power to impose their will on them. But long before these corporatist examples, there was sexual assault taking place in literature and tales that were being fed to American children, and the story of Pocahontas and John Smith was but one of them. The three examples provided prove this to be the cast.

But wait: there's more: "Pocahontas Did Not Sneak Into Jamestown to Warn John Smith About a Death Plot," "As Colonists Terrorized Native People, Pocahontas Married and Bccamc Prcgnant," "Pocahontas Was Kidnapped, Her Husband Was Murdered and She Was Forced to Give Up Her First Child," and "Pocahontas Was Raped While in Captivity and Became Pregnant With Her Second Child." Real-life tragedy turned into a fairy tale by the white man, a tale that has traveled through hundreds of years.

And one more thing: "Pocahontas had a Native husband and Native child; never married John Smith." The white man can win only when he tells the story. He can overcome entire cultures, outfight entire races of people, always get the girl and out think everyone – when he is in charge of the narrative. And Trump was in charge of the narrative when it came to his attacks on Elizabeth Warren and the label, "Pocahontas."

The racism continued and this time it was a jab, via Tweet, at Native Americans. On May 23, 2016 Trump said, "Goofy Elizabeth *Warren, sometimes known as Pocahontas, bought foreclosed housing and made a quick killing. Total hypocrite!"* The fact is, *n*obody but this racist megalomaniac ever referred to Warren as "Pocahontas." But his racism morphed into sexist allegations as he continued his rant by charging her with crimes relates to real estate and housing:

> Donald Trump lashed out at Sen. Elizabeth Warren, D-Mass., for
> being a hypocrite after Warren attacked Trump for saying, before

the housing bubble burst in 2008, that he hoped to profit from a downturn in home prices because of a real estate bubble. (As our colleagues at PolitiFact noted, Trump actually failed to predict the magnitude of the financial crisis, saying he didn't think the real estate market would "take a big hit."). (Kessler, 2016)

So not only did the charlatan Trump err when it came to predicting the severity of the housing crisis, but then he had the gall to try to turn the tables on Warren. And exactly what did he say about her? Check it out:

Trump alleged that Warren herself made a "quick killing" in the real estate market by buying foreclosed housing. Warren fired back with this tweet: "I helped family buy their homes and out-of-work construction worker relatives make a living. I'm proud of that." (Kessler, 2016)

Both of them are probably lying. When it comes to housing these white people with money "target" low income people and use the claim of "helping" as a front for justifying inadequate housing, high population density (re-segregation) and even predatory lending. Warren Buffett owns 70% of the mobile home market and he is exploiting First Nation people in Gallup, New Mexico and Latinos in Louisiana.

Flipping houses is becoming vogue for the rich and not so rich. Kessler (2016) explains,

Flipping is generally defined as buying and selling a property within six months, sometimes after extensive renovations. But Warren in her tweet said she assisted her family members (primarily an older brother and a nephew) who at the time were out-of-work construction workers. Warren came from a lower-income family but has an estimated net worth of $7.5 million, according to the Center for Responsive Politics, largely as a result of writing best-selling books and being a tenured professor at Harvard Law School. (Kessler, 2016).

In other words she had money and she used it to help family members. So how is that different than what Trump has done as he continues to spoon feed Ivanka, Donald Jr., Eric, Tiffany and Baron? Does he not help his relatives by not only supporting them but giving them positions right there in the White House that they cannot even perform? How about his son-in-law Jared Kushner, who is given all kinds of power, allowed to cavort with Russians on his father's behalf?

[Type text]

How can you describe Trump's on-going embellishments, fabrications and distortions of the truth as it relates to women of color in general and in this case, Elizabeth Warren?

> As usual, Trump greatly exaggerates. Warren twice bought homes in foreclosure, but she did not make a "quick killing." One home that had been purchased in foreclosure was held in her family for 13 years. One home bought by Warren was resold within five months — but it was not purchased in foreclosure. The overall pattern demonstrated in the 25 real estate transactions don't support Trump's claim that she made a "quick killing" out of foreclosed homes. (Kessler, 2016).

Trump's legacy of lies lingers on. And the white people who believe in him are just as guilty as he is. And as long as they are there and remain true to their racist (read: patriotic) ideology, he will continue to insult people of color, nationally and globally.

Trump Maligns the Native American "Code Talkers"

In November of 2017 Trump was at it again with the Pocahontas slur but this time he said it in front of a group of Navajo Code Talkers who helped the white man during World War II. His comments were not only insulting, but appeared under a portrait of Andrew Jackson, the racist muthafucka who hated Indians so much that he sold their skins as belts and was the author of the Indian Removal Act of 1830. It was no accident and Trump was not afraid to skin and grin in the faces of the Native Americans as he praised them, paternalistically patted one on the shoulder and said, "you're special." Only in white culture would such actions be viewed as sincere benevolence.

According to Estepa (2017)

> President Trump couldn't resist using his old nickname for Sen. Elizabeth Warren — "Pocahontas" — even at an event honoring Native American war heroes. At what was supposed to be a simple ceremony, Trump stood in front of a painting of President Andrew Jackson, who signed the Indian Removal Act, with elderly veterans of the Navajo tribe.

The white media refers to it as Trump "not being able to resist." This lack of impulse control, even when surrounded by men of color, is the prototypical example of white racism. Trump is not the first: white Presidents have insulted

[Type text]

men of all races for centuries, and the ones who are in attendance at the White House have been vetted to make sure that they're "safe and accommodating." As it relates to larger crowds, the coward Trump is not going to insult black people unless he's surrounded by a throng of secret service agents. He knows he'd get his white ass kicked. White men, to this day, fear black men.

Continuing with the event for the First Nation people:

> He didn't end up giving a speech to honor the Code Talkers, implying that earlier remarks had already covered it all. But he did have time for his quip about the Massachusetts Democrat. "You were here long before any of us were here," the president told the veterans. "Although we have a representative in Congress who they say was here a long time ago. They call her Pocahontas." An awkward silence, unsurprisingly, followed. (Estepa, 2017)

All those fake acknowledgements meant nothing when a picture of Andrew Jackson is hanging in the background. Jackson hated Native Americans so much that some background must be shared to give you the full impact of the insult that Trump imposed on this special ceremony that was supposed to honor the Code Talkers. According to one source,

> In the early 1800s, the United States government began a systematic effort to remove American Indian tribes from the southeast The Chickasaw, Choctaw, Muscogee-Creek, Seminole, and original Cherokee Nations[5] had been established as autonomous nations in the southeastern United States. This acculturation was originally proposed by George Washington and was well under way among the Cherokee and Choctaw by the turn of the 19th century … In an effort to assimilate with American culture, Indians were encouraged to "convert to Christianity; learn to speak and read English; and adopt European-style economic practices such as the individual ownership of land and other property (including, in some instances, the ownership of African slaves)." (Davis, 2008)

These are facts that far too many Americans are ignorant of. All they know is what they see in reruns of movie westerns where the Natives are depicted as "savages" and the white man and his cavalry come to the "rescue" of some white folks trapped in what were called "settlements." John Wayne, Richard Widmark, Lex Barker, Maureen O'Hara and a slew of peckerwood actors made their fortunes carving out a movie in the "western genre" that featured white men with guns

[Type text]

strapped to their sides and Native Americans staggering around talking about "how" as the white man wiped them out in the name of progress.

But what if young people learned what I just shared in the previous excerpt? What if they knew of the doggish intent and motivations behind their so-called "founding Fathers"? And yet what do they do every year? They celebrate "President's Day," "George Washington's Birthday" and then have the gall to celebrate "Thanksgiving," a day when they celebrate their backstabbing of the very First Nation people who taught them how to feed themselves and wipe their pink asses!

But that's not all:

> Thomas Jefferson's policy echoed Washington's proposition: respect the Indians' rights to their homelands, and allow the Five Tribes to remain east of the Mississippi provided that they adopt behavior and cultural practices that are compatible with those of other Americans. Jefferson encouraged practicing an agriculture-based society. However, **Andrew Jackson sought to renew a policy of political and military action for the removal of the Indians from these lands and worked toward enacting a law for Indian removal**. … In his 1829 State of the Union address, Jackson called for removal. (Davis, 2008 – emphasis added).

Trump had to know what Jackson stood for and yet the ceremony was in a room of the white house with Jackson's huge portrait prominently displayed. But that insult was not enough. He then turned to Warren – who is a piece of shit herself in my book. After all, according to Politifact (December, 2017), Warren's central offense dates back to the mid 1980s, when she first formally notified law school administrators that her family tree includes Native Americans. Warren said she grew up with family stories about both grandparents on her mother's side having some Cherokee or Delaware blood. That genealogical claim has zero documentary evidence to back it up, according to a PolitiFact review of news and newsletter databases back to 1986.

So this white bitch lied with her claim and Trump merely capitalized on the lie. She got away with it and Trump is being blamed for being a racist, which really reinforces her lie. How can she be called those names when she isn't even a Native? At any rate,

> Trump has frequently called Warren – who claims to have Native American heritage and has faced criticism for those claims – by the name Pocahontas, a reference to the daughter of a Native

> American chief in the 17th century. Yet the formal setting for the
> unscripted jab drew immediate backlash, including Warren, who
> called the latest quip "deeply unfortunate." (Estepa, 2017)

What is "unfortunate" is that this white bitch claimed to be part Native American when she wasn't. That's how she jump started her career – with a lie. So what she gets she deserves. Now she's trying to be some kind of activist for the downtrodden when, like Hillary Clinton, this bitch makes her money in real estate, and that includes bilking those who are dumb enough to rent her properties. She follows the model established by Warren and Susie Buffett: that of the poverty pimp.

So when the ceremony for First Nation people was held, Trump took his shot at her at their expense. And those red bastards stood up there like a bunch of apples (red on the outside, white on the inside) and didn't say shit. At least the old guard that was being honored didn't. But some of the young bucks had plenty to say:

> Navajo Nation President Russell Begaye said in a statement that he
> didn't want to engage in the feud between Warren and Trump. But
> he acknowledged that "all tribal nations still battle insensitive
> references to our people." "The prejudice that Native American
> people face is an unfortunate historical legacy," he said. (Estepa,
> 2017)

So two white people exploit the Natives in their own way and they argue back and forth. Welcome to the REAL America.

Trump Dumps Omarosa Manigault Edwards

During the December 13, 2017 telecast of "CNN Newsroom with Brooke Baldwin," the news came heavy and hard about the "drama" around Omarosa's "resignation" from the White House. It didn't sound like a resignation to me.

This is the same bitch I saw on "The Apprentice" and when I saw her for the first time I said to myself, "she's sucking Trump's dick." Later on, after Trump had won the presidency she was on television and said something to the effect, "Every critic, every detractor, will have to bow down to President Trump. Everyone who ever doubted Donald, whoever disagreed, whoever challenged him. It is the ultimate revenge to become the most powerful man in the universe."

There is no doubt that this woman has "game." She can seduce any man by appealing to his ego, which is probably how she trapped Michael Clark Duncan, that huge Uncle Tom who appeared in such degrading movies as "The Green Mile" and then played the Kingpin in the Ben Affleck flop, "Daredevil." After he croaked she has apparently latched on to some other hapless coon, John Allen Newman who is, get this: a pastor from west Florida. One pimp marries another.

She had her wedding at the Trump Hotel and then had the nerve to bring her wedding entourage to the White House for photos. More on that debacle later.

General John Kelly was brought into the White House to screen Trump's visitors. Even cabinet members had to go through Kelly and when I heard that I immediately knew that Omarosa's days were numbered. And sure enough, Kelly – on the record for not liking black women – made it clear that she was persona non grata and asked what she actually did to earn her $180,000 a year salary. More on this second situation in a minute.

According to April Ryan of Urban American Radio Network, General Kelly said he had "a tense exchange with her twice." When a white man says that it means that she was cussing his white ass out and he became afraid because as quiet as it's kept, white men are far more afraid of black women than they are of black men. They consider black men as sissies because of the degrading things they have been able to get black men to do. They have no respect for them. But that black woman, that sassy fireball – that's what the spineless white boy, regardless of rank or status, is truly afraid of. So he fired her.

According to Ryan, " It was a dual firing resignation." Ryan said that General Kelly grew tired of Omarosa's antics. Since the days of former sissy Rance Priebus, nobody really knew what Omarosa's duties were. She told Priebus at one point that she didn't have to listen to him. In other words there was something going on between her and Trump that gave Omarosa the impression that her shit didn't stink, that she was above the rules and protocols. And recall my initial impression of her: she and Trump had a salacious background while she was on "The Apprentice".

April Ryan, in her report, said that her White House sources told her that Omarosa "stirred things up." She said that Omarosa was a "mood changer." If Trump was doing something, Omarosa would march into his office, show him a newspaper clipping or say something that would set him off. On the streets we call this an "instigator." In black politics we refer to her as a "provocateur." Omarosa's "walk right in" access to Trump and the Oval Office was changed when General Kelly was brought in.

In addition, it was reported that Omarosa "did not have warm feelings with others, and she would cause problems within the White House. She would come and go whenever she wanted to. Now back to the wedding.

Not only did this bodacious bitch get married in the Trump Hotel (I doubt if she got a discount), but then had the gall to bring the bridal part into the White House to take pictures. She didn't ask permission and violated every protocol and one source said she "trivialized the White House" in doing so. Hell yeah: a bunch of black folks walking around taking pictures like they were at Disneyland, all on the invite of a woman who didn't have a lick of juice.

During the back-and-forth after her resignation she was telling reporters and anyone dumb enough to show interest in her story that she "helped elect Donald Trump" and that she "brought the black vote." That bitch didn't deliver a single vote except for her relatives and that dumb hallelujah huckster who was dumb enough to marry that slag. Black people didn't even like her. In fact, after the Charlottesville incident where Nazis and the Klan waged war on regular citizens, Trump defended the Nazis and Omarosa defended Trump!

Then there was the escapade at the National Association of Black Journalists meeting where she got into it with Ed Gordon, the moderator. She was heckled throughout by black people who knew she wasn't about shit. She embarrassed herself and even in front of all those black people she continued to kiss Trump's ass. Trump didn't show up, but he had a more than willing thrall ready to mock his every word.

And if America saw her as a villain when she was on the apprentice, why assume that black people couldn't see through her as well? We have a bunch of lyin' ass bitches in the 'hood who do the same shit that Omarosa was and continues to try to do.

On MSNBC's "Deadline: White House," Symone Sanders said that "high drama individuals are tolerated, but not her." Of course not. She's black. Despite her belief that she is some kind of "exception," nothing could be further from the truth.

With that having been said, let's dig a little deeper and get another look at one more Trump hire that got into a position and immediately began to think that they were not only above the law, but in Omarosa's case, could do what they wanted to do because she was "Friends" with Trump (read: concubine).

According to reports, after being told she was canned, Omarosa tried to go to Ivanka Trump (Donald's daughter) and ask her if she could keep her job. Ivanka must have told her to fuck off because then Omarosa tried to go straight to Trump, through the President's quarters. Alarms went off and from there she was escorted off the premises and had her security access revoked. The key words here are "escorted off the premises." She claims that she will continue to be paid through January, but if her security clearance is revoked, that means that she's being paid with taxpayers dollars for doing absolutely nothing.

Meanwhile, Sarah Huckabee Sanders, the lying bitch who has the unenviable task of defending Trump's antics, said she didn't know how many African Americans are in White House, but was quick to add that, "We have a truly diverse team, we always want to continue to grow the diversity. She also claimed, "I don't have a number directly in front of me, [but we have] … a diverse team at WH and in press office. We strive to grow to be more diverse …" Such bullshit and it's not even convincing bullshit.

According to MSNBC, the 22 highest paid people at the White House are white and Omarosa is the only black woman on the list.

Now she's going around claiming that she has "a story to tell." She's talking about what she heard and saw at the White House and how much of it disturbed her and her alleged concerns for "my people" and "my community." This bitch doesn't consider herself a member of the black community, in the same way that Vanessa Williams turned her back and was dating white boys. But when that bitch did that Penthouse layout, butt naked, and white folks stripped her of her Miss America title, that cute green-eyed, yellow bitch came running back to black people.

Omarosa is either shopping a book deal, a reality TV show or some kind of movie. She's just as egocentric as Trump, but as a black woman she's going to have to take another road. She's pretty enough to go into movies, but her attitude is going to alienate her from the decision makers. She probably figures that if she gives them head then the least they can do is allow her into the hallowed halls. She still hasn't learned yet that white men are duplicitous – just like she is.

In the movie "Outlander," these Scottish assholes are supposedly immortal and down through the years they may meet and battle one another to the death. Their motto? "There can be but one." This seems to be the philosophy of white folks in general but in this case, the doctrine of Donald Trump when it comes to black people in high places. If there are going to be any at all they have to be easy to control, willing to jump through hoops and willing to turn their backs on their own people. And even those of this misguided ilk are suspect, which is why, "there can be but one."

Trump and Recurring Racist Insults

During a September 15, 2017 segment on CNN's "At This Hour With Kate Bolduan," Keith Boykin, CNN Political Commentator, said that he kept a record of the people who Trump considered to be "racist", according to his (Trump's) Twitter feed. These people were Barack Obama, Ture, Tavast Smiley, and even the movie "Django Unchained." These are Trump's example of racists?

That two-faced sonofabitch was kissing Obama's ass on the day of the Inauguration and to this day continues to have some kind of obsession with him. And it's not because Obama is racist because black people can't be racist, although Obama could have been had he wanted to. Obama killed more black men and deported more Latinos than any other president. As for Ture, I don't know who in the fuck that is. But the movie "Django Unchained" was a piece of shit that at very least showed the way white slave-owners abused those they had power over. The racist was that slack jawed muthafucka Quentin Tarantino who never hesitates to use the word "nigger" in every movie he makes, from "Reservoir Dogs" and "Pulp Fiction" to the aforementioned "Django Unchained." In fact, the status of black people in that movie is just where people like Trump would like to see most of us, especially under that "Make America Great Again" bullshit that is nothing but a façade for intensified white nationalism.

Dana Milbank of gatehousemedia.com offered a July 18, 2016 article titled, "For Trump, It's White America First." Following are the main parts of the article and my views and analyses on the content of same.

> WASHINGTON — It was just another week in Donald Trump's (white) America First campaign. At least twice, Trump alleged that people have called for a "moment of silence" for the madman who killed five police officers in Dallas at a Black Lives Matter protest. It was an incendiary accusation, bound to stir racial hatred. Like Trump's accusation that New Jersey Muslims cheered the 9/11 attacks, this, too, was categorically false. There was no sign of such calls, and a top Trump adviser couldn't corroborate the allegation.

Even the news report was biased. That was no "madman" who gunned down those Dallas cops. You have to live in Dallas to understand how racist their police are. A lot of the dirt that these cops do never makes the pages of the Dallas Morning News because, like the Omaha World Herald and the Milwaukee Journal Sentinel, these newspapers kiss the asses of the local cops so that they (the papers) can gain access to police files. That kid knew what he was doing and he knew who was the source of the problems of his people.

Trump had already lied by claiming that he "saw" crowd of Muslims dancing and partying after the planes hit the World Trade Center. There were no such tapes, no such airing of any Muslims celebrating those attacks. Trump, as we now know since he's been elected, is a pathological liar. Link that with the fact that he is also a racist and you have the perfect recipe for the perfect white man. The American history books were written by men who suffered from the same twin maladies. Trump is no exception: he is the prototype.

The article continues by offering the following:

> Yet what was remarkable about the reckless accusation was how unremarkable his appeals to racist division have become. Days before and after this, Trump snubbed the NAACP, saying he wouldn't appear at the group's convention. Declared in response to racial unrest that "I am the law-and-order candidate" — an echo of Richard Nixon's response to violence following the Martin Luther King Jr. assassination.

In all fairness to the racist Trump, by "snubbing" the NAACP he was doing conscious black people a favor by showing the world that the NAACP is no threat to anyone but themselves. An old saying says that, "There are old quarterbacks and there are bold quarterbacks, but there are no old, bold quarterbacks." The NAACP boasts of being "the oldest civil rights organization," but such a title means nothing in American society. The word "civil rights" has become synonymous with black people but in recent years, others have joined in: white women, homosexual gay men, lesbians, the handicapped, left-handed quarterbacks – you name it. The NAACP has no juice any more. Along with the National Urban League, it should be disbanded.

At Trump's rallies supporters would hear the name Barack Obama and immediately begin shouting, "He's a monkey!" and when they heard Hillary Clinton's name they'd shout, "Hang that bitch." Did Trump intercede? Hell no. These people were shouting just what Trump believed in. His aides and others were doing the same thing. For instance, in regard to black female attorney general Loretta Lynch:

> There was also the deleted tweet by prominent Trump surrogate Carl Paladino, who said of the African-American attorney general: "Lynch @LorettaLynch." Paladino said it was a mistake, and maybe it was. Republicans trying to justify their support for Trump

would like to believe each incident is a misunderstanding. But they can't all be.

Jews are not a "race," but they represent a white ethnic group that has long been maligned by the world. Therefore it was no surprise to me when Trump went after them as well:

> As Republicans head to Cleveland to nominate Trump for the presidency, here, for easy reference, is a compilation of what they'd like to ignore. Trump tweeted an image, previously posted to an anti-Semitic message board, of a Star of David atop paper money; he later objected to his campaign's decision to remove the image. Trump told Jewish Republicans, "You're not going to support me, because I don't want your money."

This lying bastard may not have wanted it THEN, but I started reading his book, The Art of the Deal, and the first forty or so pages are the names of people that he got money from or entered deals with and nearly every surname was a Jewish one. And after being elected who was one of the first people that he went out to appease: Israeli Prime Minister Benjamin Netanyahu.

But unlike black people who sit on their ass and allow negative images to be imposed on us, the Jews immediately fight back because they don't want the exposure. Jenna Johnson (2016) in her article, "Trump: It's 'Ridiculous' to Compare His Pledge to a Nazi Salute,' wrote:

> He had supporters raise their hands in a loyalty pledge that the former head of the Anti-Defamation League called a "fascist gesture." He said, "I don't have a message" for supporters of his who threatened anti-Semitic violence against a Jewish journalist. The journalist had criticized Melania Trump, who said the writer "provoked" the attacks.(Johnson, 2016)

Jews have a long history of thievery and deception themselves. They have been kicked out of a number of countries because of their banking practices. In recent years in America, they have somehow made themselves out to be victims. Through their control of the east coast media, Hollywood and much of Congress, they are able to define 'anti-Semitism" as any act or word spoken against Jews without their permission.

Jews in America are a kind of oppressive force in and of themselves. At the Congressional level they have this group called AIPAC – American Israeli Public Affairs Committee. They wield awesome power and if they don't like you they

[Type text]

will raise money and distribute negative information about you. In fact, the U.S. Government contributes $4 billion every year in "foreign aid" to Israel, and as stated earlier, the east coast newspapers, along with CNN, CBS, ABC, NBC and even National Public Radio are all controlled or heavily influenced by Jews.

For the most part they do not like some of Trump's actions (the ones that don't benefit them, that is). For instance,

> His "America First" campaign slogan was the name of the isolationist, anti-Semitic organization that opposed involvement in World War II. Trump has banned news organizations such as The Washington Post from covering his events but credentialed the host of a white-supremacist radio show. He repeatedly declined to disavow David Duke and the Ku Klux Klan in a CNN interview. (Johnson, 2016)

Trump was voted in by groups of people who are as stupid as he is. Why does America act shocked? These are the same peckerwoods who benefited from racial segregation, restrictive covenants and racial profiling. And they are the descendants of the same people who wiped out hundreds of thousands of First Nation people, Latinos and of course enslaved African people for over three and a half centuries. Why then, should people act shocked when there are recurring insults against people of color and for that matter, even white ethnics such as the Jews?

When you ban a news organization you are banning Jewish influence. But this is not what is being broadcast to a silly American public. Jews remember the so-called "Holocaust" and claim that six million Jews were killed by Hitler during that time. And their slogan is "Never forget." That is why some of Trump's actions in 2016 raised their ire:

> The Trump campaign chose a white supremacist as a delegate, then blamed a database error. Trump retweeted a message from @WhiteGenocideTM, phony crime statistics that originated with neo-Nazis, a quote from Mussolini and a message from a supporter who embraces a "right-wing death squad" label. (Johnson, 2016).

Remember the information I shared about the "white supremacist" scam: all white people are white supremacists. The ones in power simply do not like that fact being advertised by groups like the Nazis and the Klan. Let me take some time to explain why the Jews don't like these "white nationalist" groups and how pervasive these groups are.

[Type text]

On July 25, 2014, Spike TV aired a segment of "Lockdown" that featured the Aryan Brotherhood of Texas. According to the information provided, The Aryan Brotherhood of Texas runs a lot of prisons in Texas. Having lived in Texas, I know for a fact that Big D – the name for Dallas - is called "predominantly rich and white" and the show added that its also a cover for the ABT, the perfect hidelout. The show says that there is ABT in every town in Texas and claims that "ABT has invaded these neighborhoods and the social fabric of these cities." A white woman says, "they can clean themselves u0p and look just like you and me."(Lockdown, July 25, 2014).

One of the ABT members interviewed said "its not a psychotic behavior." Another said that laws don't apply to him. His name is Tiger, drinking by age six, smoking cocaine when he was 13. He went in a petty criminal and became a gangster criminal, the show reports. They call it a gang based on racism. The essence of the Aryan Brotherhood of Texas was planted I the early 1960s. At the time the prison system was run by a man who believed in the'tender system," giving exemplary inmates special privileges. These were white boys given total control. They had blackjacks, knives and did whatever the warden told them to do. David Ruiz filed a lawsuit alleging abuse and in 1980 a judge ruled to end the "Tender" system.

The Texas Department of Corrections was then, as now, divided along racial lines. The favored whites found themselves in the minority. In 1982 a small group of pecks reached out the ABT in California, started in San Quentin decades earlier. ABT in Cali was 1 percent of the population but was responsible for 18 percent of the murders. The New Group became the ABT. A constitution was drafted, unbreakable rules that the members had to abide by. The organization didn't take child molesters, snitches or people of that ilk. They were there in the prison system to protect themselves from other races. One member said that the group was , "On the front line to re-instate the white man to his rightful position of power," and the group's members moved from the prisons into the community once released.

Now you might ask what this has to do with Donald Trump, his racist ways, his views of immigrants and Jews. It should be clear: what the Aryan Brotherhood stands for is the same thing Trump is promoting in his own way. And the Jews can see it and they are afraid.

Like the ABT, Trump hates all people of color as well:

> Trump launched his campaign saying Mexico was sending
> "rapists" across the border. He called for mass deportation of 11
> million illegal immigrants, "half" of whom are criminals. He said
> the American-born judge in a fraud case against him could not be

impartial because of his Mexican ancestry. He tweeted a photo of himself eating a taco bowl and wrote "I love Hispanics!" He kicked Jorge Ramos out of a news conference and said Univision "takes its marching orders" from Mexico. (Johnson, 2016).

The title of this section is "Trump and Recurring Racial Insults." Something can be "recur" unless it is repeated. When it comes to a white man spotting a person with skin color and the immediate reaction is disdain, then what comes out of his big mouth is based on what his attitude is. Trump is a white racist and a white nationalist, although he lacks the courage of many of those who claim to belong to such a group. All white people are white supremacists because they benefit from it by way of white privilege. But as far as Trump and his insults, they became most obvious during his bid for the Presidency:

He used broken English to mock Asians. He used a fake Indian accent. He referred to Elizabeth Warren, who has claimed Native American ancestry, as "Pocahontas." He asked a Texas-born Asian American at one event: "Are you from South Korea?" (Johnson, 2016).

Trump is a coward because he knows that the people he makes fun of cannot get to him to retaliate. Like most rich white boys they have bodyguards and security personnel around them all the time. Just like his ancestors, they hurled their insults and then used mobs, white citizens' councils, neighborhood associations and other "civic groups" for protection. In addition, they had racist national and local laws standing behind them.

The ultimate insult, to many people, was the one he used against former President Barack Obama, an insult that he carried with him for years and one he never formally apologized for. Remember?

Trump said last year that "I really don't know" if President Obama was born in the United States. He implied that Obama was responsible for the Orlando mass shooting. He let stand the remark by a questioner at one of his events who called Obama a Muslim. There are many more, but this column is 750 words — far shorter than Trump's catalogue of racial animus. (Johnson, 2016).

And so it goes. And he has tens of millions of followers because of his disdain for and willingness to oppress and target people of color. This is the REAL America and this is just one more reason why Donald Trump is a white male prototype.

[Type text]

Trump as Master Warmonger

What could this fat, spoiled orange-colored white man possibly know about combat, war or for that matter fighting of any kind? His claim to fame in the area came on April 1, 2007 at "Wrestlemania 23" when he and WWE owner Vince McMahon had one of the most staged and fake "battles" of all time (outside of the ring). The event took place in Detroit, a city that Trump has continually ignored and oftentimes downgraded during his Republican campaign.

That's it. A fake wrestling match with another white man dubbed as "battle of the billionaires." Let's take a look at this big mouthed war-monger and check out a bit of his record on "war." Remember: a warmonger need not necessarily be a warrior and can, in fact, be a coward. A warmonger is defined as someone who, "a person who encourages or advocates aggression towards other countries or groups.(Merriam-Webster, 2017).

Trump's main focus seems to be on North Korea's Kim Jong-un. And Jong-un used the term "warmonger" in one of his counter-insults that was aimed at Trump on November 11, 2017. Check out the scenario:

> North Korea said on Saturday that the comments President Trump has made during his trip through Asia "begged for a nuclear war on the Korean peninsula."In a statement released to a state-run media outlet, a spokesperson for the regime's foreign ministry said, "Trump, during his visit, laid bare his true nature as destroyer of the world peace and stability and begged for a nuclear war on the Korean peninsula." "His current trip to our surrounding region is a warmonger's visit for confrontation to rid the DPRK of its self-defensive nuclear deterrence," the ministry also argued, reports Al Jazeera. "It is also nothing but a business trip by a warmonger to enrich the monopolies of the U.S. defense industry by milking the moneybags from its subordinate 'allies.'" (Geobeats, 2017).

Trump has been incessantly engaged in "war-oriented" name calling with Kim Jong-un, who has been in power in North Korea since 2011. Trump called him "Little Rocket Man" and Jong-un fired back with "lunatic old man." It should be clear that Jong-un's insult was far more accurate and fitting than Trump's. But now let's take a step back to 2016 and check out the following article by Maggie Haberman and David E. Sanger of the New York Times. Published on April 9, 2016, the article gives us a good idea about Trump and his views on war. The headline of the article was, "Donald Trump's Trial Balloons are Catching Up to Him." Following are his views and mine.

> WASHINGTON — Two weeks ago, Donald J. Trump said he could live with a nuclear-armed Japan and South Korea if it meant they could defend themselves against North Korea without American aid. "I'm not sure that would be a bad thing for us," he said. (Sanger, 2016)

It is clear that this peroxide-dyed hair wearing idiot has no idea about the nature and scope of a nuclear bomb. He talks about the existence of nuclear arms as if it was nothing more than a crate of hand grenades. Add that to the fact that the nations he mentioned above – South Korea, North Korea and Japan – are all nations of color, then you can better understand his nonchalance. Trump is a long-time racist and the more he can get people of color to do America's dirty work, the more he can lay back and work with Vladimir Putin to find more places where they can dig fork oil.

No one takes Trump seriously, but he fear of his idiocy and mentally retarded tendencies to have the world on guard. For instance,

> Since then he has changed his tune. After Japanese and South Korean officials raised fears of an Asian arms race, and President Obama ridiculed his remark, Mr. Trump began to say he did not actually want the two countries to obtain nuclear weapons — but that, because of American weakness, "at some point it could happen anyway." . (Sanger, 2016)

Admitting that America is "weak" is just a trap and a lie. He wants the world to think that America is becoming weak so that he can justify linking up with Russia, his white counterpart. As I predicted in a 1979 article in the World Herald as a member of a panel on Third World Nationalism ("Panelist Foretells Worldwide Race War"), it was all going to come down to the white folks and the nonwhite folks waging war. The majority of the world is "colored" and white people are becoming increasingly fixated on their global "minority"status. That fear prompts them to create straw men and fake scenarios to convince their cowardly populations in Europe and North America that "they're out to get us." Add to that the changing demographics of America, which is becoming increasingly brown and black, and these peckerwoods elected somebody who they believed would not be afraid to wage a campaign of race-based genocide.

Ignorance of the law is no excuse, or so the cops tell us. That also applies to Trump as you read the following excerpt:

> It was not the first time Mr. Trump has hastily added deflating caveats to his headline-grabbing trial balloons. In a debate a month ago, he declared himself in favor of torture if it would extract information from terrorists, then issued a statement saying he would respect the law, then followed it up by saying that the law must be changed. . (Sanger, 2016).

Torture is the white man's favorite weapon and one that he has used with much success, for centuries. But as you read the words I share with you, keep in mind that there are tens of millions of white people who see this bastard as some kind of hero, as a "man" who has come to their rescue. The "Trump style," now referred to as "Trumpism," is rooted in stupidity, racism and statements steeped in brutality. Put another way,

> None of this seemed to matter much until recently. But the Trump style — long on gut instincts, short on briefing books — has taken a toll. His opponents have called him reckless and unfit to be commander in chief. Mr. Obama has said Mr. Trump "doesn't know much about foreign policy, or nuclear policy, or the Korean Peninsula, or the world generally." Mr. Trump did not respond to repeated requests to speak with him. His aides say that he is continuing to build out a policy team and will soon give speeches. . (Sanger, 2016).

Under ordinary circumstances, Trump wouldn't have to know much about the world. If he hadn't fucked up the various administrative positions in the government, he'd have trained people informing him, just as Obama, both Bushes, Clinton and Reagan did. They sounded intelligent and worldly because of their consultants, their various diplomats and world ambassadors. But Trump is of the "lone wolf" variety and wants to act on his own, even if his actions are those of a retarded circus monkey. You have to have a conscience in order to give a shit about people's opinions and it is clear that this is yet another area where Trump is sorely lacking. What most people refer to as "reckless" and "unfit to be commander in chief" appears to be compliments to Trump.

Trump must not remember that America dropped two atomic bombs on Japan, and that the Korean War led to the deaths of hundreds of thousands of people on both sides during that conflict. Did he think these people forgot about that? Does he think that the white man is going to get away with his perennial

[Type text]

global crimes and that there won't be any comeuppance? Just look around: why do you think all these camel jockeys and other Asians are blowing shit up, killing Americans and destroying American institutions all over the world? What do you think that attack on the Twin Towers was all about? In sum, *these are the orphans of the people that America murdered in decades past.*

Instead of studying the principle of the boomerang, Trump just ambles along making tactical error after tactical error:

> But Mr. Trump's rhetorical journey on letting Japan and South Korea build their own arsenals was instructive. He first suggested that he was open to arming the two nations during an interview with The New York Times. He also began saying that he would pull out of NATO if European members did not pay a greater share of its costs. "If it breaks up NATO, it breaks up NATO," he said at a rally in Racine, Wis. . (Sanger, 2016).

Two yellow nations armed with nukes so that they can "help" the white man? Has he lost his damn mind? Or does he think so little of people of color that he believes that America can do all the dirt it has done, from exploitation of Asian women and eugenics campaigns to the media-based creation of "the Jap Rat" and the "Charlie Chan" stereotype, and get away scot-free?

Again, Trump is no exception. White supremacy and arrogance have most of the Caucasian decision makers think that their bullshit "seductions" of people of color around the world has turned them into "allies" and "partners." For instance,

> "Our allies magnify our power," Mr. Burns said. "Our trans- Atlantic and Asian alliances are a significant power advantage over China and Russia, who don't have real allies in the world." Yet Mr. Trump's analysis — like his campaign — cannot be dismissed simply because it violates the Washington consensus. Such defiance has attracted supporters. And, without question, there are strands of his frustration to be found in the mainstream discourse of both parties these days. . (Sanger, 2016).

They want to link China and Russia while at the same time kissing the asses of both? How can they be both enemy and friend be? China has more people than anywhere in the world and is leaps ahead in technology. Russia and its kleptocratic government has a hold on Trump and therefore controls him. But Russia, like Trump, is white and anti-immigrant. China is nationalistic but hides that fact to appease America. Trump can be flattered and led to believe that kissing the asses of China and Russia is giving the United States "a significant power advantage"

[Type text]

over them when, in reality, the opposite is the case. America's arrogance, led by Trump's mental instability, is going to be its undoing.

American policy is dictated by the belief that they are calling the shots. They think that because people of color smile in their presence, spend all kinds of money during meetings of the United Nations, fall for, have sex with and marry American white women, that the world is nothing more than America's willing thrall. Check out the following statement about "return on investment" made by Defense Secretary Robert M. Gates just before he left office in 2010 when he,

> …. blasted the Europeans as having driven NATO into strategic irrelevance by failing to put their money where their interests were. "If current trends in the decline of European defense capabilities are not halted and reversed," Mr. Gates warned in one of his last major speeches, "future U.S. political leaders — those for whom the Cold War was not the formative experience that it was for me — may not consider the return on America's investment in NATO worth the cost." . (Sanger, 2016).

The white man has a mindset that if you dangle enough money out front, you can make people like you. While there is little doubt that people will PRETEN D to like you, money is not the "end all" that whitey thinks it is. The North Atlantic Treaty Organization was an idea that would consolidate white power, but the reason why it fades is because the rest of the world is growing and becoming increasingly aware of the white man's history and his ways. They can therefore pretend to want to "join" or "become allies," but that is nothing more than an infiltration tactic. And the white man's ego keeps him from believing that a person of color could EVER out-smart or out-finagle him.

Until it's too late (can you say "Twin Towers attacks"?)
In spite of all this,

> Mr. Gates's phrase — "return on investment" — goes to the heart of the emerging Trump doctrine: Allies who will not pay their share, and defend themselves, will not be allies. The difference is that Mr. Obama, Mr. Gates and Mrs. Clinton are all urging gradual change. Mr. Trump is declaring, perhaps for effect, that he would reconsider the entire structure of postwar alliances. . (Sanger, 2016).

In my educated view, I think that "return on investment" has been mis-diagnosed by the white man. People like Warren Buffet, Bill Gates, Donald Trump – they view this concept in purely financial or economic terms. But some people see it differently: return on investment is another way of saying "reap what you sow," and when it comes to that concept, the white man is in debt to the world. Remember the words of Malcolm X, although the context may be different, but the culprit and the debtor remains the same. In the book By Any Means Necessary, Malcolm explained the following:

> "If you are the son of a man who had a wealthy estate and you inherit your father's estate, you have to pay off the debts that your father incurred before he died. The only reason that the present generation of white Americans are in a position of economic strength...is because their fathers worked our fathers for over 400 years with no pay...We were sold from plantation to plantation like you sell a horse, or a cow, or a chicken, or a bushel of wheat...All that money...is what gives the present generation of American whites the ability to walk around the earth with their chest out...like they have some kind of economic ingenuity. **Your father isn't here to pay. My father isn't here to collect. But I'm here to collect and you're here to pay."** (By Any Means Necessary, New York: Pathfinder Press, 1970, page 123 – emphasis added.)

Do you think the white man doesn't realize what he's done to the world? Malcolm was talking about reparations for years of enslavement. When the white man fought his brother and had fucked up the European economies, following World War II America developed a plan where the U.S. gave over $13 billion in economic support to help rebuild Western Europe. White folks helping out other white folks. And this was in the 1940s.

What about the nations of color he's raped and stolen from? What about the under development of Africa? How about his respective invasions of Vietnam and Korea? What about the returns on THOSE investments, white boy? But again, race is what Trump is concentrated on, which is the goal of the white nationalist. As Sanger (2016) put it,

> His impulse also ignores the tangible return on the nation's investments in alliances: the winning of the Cold War; the sharing of one another's deepest intelligence secrets by the United States, Britain, Canada, Australia and New Zealand; the counterterrorism partnership with France and Germany; and the collaboration in cyberespionage with Israel against Iran.

All white concerns, from New Zealand, Israel, Canada and Britain to France and Germany. These peckerwoods are consolidating their power and Trump is

[Type text]

trying to horde as much of it as he can. But in either case, it's all about white nationalism and its maintenance. The "colored" nations – Iran, Iraq, Saudi Arabia, Syria, Asia, and Africa – they are, on varying levels, the enemies of the white man, who is colorless in a world where skin color is the overwhelming norm. Don't you get it? Even the melanin-deficient Trump sees that, which is why he tans his skin!

It's about global white unification, plain and simple. Put another way,

> Alliances move incrementally because getting nations to rethink
> their core national interests takes time, persuasion, and often
> coercion. And while it is tempting to issue ultimatums, it was Mr.
> Gates, a former C.I.A. director, who observed that three of the
> least-uttered words in Washington are, "And then what?" .
> (Sanger, 2016)

Rethinking "core national interests" may apply to many things. But when it comes to these white nations there is one subject that they all are in agreement on, and that is, "What are we gonna do about all these niggers?" And when they use that word it is not only black people, but anyone who is not white. And if that is too hard to believe, just look at the history of the white man here in America.

A coward who remains a "master warmonger." And that is the most dangerous kind of person: someone who is so spineless that he can and will "push the button" at the drop of a hat. The violence starts at the top and the attitude is pervasive – even at the rallies he has held and continues to sponsor. And since "like takes to like," the scum that permeates the Trump makeup and those who are like him filters down to the people who vote for and follow him. Just check out the following.

Trump and the Violence at His Rallies

Trump's rallies were mainly made up of rednecks and other hicks, but every now and then some people of color would attend. At one rally in Dayton agents rushed the stage to protect Trump from a man who had gotten on stage. Trump tried to make himself look like a super hero, as you will see in the following March 12, 2016 article that appeared on MSN.com. under the headline, "Agents Rush Stage to Protect Donald Trump at Dayton Rally."

According to the article:

> Security guards rushed the stage to protect Donald Trump at a rally
> in Dayton, Ohio, on Saturday, less than a day after thousands of

[Type text]

> protesters forced him to postpone a rally in Chicago.Trump
> appeared to be have been alerted by a member of the crowd that
> someone was behind him, and he immediately jerked his head
> around as four agents surrounded him to provide a protective
> shield. (Cirrill, 2016).

Trump is a coward who has probably never had a fist fight in his life. He talks a lot of shit because for the most part he's always had his own security staff. This is the kind of person who is always willing to assault or drop bombs on other people. And the reason for that is simple: he's never been tested. In mid-April he dropped a 22,000 pound bomb on Afghanistan. This came on the heels of his firing 59 cruise missiles into Syria even as he ordered Naval ships to creep ever closer to another maniac, the leader of North Korea. Cowardly people are always the first ones who start wars, or so it seems.

According to the accounts of the Trump rally, "A man attempted to breach the secure buffer and was removed rapidly and professionally," Trump spokeswoman Hope Hicks said in an e-mailed response, directing further inquiries to the Secret Service. (Cirrill, 2016). Trump was reaping what he had been sewing; he wanted to come off like a bad ass, call people names, curse in front of audiences and instigate, but his cowardly ass took a powder when things appeared to be getting too troublesome.

Continuing:

> Trump continued with his speech after the incident as the crowd
> chanted "USA, USA." He gave them thumbs up. "Thank you for
> the warning," Trump told a member of the audience in the front
> row. "I was ready for 'em, but it's much easier if the cops do it,
> don't we agree? What a great job. What a great job. And to think
> I've had such an easy life. What do I need this for? What do I need
> this for? I've done great. I love this country. We're going to make
> this country great again. It's payback time. These guys are so
> fantastic." (Cirrill, 2016).

It's payback time? For what? All he's done is rip off one sector of the market after another. All he's done is live a sheltered life and go through the motions of being a "tough guy." There is nothing in Donald Trump's listless life that shows that he knows how to fight, that he can fight or that he'd know what to do if he ever got in one. And yet he stumbles into the Republican nomination for President and then gets in front of stadiums filled with uneducated rednecks and talks that "make America great again" bullshit, implying that America has gone

[Type text]

under because for the previous eight years a black man was at the helm. That is the unspoken message.

He says it's a "great job." Of course it is: any job that you can get where you don't have to do any thinking or manual labor is a job made in Heaven. You make all that money, receive international and national attention for things you didn't do, tweet shit off the top of your head and have the entire world shaking, flying back and forth from one hotel to the next and pretending that you're "working" – that's a "great job," alright. In his own words, he's had such an "easy life." It's easy because he takes short cuts and has other people doing the real work. Remember the old saying by Napoleon Hill: "All rivers and most men are crooked because they choose the path of least resistance."

Agitation is all this provocateur knows. His life is listless unless there is someone or some group that he can degrade or run a scam on. His rallies are a reflection of the people who are the most likely to fall for his line of bullshit, all the while knowing what he's done in the past. Continuing with Trump's rallies and the violence that continued to be an integral part. Continuing to play the role as the defender of the downtrodden and as a victim himself, check out the following:

> Trump also said that the activist group MoveOn.org was responsible for organizing the protests. "These are bad people. Let me tell you, these are people that truly don't want to see America great again. I'm telling you that," Trump said. "We have got to toughen up now. We don't like it," Trump said. "By doing what I did -- that story is all over the world right now that we made the right decision under great pressure." (Cirrill, 2016).

Trump is what we used to call a "provocateur" back in the 1970s. These were sellout black people who would be working for the system who were sent to infiltrate black organizations and stir up shit so that the cops could raid, harass and shoot down black militants. That is what Earl Anthony and Louis Tackwood did and were successful at. Trump is working for Vladimir Putin, make no mistake about it. His job is to divide America, stir up a lot of shit, keep people in a state of outrage, and have these crazy silly Americans (both black and white) pointing their fingers are peripheral issues and keeping their minds off of the kleptocracy that Trump is seeking to create – just like his boyfriend Vladimir has done in Russia.

The violence brings attention and dupes Trump followers into thinking that he's a real "cowboy." Check it out:

> Friday's cancelled rally followed weeks of escalating tensions between protesters and some attendees at Trump's rallies, scuffles

that have gone viral on social media. Last week in New Orleans,
local police struggled to remove dozens of protesters, and Trump's
personal security had to assist. In St. Louis on Friday, hours before
the protests erupted in Chicago, more than a dozen local police
struggled for more than 10 minutes to remove a group of protesters
who chanted that Trump was a racist. (Cirrill, 2016).

It would not be beyond Trump to sabotage these "rallies," have them
cancelled and in doing so be able to blame the cancellation on "unruly protesters."
In that way he could avoid a possible confrontation and also be able to tease the
media into making a story out of a non-story. Trump's effective use of the media is
one reason for his on-going public persona, even as President. Even when he is as
guilty as sin, which is in most cases, the media wants to break down the action or
the terminology, use psychological assessments and then bring on a slew of other
white "experts" to provide analysis and commentary. In doing so, the media sells
advertisements and promotes itself. In the newspaper business we had a slogan: "If
it bleeds, it leads." This means the more violent the story, the higher on the front
page it will appear.

And despite his "concern" for the alleged violence, Trump kept on stoking
the fires and flames of fanaticism:

> Trump mused that he would be open to holding more town hall
> rallies, venues that are smaller to accommodate more personal one-
> on-one interaction between the voter and candidate. "I'd actually
> like to have a couple of town hall meetings," Trump said. (Cirrill,
> 2016).

This coward never did that. If he held a townhall meeting it would have been
pre-planned; those in attendance would have been screened and the place would
have been packed with Trump's flunkies. Trump doesn't have the guts to stand up
to people with opposing points of view. Even during the Republican debates, he
was on stage with white men who were similarly fucked up in thinking and values,
and even one black (Ben Carson) and two Latinos (Ted Cruz and Marco Rubio)
who were not going to give him much push back. It's like a pillow fight when
these Republicans differ and they are trying to sound "professional" and they pull
punches and refuse to confront each other because they all have skeletons in their
closets.

Trump can therefore tee off on them and in doing so, increase the violence at
his rallies that consist of people who see him as a real "macho man."

[Type text]

In sum, keep in mind that violence at Trump rallies were a precursor of things that were yet to come. The violence pitted his redneck supporters and those "Make America Great Again" peckerwoods against anyone who wasn't male and pale. They even attacked their own fellow white females. And look around: what is taking place as of the end of the year 2017 as white women wage war under the banner of "sexual misconduct" and Uncle Tom negroes continue begging Trump to treat them the same way he treats white citizens. Trump has accomplished the goals of his boyfriend Vladimir Putin: divide America and pit American institutions against one another.

And speaking of Putin, let's take a look at the Trump-Putin relationship: are they barbaric buddies or outright booty bandits?

Donald Trump's Homoerotic Love Affair With Russia's Vladimir Putin

There is something going on between Donald Trump and Vladimir Putin, and it's not just political. It's deeper than a "bro-mance" and it borders on homoerotic fixation – at least when it comes to Trump's feelings for the Russian ruler. In my view Trump has an obsession/attraction to a number of men, including former President Barack Obama. But with Putin there is something more: something that forces Trump to literally submit to the Russian leader whenever he is in Putin's presence.

Let's take a look at my theory, based on an article in the June 17, 2016 issue of the *Washington Post* titled, "Inside Trump's Financial Ties to Russia and His Unusual Flattery of Vladimir Putin. The article, written by reporter Tom Hamburger, begins as follows:

> Donald Trump was in his element, mingling with beauty pageant contestants and business tycoons as he brought his Miss Universe pageant to Russia for a much-anticipated Moscow debut. Nonetheless, Trump was especially eager for the presence of another honored guest: Russian President Vladimir Putin. (Hamburger, 2016).

The year was 2013, and Trump was over in Russia kissing ass and keeping most of his dirt undercover – sometimes literally. He was already married to

Melania and yet he was cavorting all over the place for his "business" and she evidently didn't give a damn. After all, it's not as if they're having sex or sleeping together, right? Why doesn't the media probe their personal lives the way they did Barack, Michelle and their kids' lives?

Trump acts like a love-starved teenager whenever the name Putin comes up. He even acts like a child. For instance, note the following:

> Trump tweeted Putin a personal invitation to attend the pageant, and a one-on-one meeting between the New York businessman and the Russian leader was scheduled for the day before the show. Putin canceled at the last minute, but he sent a decorative lacquered box, a traditional Russian gift, and a warm note, according to Aras Agalarov, a Moscow billionaire who served as a liaison between Trump and the Russian leader. (Hamburger, 2016)

Like two lovers: communicating by phone, invitations and then sending a cordial gift when the "date" is cancelled. What is this shit all about. Trump was not even the president but he was currying favor with this Russian asshole who was known for locking up journalists, killing off his competition and doing everything in his power to divide America's institutions – the way he has effectively done in order to get his "boyfriend" Donald Trump elected. And what was the need for that move to be made? Because, as Hillary Clinton made clear during the Presidential debates, Trump is Putin's puppet. And when she said it, all Trump could do was respond in a bitch-like manner, "No, YOU'RE the puppet." You know, that "I'm-rubber-you're-glue" type of bullshit.

But Trump got paid and remember that this was rooted in a need for Trump to build a Trump Tower in Moscow. And Putin wanted to have access to oil in certain areas which meant America would have to drop its sanctions. But before that there was something going on between Trump and Moscow's oligarchs:

> In 2005, Trump signed a one-year deal with a New York development company to explore a Trump Tower in Moscow. Bayrock Group found a site — an old pencil factory — but the effort fizzled again. Trump claimed in a later court proceeding that Russian investors were spooked when a 2005 book questioned his net worth. But the Russia quest continued. In his 2008 speech, Donald Jr. announced that he had traveled to Russia six times in the previous 18 months. But, he said, Russia presented enormous challenges. "As much as we want to take our business over there, Russia is just a different world," the younger Trump said. "It is a

> question of who knows who, whose brother is paying off who. . . .
> It really is a scary place." (Hamburger, 2016)

And Trump Tower in Moscow was what Putin and Trump saw as a major financial achievement:

> Trump has long aspired to build a Trump Tower in Russia — a
> market that first gained his attention in the 1980s as the Cold War
> was ending and the Soviet Union began to open more to outsiders.
> "Russia is one of the hottest places in the world for investment,"
> Trump said in a 2007 deposition. "We will be in Moscow at some
> point," he promised. (Hamburger, 2016)

With all this information, why would Trump have the gall to run for office – unless there was an incentive, unless he was prompted to? This white man seeks more money and as a result, the bid for the Presidency was, in my view, the fulfillment of a promise that he had made to his boyfriend Putin. Putin, more likely than not, wanted proof or the "commitment" that Trump had to various projects in and around Russia. Even when rejected for some of those projects, Trump continued to press on, like the rejected girlfriend who wants the "ex" to give her another chance to "prove" herself.

But the love affair goes much deeper than that. The bottom line was that Putin knew that the two could help each other in their tryst, but that he (Putin) would be the ultimate winner, because even with Trump under his control, anything that Trump was in control of would inevitably belong to Putin. After all, it was a twisted version of "community property" like in a twisted marriage. "What's mine is mine and what's yours is mine." You know – the way the se housewives do the tricks … oops I mean the "men" that they dupe into marrying them.

In other words, the two could help each other, and that is what it was about: quid pro quo between a kleptocrat (Putin) and a wannabe autocrat (Trump).

Pay close attention to the following:

> Still, the weekend was fruitful for Trump. He received a portion of
> the $14 million paid by Agalarov and other investors to bring the
> pageant to Moscow. Agalarov said he and Trump signed an
> agreement to build a Trump Tower in the heart of Moscow — at
> least Trump's fifth attempt at such a venture. And Trump seemed
> energized by his interactions with Russia's financial elite at the

pageant and a glitzy after-party in a Moscow nightclub.
(Hamburger, 2016)

Trump had been sued for tens of millions by Americans he had bilked, from that scam Trump University to non-payment of employees who worked on various Trump Towers. He wouldn't pay cooks, janitors and definitely not the construction workers. And even after winning the Presidency, the cheap sonofabitch used taxpayers money to travel to his hotel in Mar-A-Lago and would charge visiting dignitaries to stay in his hotels and upped the membership from $100,000 a year to $200,000 a year. And remember: tens of thousands of Americans knew about a lot of this stuff and continued to kiss his ass and attend his rallies. Little did they know that Trump was under the control of Vladimir Putin.

Look at how long Trump's been infatuated with Russia:

> "Almost all of the oligarchs were in the room," Trump bragged to Real Estate Weekly upon returning home. Trump's relationship with Putin and his warm views toward Russia, which began in the 1980s when the country was still part of the Soviet Union, have emerged as one of the more curious aspects of his presidential campaign. (Hamburger, 2016).

Trump's tendency to brag about issues that he believes makes him look good is going to prove to be his undoing. But remember: he's a white male and so is Putin. Brothers may fight, but brothers will still be brothers (recall the American civil war). And so it goes: he boasts that he's tight to the second existing "super power" and between the two of them he believes that can be some future long-term linkage. Trump doesn't give a damn about what the experts say or what the average American thinks. The long-time hatred of Communism was a trick, since the controllers of Communism, like the ones who control and work to spread "democracy", were both peckerwoods.

Trump loves Russia and Putin no matter what the track record. For instance,

> The overwhelming consensus among American political and national security leaders has held that Putin is a pariah who disregards human rights and has violated international norms in seeking to regain influence and territory in the former Soviet bloc. In 2012, one year before Trump brought his beauty pageant to Moscow, then-Republican presidential nominee Mitt Romney called Russia the United States' top geopolitical threat — an assessment that has only gained currency since then. (Hamburger, 2016)

You can't tell a man who is love with a woman anything negative about that woman that he is bound to believe. That's the way it is between Trump and Putin. Trump is the effeminate one with Putin being what Eldridge Cleaver would have called "The Omnipotent Administrator." In other words, Trump's job is to defend the one that he loves by any means necessary and that is what he has done for decades.

For instance, do you remember that February 6, 2017 interview with Bill O'Reilly on Fox News? Let me refresh your memory, and note closely the words of the future President Donald J. Trump:

>)President Donald Trump appeared to equate US actions with the authoritarian regime of Russian President Vladimir Putin in an interview released Saturday, saying, "There are a lot of killers. You think our country's so innocent?"Trump made the remark during an interview with Fox News' Bill O'Reilly, saying he respected his Russian counterpart."But he's a killer," O'Reilly said to Trump."There are a lot of killers. You think our country's so innocent?" Trump replied.(Tatum, 2017).

So Trump is so in love that he would castigate his own country to defend Putin. Don't get me wrong: America is fucked up, cowardly and definitely has a history of killing, but that's not the point. Take note that nowhere does Trump agree that Putin was also a killer. It is easier for Trump to indict American history, his racist forefathers and the like than to say a negative word about Donald Trump. Do you know what this reminds me of? The lyrics from the old classic March 1966 cut, "When A Man Loves a Woman" by Percy Sledge. In particular, the following:

> When a man loves a woman
> Can't keep his mind on nothin' else
> He'd trade the world
> For a good thing he's found
> If she is bad, he can't see it
> She can do no wrong
> Turn his back on his best friend
> If he puts her down

Simply omit the gender distinctions: is this not the way Trump acts whenever the subject of Russia or Vladimir Putin comes up? "Can't keep his mind on nothing else" seems appropriate because Trump is busy defending every action and policy that Putin advances. "He'd trade the world for the good thing he's

[Type text]

found." That is what Trump is in the process of doing as he withdraws from NAFTA, the Paris Climate Accords, and UNESCO, to name but a few. Trump has literally "traded" the world in his defense of Putin and Russia. "If she is bad, he can't see it/She can do no wrong." Look at the Syrian situation and the Russian invasion of the Ukraine – Trump turned his head and his back on the world so Putin could do his dictator thang. "Turn his back on his best friend/If he puts her down." Trump and Reilly were friends. Trump is the leader of America. And yet he rejected both of them when the subject became Putin as a killer. Trump's answer: "Are we so innocent"?

Russia controls Trump in a lot of ways and most of them are linked to money, which Russia has tons of (theft from the masses and amassing wealth through its kleptocracy). Put another way,

> Trump has conveyed a different view, informed in part through his business ambitions. Since the 1980s, Trump and his family members have made numerous trips to Moscow in search of business opportunities, and they have relied on Russian investors to buy their properties around the world. "Russians make up a pretty disproportionate cross-section of a lot of our assets," Trump's son, Donald Jr., told a real estate conference in 2008, according to an account posted on the website of eTurboNews, a trade publication. "We see a lot of money pouring in from Russia." (Hamburger, 2016)

His own son's words should put an end to Trump's presidency because it proves treason and collusion. Let me repeat what Donald Jr., said above: "Russians make up a pretty disproportionate cross-section of a lot of our assets." This is the financial link that helps to keep Trump beholden to Russia and keeps Russia in the driver's seat. As the saying goes, "The hand that feeds, controls."

Add the money to the bitch-like response of Trump to a simple "compliment" and it should be clear who is calling the shots. In fact, Trump said as much himself, remember?:

> The back-and-forth has continued. In a mid-June rally, Trump cited those comments as the reason he will not reject the Russian leader. "A guy calls me a genius, and I'm going to renounce?" Trump said. "I'm not going to renounce him." The next day in St. Petersburg, Putin again called Trump a "colorful person" and said he welcomed Trump's proposal for a "full-scale resumption" of U.S.-Russia ties. (Hamburger, 2016)

I saw a clip where Putin denied calling Trump a genius. But Trump is prone to embellishment (lying) and blowing up things – like when he got spineless Sean Spicer to say that a photo shows hundreds of thousands of people at Trump's inaugural in an attempt to make it appear as if Trump had more people than Barack Obama did (Obama had many times more). Calling Trump "colorful" is no compliment. To be "colorful" is to be "exciting or lively." So what? A retarded child with ADHD is "colorful" but the question is: does he know his ass from a hole in the ground?

Of course Putin would "welcome Trump's proposal for a full scale resumption of U.S.-Russian ties" because that is the key to expanding Russia's control. Such an arrangement is nothing more than a farmer welcoming the coming of an extra mule to pull the plow: the mule gets nothing but helps the farmer with HIS territorial development! The linkage is clear and it is based on the one-way love affair that Trump has going with Putin:

> On the campaign trail, Trump has called for a new partnership with Moscow, overhauling NATO, the allied military force seen as the chief protector of pro-Western nations near Russia. And Trump has surrounded himself with a team of advisers who have had financial ties to Russia. (Hamburger, 2016)

That is why so many positions in the White House have not been filled. That is why Trump surrounds himself with idiots and "yes" men. That is why Trump continues to defile and denigrate American institutions such as law enforcement, the media, the military and others. Such degradation pits American institutions against the executive branch and as we know, "A house divided against itself cannot stand." And Putin and his boys are at the ready, willing to provide as much money as may be needed. As Hamburger (2016) wrote,

> The coming together of Trump's business and political agendas was evident during his 2013 Moscow trip, in which he was seeking deals at the same time he was starting to ponder a presidential run.

Did you read that? He never lost sight of making money being a priority – the Presidential bid was just another avenue he would use in order to generate the revenue. The same mentality he had when he opened up that scam school Trump University and all those other bullshit initiatives he had. He puts his name on a building that someone else builds or pays for and then tells people its his building. He sells his brand, he doesn't sell any skill because he has no real skill to speak of.

Just a big mouth, the ability to lie at the drop of a hat, and white skin which in America, is a key to open up a myriad of doors.

Hamburger, 2016) further explains,

> Russia has signaled a deep interest in the U.S. election and in
> Trump, in particular. The Russian ambassador to the United States,
> breaking from a tradition in which diplomats steer clear of
> domestic politics, attended Trump's April foreign policy speech in
> which he called for ending "this horrible cycle of hostility"
> between the two nations. (Hamburger, 2016).

That sounds so nice, doesn't it? But remember that these are white men who are colluding,planning, plotting and conniving. These are white men who want to amass power so that they can rule the majority of the world, which consists of people of color. But while Trump is a punk and wants to tow the line with Putin, the Putin plan is much different: pimp the hell out of Trump, use his access to world resources, take over those resources, expire the Soviet empire, and then use the threat of nuclear missiles to ward off any kind of response or retaliation.

And so it would come to be. The white men used technology and computer knowledge to infiltrate the American political system. Not that black people would have noticed a difference between lying ass Hillary Clinton or the even worse con man Trump. But for the sake of the rest of the nation, the die was cast. And America was so busy with video games, watching pro sports, seeing what the latest fashion craze was and falling for the lie that "education is the key to success," they couldn't see the game that was being run on them by Trump and Putin, even though Trump was telling them, in coded language, all along.

Again, Hamburger:

> And in the past week, The Post reported that hackers tied to the
> Russian government had gained access to the Democratic National
> Committee's opposition research file on Trump.A spokesman for
> the Russian Embassy said that Ambassador Sergey I. Kislyak's
> attendance at the Trump speech should not be considered an
> indication that Russia is partial to Trump. "There is no preference,"
> the spokesman said. Still, the relationship is setting off alarms in
> pro-Western capitals — and in the U.S. foreign policy community.
> (Hamburger, 2016).

Remember that the article just quoted from was published in June of 2016. And today in November of 2017, these peckerwoods are still fist-fucking around looking for "evidence of collusion," "proof of infiltration" and shit like that when

[Type text]

the writing was right on the wall. The hate that these white men held for Barack Obama, which had them blocking everything he proposed, and had Trump cancelling out all that was done, paved the way for the racial divisions in this country today. White people will forget but black people won't. But black people are so damn naïve and pro-American, they don't have the guts to challenge the system even when it is clear that the damn system is broken.

Trump is in love with power and men who wield it without mercy. At the top of that list of dictators that Trump admires is Putin. Putin, in turn, wants to enjoy some of the American materialism that Trump hotels and other enterprises are known for. Put another way,

> Part of the allure was what Trump and his associates saw as a huge opportunity — **the chance to market American-style luxury apartments to the wealthy elite in a place that still mostly offered utilitarian Soviet-style construction.** The Russian market had "natural strength, especially in the high-end sector," said Donald Trump Jr. in his 2008 real estate conference speech. Moscow held special appeal because wealthy people throughout the region wanted to own real estate in the capital city, he said. (Hamburger, 2016 – emphasis added)

Two power hungry white men pretending to be on the opposite ends of the ideological spectrum – one Communist and one Capitalist – but in reality when it comes to black people, they share the same views: let's keep the niggers contained and powerless. Both countries were involved in the pillaging of Africa and both nations have a hatred for brown immigrants. Both nations trot their women out as whores for the world to gawk at and use them for political gain. And these bitches are aware of it but try to play dumb the way they are now doing with all this talk about "sexual misconduct." These bitches will gladly endorse such misconduct when they can get paid. And don't you forget it.

Trump's 'Attraction' to Men: Obama, etc.

There is no doubt in my mind that Donald Trump has been involved in gay relationships before. You can look at the way Melania stares at him and refuses to hold his hand to see that he's not screwing HER. He hires men who he sees from a distance, as was the case with a man named Allen Weisselberg:

<blockquote>
Allen Weisselberg, the organization's chief financial officer, started off as an accountant for Mr. Trump's father. Matthew Calamari, the organization's chief operating officer, was recruited in 1981 after Mr. Trump saw him eject some hecklers while working security at the United States Open tennis tournament. (Twohey, et. Al. 2016).
</blockquote>

As I make clear in this book, Trump's male obsession with Barack Obama is clear to anyone. His talk about the size of his penis, a joke in and of itself, clearly shows a sexual obsession. The way he spoke about how he treats women – grabbing them by the pussy – shows the art and style of a brute, not a man who has any feelings about women. In my view, all the pussy he's gotten he's paid for directly. But as I wrote below, he has the characteristics of a "rejected ho." Check out my following essay:

TRUMP AS THE "REJECTED HO": 10 EXAMPLES

By: Matthew C. Stelly
August 16, 2017

Donald Trump's problem is that he has a homoerotic fixation on former President Barack Obama and it is beginning to manifest itself in a myriad of ways. Following is an analysis of how Trump displays many of the characteristics of a rejected girlfriend. In other word, a bitch.

As a scholar and master investigator, my interest flared when I read about the "Steele dossier" that had been circulated about Trump's link to Russia. Inside the dossier, in addition to information about alleged schemes to rig the election, were inferences that Trump was in Russia and stayed at the Ritz-Carlton, the same hotel that former president Barack Obama and wife Michelle stayed in.

According to the information, Trump wanted to stay in the same room that Obama stayed in and then got Russian operatives to hire prostitutes to stand over the bed that the Obama's had slept in and, get this: piss on it while he (Trump) watched. Now fast forward to August 24, 2017 where Trump circulates a damn meme about him "eclipsing" Obama. According to ABC News:

<blockquote>
President Donald Trump today retweeted a meme a picture of him gradually blocking an image of former President Obama, with the caption "The best eclipse ever!" The meme was originally tweeted at Trump by a Twitter user who identifies himself as Jerry Travone, "a YouTube actor and political junkie" and "proud Trump
</blockquote>

supporter and pushback against liberalism," according to his
Twitter bio.

So you see the two of them and slowly Trumps photo appears in front of Obama's and finally covers him totally. This, in my view, is a homoerotic reference. Trump is obsessed with his African American predecessor, feels inferior and in all likelihood, dickless by comparison. Obama is smarter, better looking, funnier, had a finer wife, more beautiful and well-behaved children and is more loved in most parts of the world. By comparison, Trump feels impotent.

This, in my view, was a version of "beat up my boyfriend" or "I'm gonna screw you in the same bed that my ex and I used to have sex in" scenario that some of us have heard about from time to time. Hence, my idea about Trump's homoerotic fascination about Obama, who is black. More than a few white men have had that "I wish I was a nigger" fantasy in their lives, mostly wanting the sexuality associated with black men. Malcolm X said that when he was a pimp, the service he was asked to perform most by white "tricks" was to screw their wives while they watched.

Let the juxtaposition begin.

To begin with, lies about the background of the "boyfriend" who rejected you. All of a sudden the boyfriend who you admired from afar is seen in a different light. Now as you seek to move on with your life you find that life is more difficult than it appeared to be when you watched the "other guy" do it. You feel inferior and overwhelmed. All of this makes you tense and you need someone to blame. Your narcissism won't help because all your life you took credit for what other people did. Now it's on your shoulders and you simply can't hang. You don't have the necessary skill set. This sets the stage for the "rejected bitch" scenario I am about to unveil.

Secondly, lies about the former boyfriend regarding the things you used to believe and boast about and told your friends that he was "a great guy." Now all of a sudden he is the bane of your existence. Remember just after the inauguration during the transition? Trump shook hands with Obama and appeared to not want to let go. He told the media that Obama was "a great guy" and that he liked him and all that. This changed almost immediately because when all is said and done, he didn't really mean it. Trump was lying once again. He knew the Obama was beloved and he was trying to feed off of some of that emotion. But it fell short. Way short.

Third, Trump – like the rejected girlfriend – is jealous over the fact that Barack's main squeeze, Michelle, has more beauty and class than his bitch,

Melania. Just compare the two. One can barely speak English, has photos all over the internet posing like a ho, and has a cold blooded stare that she directs at Donald when he's not looking. Michelle was all class and so smart that Melania had to plagiarize one of her speeches. The white press just glossed over it as if it never happened. But we know that it did.

Fourth, as the rejected bitch, Trump now travels and goes out of his way to prove that he is "desirable" by throwing himself at other women, forcing himself on them and making claims about his exploits that simply are not true. This is what the rejected girlfriend does, hoping that the "news" will get back to the ex boyfriend who, in reality, could care less. Like that rejected girl, Trump can dye his hair, maybe add a few extensions, get a tan and wear high-end suits. But it simply doesn't work: he has to PAY for sex as most white men tend to do. In fact, as most men do: what do you think a housewife is?

Fifth, the rejected girlfriend blames the former boyfriend for things that he did not do. Remember Trump said that Barack bugged Trump Tower? Remember when he said that Barack was responsible for the creation of Isis because he "pulled out too soon"? (No pun intended). The rejected girlfriend will spread rumors in order to make the ex look bad and make her appear to be a victim. Witness the spate of domestic violence charges that are filed after the fact. No restraining orders. No police reports. Just rumors about "what he used to do" when they were together. No evidence – just like there was no evidence of Trump Tower having been bugged. No evidence of a team of investigators having "proof" that Obama wasn't born in America. Remember THOSE lies?

Sixth, the rejected girlfriend seeks to destroy all material reminders of the ex-boyfriend through destruction. The burning of gifts, bleach on clothing left behind and "cleansing" of the apartment are a few examples. This is what Trump is doing in his homoerotic fixation on Barack Obama. He is trying to "cleanse" the government record of Barack's accomplishments because he cannot stand being constantly reminded of Obama's accomplishments. Mitch McConnell had vowed that he and his white buddies would reject every bill that Obama sent for them to consider. Trump went one step further and worked to take Obama accomplishments off the books permanently.

Seventh, the rejected girlfriend enlists the aid of her girlfriends to "get payback" on the boyfriend who is long gone. They will do things like shoot up his car and then run for the bushes, they will spread rumors about him and even go so far as to make claims like "he's got AIDS" and so on. This is what Trump did. The AIDS claim or the claim by the rejected girlfriend that the ex is gay is analogous to saying Barack was not born in America. The shooting up of cars and running for the bushes is just what Trump is doing to this very day as he exhibits "hit and run" tactics against Obama's global peace initiatives, his punishing of Putin and Russia and his closeness to countries of color.

In addition to seeking the aid of her girlfriends, the rejected woman also looks for guys to beat up the ex. This is done through finding a big dummy who is hard up, giving him some booty and while he's lying there in a cum-stained stupor, telling him that the ex "raped" her or perhaps one of her children. Trump has found black lackeys in the Black Republicans, Republicans for Trump and coon preachers who he tells stories to and who, after being paid, spread the word through churchgoers about the "sins" that Obama committed because, after all, he's not a Christian – he's a Muslim!

Similarity number nine is what takes place when the rejected female finds out that her ex is far more popular and acceptable than she otherwise knew. So she simply flips the script: that "niceness" was a front for the outside world but behind closed doors he used to beat her with a pick axe. When asked why there were no bruises, she simply tells people that she covered them up with makeup. When asked why no police report could be found or why no restraining order was filed, she says she was "afraid" because he threatened "to do something to her" if she made those moves.

Trump has committed similar atrocities against a man who he has a homoerotic attraction to. Even with Barack long gone and vacationing with his beautiful wife and daughters, Trump's obsession has him cooking up more and more lies: Obama was in collusion with Hillary during the election, Obamacare must be repealed and replaced. He covers up his lies with more lies using fake data, false statistics and outright lies in a more modernized and sophisticated version of "see – the nigga did it!"

Tenth and finally, now rejected, the female seeks a substitute, one who looks like the ex, is more accomplished than the ex, but who she can control more easily. Then she can parade this charlatan around, a guy who doesn't even know he's being used, and hope that the word gets out that she's "moved on." Why do you think Ben Carson is in the cabinet? What role do you think Omarosa Manigault plays in the west wing? They are nothing more than window dressing on the set, an attempt to replace the "ex" with someone who has a similar appearance but who is grossly lacking in essence.

Trump is a ho. He's taking it up the ass from Putin who, by the way, has also screwed Melania more than once. Trump is screwing his daughter Ivanka and those kids are probably his. Jared Kushner, in case you haven't taken a good look, is as

[Type text]

gay as the day is long. Those two mannequins, Don Jr., and the other son, are nothing more than impotent imitators of their impish father.

Trump as White Male Prototype: Gender Bias/Misogynist

Before getting into the gist of this section of the book, let me give you a general and most diabolical example of the low regard that Trump has, not only for women but for human life and human rights in general. Recall with me if you will, the following:

> In a television interview on March 30, he suggested that women who have illegal abortions should face "some form of punishment," then reversed himself in another carefully worded statement, then suggested in an interview that abortion should remain legal, then effectively clicked "undo" with another written statement. In each case, Mr. Trump appeared to be seeking a sort of shelter somewhere between his original remark and the wave of objections it set off. . (Sanger, 2016).

It matters not if he meant it or not. Just the mere fact that an asshole with that much power would even attempt to believe that a woman's right to life should be punished clearly shows why he is thrice divorced and has to grab women's pussies (his words) for a cheap thrill. This is the perfect overview for what you are about to read when it comes to Trump, a master misogynist and so typical of most white men despite the way the media attempts to make him appear to be "an exception."

<u>Donald Trump: A Misogynist Overview</u>

From outright insults and an apparent fear of their blood to a public claim that women who have abortions should be punished, Trump's misogynistic claims say far more about his previous wives than they do about him. They knew he was an asshole when they dated, lied to him, took his money and made a living off of him after they divorced him. So they aided and abetted him in his on-going crimes of stupidity being perpetrated on an equally stupid American public. These women cannot feign ignorance and get away with it. So let that be clear.

Furthermore, you would think that Donald Trump would be able to "relate" to women since, in my view, he's a bitch himself. He has all the characteristics of a scatter-brained old woman who has been jilted by a lover and now just lashes out at everyone within hearing distance. Were he not a white male prototype – that is, talking out of both sides of his mouth while wielding power over the ignorant and rednecked – he would be a cartoon character worthy of Disney.

A thin-skinned, name-calling, cosmetically covered, orange-tanned woman in a man's body and with a typical male mentality

Brennan (2003) provides us with important general insights when he writes,

> Now and throughout history, pejorative language has played a major role in the longstanding victimization of women … It [his study] concludes with observations about how this pernicious anti-female lexicon of derogation is part and parcel of a pervasive seamless shroud of anti-life rhetoric called upon to rationalize violence against other victims (born and unborn) in contemporary society and in times past.

The anti-female lexicon permeates American society just as does a color-coded lexicon that I have addressed in several of my other writings. Trump, again, is no exception and in fact, is the prototype when it comes to the maltreatment of women. He is the image that the policy makers had in mind as the definition of what constituted "sexual harassment" was being developed. There are a plethora of examples of this being the case.

I won't even begin with the way that he has treated and continues to treat his daughter Ivanka. I actually saw that edition of "The View" on television the day he told the host that he would date her if she wasn't his daughter. (addressed later in this book). This was more than a decade ago and I was appalled at it then. As the father of three beautiful daughters I have never at any time sought to date any of them. I have seen a picture of Trump sitting with Ivanka when she was only 15years old, clad in a mini-skirt, being tightly hugged by her "father." And even today, in 2017, she appears to be more of a wife in terms of her body language than the rather seductive Melania.

The wolfing continued. In March of 2016, a Washington Post editor said that Trump called her "beautiful." In my view, so what? These white bitches put on dresses that are up to their vaginas, wear low cut blouses – and this is workforce attire! If someone calls you beautiful, that is what you were seeking, wasn't it? At

[Type text]

any rate, this is an extension of the "nigga raped me" stuff that has taken place historically at the hands of "Miss Ann." But this woman was conservatively clad and Trump nevertheless felt the need to make unwarranted comments.

At any rate in March of 2016 here is what was described in the Boston Globe story:

> A Washington Post journalist said Donald Trump called her "beautiful" after she asked him a policy question during a meeting with the paper's editorial board Monday. In a piece published on the Post's website, Karen Attiah, deputy digital editor for the publication's opinion section, wrote that she was "stunned" by the incident. (Reiss, 2016).

These white bitches always turn out to be somehow "victims." This woman is a black woman and she's the Global Opinions Editor of the Washington Post. So what if he called her "beautiful"? She's just trying to become a part of the story. Like far too many black men, her hair has been straightened and it is very long, as if extensions were added. Why does she do that? So she can "fit in to get in." Now that she's in – on the white man's turf, mind you – she's complaining because a known pussy-chaser called her "beautiful." Why therefore, would she be "stunned" when she got the desired male response?

Continuing:

> Attiah wrote that during the meeting, she pushed Trump to answer questions on his message of racial inclusion. According to a transcript of the conversation posted on The Washington Post's website, Trump told Attiah that he is "the least racist person that you will ever meet." She then pressed him on his rhetoric and how it might be divisive for the country. (Reiss, 2016).

This is vintage white male rhetoric. He is being pushed on an issue that he is obviously ignorant of and he's talking to a black woman whose physical appearance is the epitome of self-induced aesthetic assimilation. He therefore spots a weakness: she wants to appear white, she's a high ranking black person, most black people I know are sellouts, therefore she must be a sellout too, Attiah should have been attacking that remark about him being the least racist person that she would ever meet, which implies that he knows her on a personal level. Instead, she attacks a compliment and wants to make her physical appearance the issue. That's how I see it.

Attiah's recollection of the incident continues:

[Type text]

> He responded by noting that he has had "Muslims call and tell me you're right with the Muslim thing, I think it's a serious problem . . . you know you may think of it as negative, many people think it's very positive." At the meeting's end, Attiah wrote that after she thanked Trump for taking her questions, he said he hoped he had answered them, "and added casually with a smile, 'Beautiful.' "(Reiss, 2016).

And then,

> Attiah wrote that she was stunned. "I stayed in the conference room for a few minutes as it sunk in that the potential GOP nominee for president thought it was okay to comment on my appearance," she wrote. (Reiss, 2016).

What a shallow bitch. That is what these female reporters do – hope for the chance to be "noticed." Again, this was not the issue she should have been dealing with. So caught up in her own selfish interests she missed the statements he's making regarding Muslims and again, missed out on his inference that he knows who she knows. This mentality is the same one shared by Megyn Kelly

> "In Trump's world, commenting on a woman's appearance in a professional setting is fair game," she continued. "At least now I know, firsthand, that the sexism that Trump puts on display against Megyn Kelly under the lights of national TV is not that much different from how he is in real life toward female journalists." (Reiss, 2016).

Insulting women would be one thing if that's all he did. But this cowardly sonofabitch has the nerve to be thin-skinned, and if someone retaliates or says something about any of the many physical or mental flaws that he has, he has a damn conniption fit and lashes out like a child.

The attempts at "womanizing" continued as Reiss (2016) reported in a Boston Globe article on March 22, 2016, titled "Washington Post Editor Says Trump Called her 'Beautiful'."

<u>"To the Victor Goes the Spoils"</u>

This statement was made several times during the Republican Presidential contest and repeated by Democrats as an example of everything immoral that they

[Type text]

could get their hands on. Everything but one, and in my view it is the most important. It is military and political in its generic nature, but it is also sexist and misogynistic in its real-world application

The concept of "To the victor goes the spoils" is a term that applies to war. Whoever comes out on top gets the natural resources of the people that they've conquered. In fact, that was the source of the topic being raised by the Republicans. Trump spouted that if he would have been in charge during the war in Iraq, he would have "taken their oil." When asked about it and told that such an act was a violation of international law, he shrugged it off and kept repeating it. He believed that since oil was how the war was funded, and how subsequent rise of ISIS, to take the oil would have been depriving the Iraqis of their primary funding source.

But that's not all that "the spoils" refers to: it also refers to the women.

This may sound like a generalization, but I'm going to say it anyway: there are far too many men and far too many cultures that seem to endorse rape. They seem to think it's alright to snatch a woman and take the booty. Trump himself said that he would grab women by the pussy and just walk up and kiss them – both forms of sexual assault. So if the winner of a conflict wins additional benefits, then those benefits include the free access to the women of that tribe, country or culture that the victory has just overwhelmed.

This is Trump's philosophy as was made clear when women came forward with charges of sexual assault. This was the style of Gary Hart and his lies about having an affair with women and daring the media to follow him; this was the style of John Edwards who was getting booty while his wife was dying of cancer. You may believe that there is a difference between womanizing and rape. There is, but it is merely a difference in "tactics," not in intent and philosophy.

If the "victor" is a millionaire or a billionaire and the people that he controls are poor, then he can use his superior economic position to impose himself on the women of those poor people. Remember slavery? Black men were powerless when white men staggered into the shacks and started snatching up black women and sometimes raping them right in front of the men.

<u>Trump and Menophobia</u>

Menophobia is the fear of menstrual blood – the blood that comes from women when they are on their periods. I don't know about you, but when a woman tells me she's on her period that is good news because it means that she's not pregnant. The playas out there know what I'm talking about. But the fear of period blood, according to the research, goes back to Biblical times. As Moss (2015) notes, "The sociologist Emile Durkheim actually hypothesized that religion developed as a partial response to the "repulsing action" of menstruation." That's how far back it goes, folks. So let me provide some background and evidence so you can see that Trump is nothing unique; he is but one of hundreds of millions of men, black and white, who have a subconscious fear/hatred of women because they bleed once a month.

This brings us to what one writer referred to as "Bloodgate" as it relates to Donald Trump and his comments about former news reporter Megyn Kelly. Moss explains the situation as follows:

> By now we have all been caught up in #Bloodgate. Donald Trump's chauvinistic gaffe about Fox News anchor Megyn Kelly menstruating has (slightly) damaged his reputation among Republicans, leading to retracted invitations and the implausible explanation that he was referring to her nose. "I cherish women," Trump later added.(Moss, 2015)

Trump is not unique. White men have long feared the woman's menstrual periods and this goes back to the Bible. For you holy rollers who kiss the ass of every single person who talks that Christian bullshit, just think about what your own Bible says about a woman's monthly cycle. Leviticus, versus 19 through 33 lays down the (sexist) law. Let's go through it and you can see that Trump, like most male Christians, is one misguided sonofabitch.

The passages begin, thusly:

> **19** "Whenever a woman has her menstrual period, she will be ceremonially unclean for seven days. Anyone who touches her during that time will be unclean until evening.

Seven days? Can you imagine the stigma and shame that these women had to undergo because men were afraid of their blood? Oh sure, they were good enough to screw in the butt, get head from and perhaps have sex with hanging upside down, but actually blood?! This is where the inferiorization of women got a major boost in patriarchal culture. Let's read on:

> **20** Anything on which the woman lies or sits during the time of her period will be unclean.

So it appears as if the Bible is implying that a woman's vagina is contaminated. That she must be shunned. She cannot even sit on her ass without someone shouting, "She's got the cooties!" What the fuck? Trump is hailing back to what is ancestors started and since he claims to be a Christian, he is falling in line with what hundreds of millions of men, black and white, have accepted as Christian policy. Can you see why women hate men's guts?

Continuing:

> **21** If any of you touch her bed, you must wash your clothes and bathe yourself in water, and you will remain unclean until evening.

Wow. This is an early version of "the scarlet letter" in a much different context, is it not? The woman gets the blame for everything, even those physical things that take place naturally. She carries life inside of her and raises the children in many cases, but if she bleeds once a month, she must be avoided. Of course to the cockhounds of the world, she had BETTER get a period or else it's a sign she might be pregnant and if that happens, it's time to get the hell out of Dodge, right?

> **22** If you touch any object she has sat on, you must wash your clothes and bathe yourself in water, and you will remain unclean until evening.

You can't even touch an OBJECT she touched? The so-called Holy Bible is laying this kind of shit out as a matter of law? How many billions of Christians believe this shit? Even women fell prey to the belief that they were somehow "dirty"?

> **23** This includes her bed or any other object she has sat on; you will be unclean until evening if you touch it.

So she can't get any dick. Oh sure, she can give up head behind closed doors and is there any doubt in your mind that this is still taking place all over this country among women who still get their periods? Remember those thick-ass Kotex pads? Women were walking around looking like middle linebackers and you could tell they were "on the rag" as we called it. Yes, I was a part of this sick shit and it is truly twisted. Speaking of the combination of sex and blood, check out the following:

> **24** If a man has sexual intercourse with her and her blood
> touches him, her menstrual impurity will be transmitted to him.
> He will remain unclean for seven days, and any bed on which
> he lies will be unclean.

Wow. A man becomes "contaminated" if he lays with a woman who is on her period. This sounds like the beginning of the basis for the spread of venereal disease! Don't worry about gonorrhea, syphilis, crabs or any sexually transmitted disease: worry about getting blood on the tip of your dick! And you wonder why these Catholic priests are screwing little boys in the butt: they've got an entire religion based on avoiding women altogether!

> **25** "If a woman has a flow of blood for many days that is
> unrelated to her menstrual period, or if the blood continues
> beyond the normal period, she is ceremonially unclean. As
> during her menstrual period, the woman will be unclean as long
> as the discharge continues.

"As long as the discharge continues" the woman is to be shunned and treated like shit. This is basically what YOUR Holy Bible is promoting to these men who stand in front of crowds of people and congregations of the dimwitted and promote this shit within ear shot of grown women and young girls. Women teach their daughters this shit and in doing so lend additional stigma to that which comes naturally. The fable teaches that the young boy asks his father, "You teach me that the lion is the king of the jungle and yet in each story the hunter wins. Why is that?" The father tells his son, "That's the way it will always be – until the iion learns how to write.

And so it shall be done. Women were continually suppressed with this Bible section being a part of the support system, and laws were developed to maintain their suppression. This was carried on when the peckerwood left Europe and brought his diseased ass to American shorts. She continued to get dogged and inferiorized and didn't even get the vote until August of 1920. And now she appears to be devoting her numbers and growing political power to "discharging" the male of the species!

> **26** Any bed she lies on and any object she sits on during that
> time will be unclean, just as during her normal menstrual
> period.

So she cannot even sleep in the very bed that she washes the sheets for and makes each morning. Before anyone, male or female, decides to join a Christian church of any kind, this particular set of verses from Leviticus should be mandatory reading. Since "the truth shall set you free," let's see how these preachers and ministers deal with these angry women who confront them with allegations and questions about how "God's word" deals with their humanity.

> **27**If any of you touch these things, you will be ceremonially unclean. You must wash your clothes and bathe yourself in water, and you will remain unclean until evening.

The previous passage was reinforcement through repetition. But the following one is an important addendum:

> **28** "When the woman's bleeding stops, she must count off seven days. Then she will be ceremonially clean.

But the bleeding is not all the woman is saddled with. Now she has to wait a week until she is deemed "clean." That means that she has three more weeks and then its back to the stigma again. In simple terms she must live in a continual state of fear and alienation. And the man is in charge, as usual: check it out.

> **29** On the eighth day she must bring two turtledoves or two young pigeons and present them to the priest at the entrance of the Tabernacle.

What are the partridge in a pear tree? What kind of shit is this? Where is a woman going to find a damn turtle dove or a pigeon. And why should she risk her neck trying to capture these two creatures of flight only to present them to some "priest"? What is he going to do with the birds – eat 'em? But this is the kind of shit that the ministers and preachers of today use to control the women of their congregation (even while screwing many of them). This is what they tell the females as they temper this bullshit with that "man is the head of the household" bullshit you find in Ephesians 5:23: "For the husband is the head of the wife, even as Christ is the head of the church: and he is the savior of the body."

Until the lion learns how to write. Now you can see why. Everything that is beneficial is in the image and interests of the male and all that is secondary and degrading is heaped upon the heads of the female. What does the priest do with the birds that the woman presents to him? Note the following:

30 The priest will offer one for a sin offering and the other for a burnt offering. Through this process, the priest will purify her before the LORD for the ceremonial impurity caused by her bleeding.

Offer it to whom? For what? Is God going to swoop down and have pigeon tartare for dinner? What the fuck? And remember: you all are so hung up on Donald Trump's on-going fuckups that you can't see that he is no exception. Before Trump there were men armed with the Bible who were promoting the kind of bullshit that would make Trump's beliefs look like the acts of the Good Samaritan!

Before the Lord? These men represent God? Is God such an asshole that he allows these dickless white and black men to front for him? Where is God when these men take advantage of these women, little boys and girls, and then continue to be forgiven by ass backwards congregations? Why does the Bible put down homosexuality when black and white ministers and priests appear to accept it when it comes to the money that fags put into the collection plate? Many are so busy taking it up the ass that they cannot see the crimes being committed against the women of their "flock"?

You should have known that the Jews were behind it. But white is white no matter what the ethnicity or religion:

31 "This is how you will guard the people of Israel from ceremonial uncleanness. Otherwise they would die, for their impurity would defile my Tabernacle that stands among them.

Who's guarding the world against the people of Israel? Who's guarding minority communities against Jewish merchants? Who was guarding South Africa against the joint incursions of the United States and Israel? Who is guarding the Palestinians against the Jews? Until the lion learns how to write, remember?

32 These are the instructions for dealing with anyone who has a bodily discharge—a man who is unclean because of an emission of semen

And,

33 or a woman during her menstrual period. It applies to any man or woman who has a bodily discharge, and to a man who has sexual intercourse with a woman who is ceremonially unclean."

[Type text]

And so it came to pass. The fear of blood is not only at Trump's door: he's a prototype but he's hardly alone. With that having been clearly established (and remember it is the Christian evangelicals who are the leading Trump ass kissers), we now deal specifically with present-day America and Trump's leadership of it.

Moss (2015) writes the following:

> As archaic and crass as The Donald is, he's not the first to see menstruation as a drain on a woman's intellect. Just this week the *Daily Mail* <u>censored</u> a picture of London marathon runner Kiran Gandhi, who dared to "free flow" during the competition. Many of us grew up on menstruation jokes, the punch line of which was 'never trust an animal that bleeds for five days and doesn't die.' This is not some modern Western hang-up: menophobia (the fear of menstrual blood) is a cross-cultural phenomenon..(Moss, 2015)

See what I mean? A male dominated society is invariably going to be a society where women receive short shrift in the same way that a white dominated society is going to prioritize the white folks and treat people of color like "second class citizens," as they say. And the Bible is not exempt from this kind of thinking. Remember (the myth of) Adam and Eve?

> In the Jewish religious imagination, blame for what is actually the primordial "curse" is often placed squarely on Eve. Eve is seen as responsible for all of the unpleasantness of the reproductive process: menstruation and childbirth included. (Moss, 2015)

Jews and that Bible. The myth of Jesus being "king of the Jews." Men hanging on crosses and dying for the sins of the world when Jews hate almost everybody in the world, but then coming back to life later on. Who writes this bullshit? We can deduce that a woman surely didn't. And we can also conclude that whoever wrote it was not a non-Jews (Gentile). And therefore if you write this male supremacy type bullshit where women are supposed to "obey" and men are supposed to be "the head," then it only stands to reason that women will be scapegoated for all that is bad. Eve got the blame for the sins of the world, Delilah got the blame for cutting Samson's hair although she didn't do it (the barbers did) and so on. Again, Trump's fear has long-time historical and social precedent.

And it's not just the Bible-toters, either. Moss (2015) explains,

> The prohibition on contact with menstruating women is not found only in Judaism. The Koran prohibits intercourse during menses (2:222) and the Hindu Laws of Manu indicate that a woman becomes purified from menstruation when she bathes at the conclusion of her period (6:66). Bathing post-period appears to have been the cross-cultural cure-all, but until menses were over women were contagious. Until 2005, Hindu women in Nepal were <u>forced</u> to live in cowsheds during their period. To this day some traditional members of Orthodox Christianity <u>abstain</u> from receiving Holy Communion during menstruation. (Moss, 2015)

This is why white people who back Trump don't care if he grabs women by the pussy or if he's afraid of menstrual blood. White men in general, appear to not have any respect for women, in general. They can date, romance, go out on dates, propose to, marry and then take care of their female mates, but look at the divorce rate and the rise in sexual assaults. These same men are kicking these women's asses knowing full well that they're not going to get away with it in the short-term. And many women are so conditioned that they "forgive" these men because "they said they won't do it again."

But they do. Look at Trump and those hundreds of millions of his misguided ilk. When black people were getting hooked on crack, the white man said it was a pathology. As soon as peckerwoods got hooked on crack and opioids, it became a "health problem." A similar scam took place when it came to the female menstrual cycle:

> But this is about more than either cleanliness or ritual purity. The idea that menstrual blood poses a health risk is evident in a variety of cultures. The ancient Jewish collection of rabbinic opinions known as the Talmud reads, "If a menstruant woman passes between two [men], if it is at the beginning of her menses, she will slay one of them, and if it is at the end of her menses, she will cause strife between them" (*b. Pesaḥ.* 111a)..(Moss, 2015)

There you have it. We have historical precedent and social acceptance on the part of far too many men and women. Trump is a prototype, but not an exception. *He is the misogynistic rule.*

<u>Trump's Attacks on Carly Fiorina</u>

[Type text]

Let's begin with the Carly Fiorina issue, which Trump also apparently got away with. In an article by Ellen Uchimiya titled "Donald Trump Insults Carly Fiorina's Appearance," the following was reported on September 9, 2016:

> Presidential candidate Donald Trump continues to test the limits of what he can say and still retain his poll-topping popularity. His derogatory comments about opponent Carly Fiorina's looks were published in a magazine piece Wednesday. (Uchimiya, 2016)

Trump was getting away with insult after insult and this should have made it clear that he was no "exception, " but the rule. Even now, these white women are squawking about "sexual misconduct" by white men in government and Hollywood and are too stupid to realize that such treatment is par for the course. Again,Trump is no exception to the rule – he IS the rule. Why do these bitches think fraternity houses, freemasonry and "men's only clubs" exist? First of all, most white men are gay but want to hide it and second of all, they don't like or trust white women. The tale about Delilah cutting Samson's hair is a metaphor: it is a lesson that women are seductive, they will sap your strength and put you to sleep. Delilah didn't even cut Samson's hair; but she was slick enough to find some barbers who would do it.

Fiorina never stood a chance against such a misogynistic onslaught. Check out the following story shared by Uchimiya (2106):

> In his <u>Rolling Stone</u> profile of Trump, writer Paul Solotaroff, who traveled with Trump for his story, described a scene on the billionaire's plane, in which Trump provided a running commentary of the television news onscreen. Scott Walker appeared on screen, and Trump's staffers laughed as he made fun of the Wisconsin governor. And then, Carly Fiorina appeared. . (Uchimiya, 2016).

Making fun of a man (Scott Walker) whose ass he would later kiss. This is Trump: two-faced and perfidious. But then the subject shifted to Carly Fiorina:

> When the anchor throws to Carly Fiorina for her reaction to Trump's momentum, Trump's expression sours in schoolboy disgust as the camera bores in on Fiorina. "Look at that face!" he cries. "Would anyone vote for that? Can you imagine that, the face of our next president?!" The laughter grows halting and faint behind him. "I mean, she's a woman, and I'm not s'posedta say bad

things, but really, folks, come on. Are we serious?" . (Uchimiya, 2016)

What gall. Look at HIS face: colored burnt orange from over-tanning, his comb-over, peroxide-dyed hair, fat face and jowls and as quiet as its quiet, the appearance of utter dicklessness. That's right, I said it. You can tell by the way he strolls across the White House lawn and the way his ties extend beneath his crotch to tell he has something to hide. His sensitivity about the size of his hands is also another indicator. And the fact that he's always been able to pay for sex means that he never had to worry about sexually satisfying the woman: he was paying for them to fake it!

And here he is with the gall to talk about Fiorina. Here's what Fiorina had to say about it when questioned by another woman who had also been a victim of some of Trump's barbs:

> Fox News' Megyn Kelly, who has herself been on the receiving end of some of Trump's insults, had Fiorina on her show "The Kelly File" as a guest Wednesday night. She read part of Trump's quote to Fiorina and asked for her reaction … "I think those comments speak for themselves and all the many, many thousands for voters out there that are helping me climbing in the polls - yes, they are very furious," Fiorina responded, adding, "I won't spend a single cycle wondering what Donald Trump means - but just maybe I am getting under his skin a little bit because I am climbing in the polls." . (Uchimiya, 2016)

Again, these white bitches miss the chance to make a social statement in lieu of salvaging their own credibility. When will they admit that hating women is as American as apple pie? What was one of the first Three Stooges shorts called? "The Woman Hater's Club." Women didn't get "the right to vote" until 1920 with the passage of the 19th Amendment, and the right to smoke until the so called women's movement of the 1920s because before that the white man told them it was "not feminine." And they went for it. Why were they left out? Because men felt superior and hated their guts, that's why. Trump is therefore a continuation of that attitude, not a pioneer of it!

Finally, bear in mind the following:

> This was not the first time Trump has mocked Fiorina - in August, he tweeted about the lone woman in the GOP presidential field: I just realized that if you listen to Carly Fiorina for more than ten

minutes straight, you develop a massive headache. She has zero chance! . (Uchimiya, 2016).

One thing is somewhat accurate: white bitches do have these "infantile" voices that squeak and grate away on your nerves. Look at some of these female news reporters: they sound like little girls. But that's not what Trump meant because judging from the way he talks about and treats his daughter Ivanka, he really LIKES little girls. It's just another insult from a 71-year old man (born under the sign of Gemini, which explains why he's two-faced) who is overweight, probably on some form of education, impotent and hated by more people than any other individual in Presidential history (can you say: "stress"?).

One more thing. On November 18, 2017, Trump tweeted that Hillary Clinton was "the biggest loser of all time." She is definitely a loser, but she is one with a positive track record. By the time Trump is finished, he will go down as the worst president of all time – by far. Now, how is THAT for being "the biggest loser of all time?"

<u>Melania Trump as "Trump Card:" What Gives?</u>

Speaking of women as "spoils," if the media and those who are really concerned about Trump had any brains, they'd do an investigation of Melania Trump. Other than her pale skin, lack of an ass, thin lips and shrunken breasts – qualities of far too many white women – what do we really know about her? Here's what she tells me about the white man's definition of beauty: he wants his women boney and looking like teenagers because at heart he's a pedophile. He wants a flat ass, small tits and no resistance – like you would get from a young boy.

His first woman looked like and carried herself like a whore. His second wife was another heavily cosmetic wearing white tramp who fit his mold perfectly and like Melania, she was born in another country. The Czech Republic. Melania is another import, born in Novo Mesto, Slovenia. All three women have the morals of the bar room maids from back in the 19th century even though they wear high-end clothing and have a ball spending his money. Donald Trump is nothing but a TRICK. He buys pussy and then pays women to keep their distance. To this very day it is doubtful that he sleeps with Melania because at age 71, it is doubtful if he can even get a boner. With that having been said, let's take a look at his wife, Melania.

[Type text]

Melania Trump looks like a whore. The bitch is so stupid that she couldn't even write her own speech but instead, plagiarized some words from a speech given by Michelle Obama during the Republican Convention (Michelle had given the speech back in 2008). Then, just this year after the Charlottesville, Virginia massacre, the bitch did it again, using Michele's words. This means that this woman has no sense of conviction or real emotion. Like her husband, she's made of stone. And like her husband, she's a damn idiot.

He boasts about his education at the Wharton School which is only partially true. He transferred there from Fordham University after two years. Before that he attended the New York Military Academy because he was so fucked up in high school, his father forced him to go. His education record is a joke – even George Bush graduated from Yale!

And how about his "better half"? The word was that she graduated from the University of Slovenia. But according to website Snopes.com,

> There is no "University in Slovenia," nor is there a "University of Slovenia." The country contains several colleges, including the University of Ljubljana, which other news outlets have reported (without citation) was where Melania obtained her degree.
> But while the claim that she possesses a degree in Architecture and Design appears on several web sites, these reports lack specific details, such as the year she graduated. (Snopes.com, 2016)

And if further information from a more credible source is needed, check out the following from none other than the Huffington Post:

> Melania Trump never earned a university degree in architecture — she dropped out of college after her freshman year, according to her biographers. Still, she claims to have a degree from "university in Slovenia." … Melania Trump hadn't been entirely truthful about. Slovenian journalists Bojan Pozar and Igor Omerza wrote in their biography on the former fashion model that she "became — and remained — a college dropout" after leaving the University of Ljubljana's architecture school following her freshman year.(Wilkie, 2016)

Does Trump know about her lack of higher education? Of course he does. But why should he care when he was a general fuckup himself and his resume is probably forged as well. If he attended the Wharton School of Business, who knows how many of those white professors he paid off in exchange for passing grades? Besides, Trump likes 'em dumber than he is so that he can run game and pay them to keep quiet.

For instance, the claim is that first wife Ivana went to the Charles University of Prague and earned a master's degree in physical education. What? He was married to her from 1977 to 1992. Then there was Marla Maples who was even a bigger and more miserable flop. According to Wikipedia, "Maples attended Northwest Whitfield High School in Tunnel Hill, Georgia … where she played basketball[6] and served as class secretary ⋯ during her senior year. Maples was crowned the 1980–81homecoming queen for her senior year (she later returned for the 1991 homecoming to crown the school's new queen."

So the first two were athletic and as dumb as a bag of hammers. One a high school graduate, and the other one from some obscure university. His current wife a college dropout from a college that may or may not have ever existed.

And speaking of third wife Melania, now comes Melania.

What I say is that Melania Trump is both the mental and physical eastern European version of beauty. She doesn't hide her feelings: she looks at Trump as if she wants to cut his fuckin' throat. His second wife, Ivania, was the same stoic-looking, cold white woman. But this is about Melania, so let's talk about her, how she met this billionaire, and a little bit about her impact. An article by Adam Edelman (January 7, 2016) titled, "Donald Trump Courted Wife Melania While Out on a Date With Another Woman in 1998, She Reveals in Interview About GOP Front-runner, provides some interesting insights:

> Before Donald Trump wanted to be President, he wanted to be a player. The bombastic billionaire was dating someone else when he first asked out the woman who would become his third and current wife, the mogul's spouse revealed in a magazine interview published Wednesday.(Edelman, 2016).

How can you be a 'player" when you don't have any game? Trump buys pussy, he doesn't "rap" his way into it the way bruthas do. He knows a whore when he sees one and the bigger the gold-digger she is, the more he gravitates towards her. There is nothing streetwise or "player-oriented" about this. He's nothing but a trick, a john waiting in the wings to spend his money on sex because in that way, he doesn't have to worry about sexually satisfying the woman. When you pay for pussy you pay for the lies that the women tell you while you're getting sexed up; they do all the work and once you're done, you get on about your business. Don't take my word for it: ask Melania, Ivana and Marla.

At any rate, when they met it seemed to me to be a case of "love at first fright." Check it out:

> **"I was struck by his energy," she told the magazine of their courtship. "He has an amazing sense of vitality.""**"He wanted my number, but he was with a date, so of course I didn't give it to him," Melania Trump told Harper's Bazaar of her first exchange with the mogul, at a Fashion Week party in 1998.(Edelman, 2016 – emphasis original).

To begin with, all that "vitality" and "energy" was probably the product of taking drugs of some kind. He was with a "date" (meaning that he was in the process of turning a trick) and she claims she didn't give him her number. She's probably lying but he still got her name and that's all a stalker like Trump needs; he has flunkies on his payroll and private investigators to " get the goods" on any woman he wants.

Continuing:

> **"He wanted my number, but he was with a date, so of course I didn't give it to him," Melania Trump told Harper's Bazaar of her first exchange with the mogul, at a Fashion Week party in 1998.** "I said, 'I am not giving you my number; you give me yours, and I will call you.' I wanted to see what kind of number he would give me — if it was a business number, what is this? I'm not doing business with you," she said. Trump then gave the Slovenia-born designer and model all of his numbers. (Edelman, 2016 – emphasis original)

What a slut. She wanted his personal digits so they could talk on a personal basis. And when that scenario took place there was no doubt in her mind that she could seduce this trick sissy. But knowing Trump he probably taped the calls and would use them to extort the pussy rather than pay for it outright. Of course, that is just conjecture – except for the parts where I charge him with being a sissy and her with being a slut.

Her story moves on:

> "The office, Mar-a-Lago, home in New York, everything," she told the magazine. Melania, then 28, was due to visit the Caribbean for a photoshoot, but called him when she returned to New York days later, she said. "I was struck by his energy," she told the magazine of their courtship. "He has an amazing sense of vitality." The couple married in Palm Beach, Fla., in 2005.(Edelman, 2016).

By the time Melania and Trump got married in 2005, they had dated for about seven years. That means seven years of him prematurely ejaculating on her and her telling him what he wanted to hear. He paid her, showered her with presents and trips on his jet, and this broke ass European bitch was thinking, "Damn, I got it made." And she sat back quietly and watched him rip off people, lie on the phone, flirt with other women and brag about it. Money in exchange for keeping her mouth shut. The small print also probably read that she would only sleep with him once a month, if that.

Four months after the previous article appeared, on April 5, 2016, Ashley Parker of *the Boston Globe* wrote an article titled, "Struggling with Women, Donald Trump Turns to His Wife." As if Trump's wife, some woman from the eastern European block who used to take her clothes off for a camera, would upgrade Trump's negative image of women. The following article clearly shows that both Donald and Melania are treacherous and should never be trusted when it comes to their claims of loving and caring for each other.

`The article begins, thusly:

> Donald J. Trump — he of the glamorous wives and high-profile romances — likes to boast of his prowess with women. But among female voters, he is having less success, with women viewing him unfavorably by more than 3-to-1, according to a recent New York Times/CBS News poll. Now, in an apparent effort to shore up his support among women after a series of missteps, Trump is enlisting his wife, Melania, on the campaign trail.(Parker, 2016)

Even the media seems to believe that what they see is what they get. "Glamorous wives and high-profile romances"? What makes these white bitches glamorous? I'll tell you what: they have money and they attend the kinds of events that white men attend and as a result, they have an elite clientele to which they can sell pussy. What makes the romances of Trump "high profile"? Because these high class prostitutes – call girls, if you will – are the type that he is attracted to. He can afford their rates, he can prematurely ejaculate all over them if he so chooses, and then get on about his business. This is not only the way of Trump: this is white men, in general.

The article says that women viewed him unfavorable by a three to one margin. I can bet you that it was higher than that. The women who viewed him favorably did so only because they saw him as a rich "trick" that paid through the nose. The ones who didn't like him were jealousy because he didn't make the offer to them! Furthermore, the women who were asked were more likely than not white women, not women of color.

Let us continue:

> Wearing a short baby-blue dress, Melania Trump joined her husband onstage at the Milwaukee Theatre on Monday night for his final rally in Wisconsin — a subdued event with a crowd that was less than capacity — before the state's primary on Tuesday. "No matter who you are, a man or a woman, he treats everyone equal," said Melania Trump, who spoke for just over a minute and read from notes, praising her husband as "a great communicator," "a great negotiator" and "a great leader." (Parker, 2016)

In other words she was looking like a slut and he was acting like her pimp. The two of them are a joke: a fat, orange-colored white man with his hair dyed blonde and a boney white woman who has posed nearly nude for a living. And there are people in this country who are readily accepting this "happily married shit. This, despite the fact that they don't live together and he has pictures with his daughter Ivanka that implies that something sexual was going on between the two of them as well.

Then she mouths the vintage "happy first lady" line: ""No matter who you are, a man or a woman, he treats everyone equal," said Melania Trump, who spoke for just over a minute and read from notes, praising her husband as "a great communicator," "a great negotiator" and "a great leader." How can you treat everyone "equal"? That is ludicrous. Does he grab men by the balls the way he said he grabbed women by the pussy? Does he kiss Putin on the mouth the way he supposedly does Melania? He doesn't treat everyone equal because no one can do that. You have to treat everyone FAIRLY – fuck that "equality" shit. All that translates into meaning is that you'll treat me, as a black man, the same way you would treat a white woman, a white man or anyone else!

Notice she had to read from her notes to add that her husband was "a great communicator, a great negotiator and a great leader." If Trump was so great, why has he been divorced twice? It's not the divorce that is so weird to me, it's the fact that there were two women that he "fell for" who didn't work out. What happened to "the art of the deal"? What happened to "the great negotiator"? Why can't he keep a woman happy enough to stay married to her? The Trumps – Donald and Melania – are liars.

Her adoration of her husband continues with the following lie: "As you may know by now, when you attack him he will punch back 10 times harder," she said.

"He's a fighter, and if you elect him to be our president, he will fight for you and for our country." You can tell from that statement that Trump doesn't deal with many black men. If we blaze on that white man, he's not going to hit us back ten times harder. That's an exaggeration and Melania is reading it because Donald wrote it. He's a fat coward; we used to take lunch money from people who looked like Trump. He can pull that stuff on his fellow whites (which is why when he visits those major cities he goes directly to the suburbs where there are few, if any, black folks), but we've been around shallow white people all our lives, and we can spot them from a mile away.

Melania doesn't have the power over her husband that other women in that position wielded. Want proof? Check it out:

> Melania Trump is a reluctant campaigner who, by her husband's telling, did not want him to run for president. But she was recently thrust into the spotlight after a super PAC supporting Sen. Ted Cruz put out an ad in Utah, aimed at the state's Mormon population, featuring a picture of the former model from a nude photo shoot. (Parker, 2016)

Why would she not want him to run for President? Perhaps she knew it would bring more attention to her own lackluster background. Perhaps she knew she would have to share some of her "modeling" secrets with the global public. Perhaps she knew that her husband, being the asshole that he is, would only bring more embarrassment to the family – meaning to her and their son Barron. At any rate he did her the same way he does everybody else who offers an opinion: totally ignored it.

Nude photo shoot? Ted Cruz is a piece of shit himself and that was a low blow. But no lower than the things Trump did and continues to do in his quest for attention. How did Trump respond to Melania's photo that showed her wrapped in a blanket, lying on her side, breasts displayed? Here's how the childish chump named Trump responded:

> Donald Trump responded by spreading a photo of his wife juxtaposed with an unflattering image of Cruz's wife, Heidi — an incident that set off a storm of criticism and that he later called "a mistake." (Parker, 2016)

Trump called it a "mistake"? That's not the same as apologizing for the action. It was a mistake because Melania probably went upside his head with one of those eight-inch stiletto pumps! It was a childish act, a selfish act, and an insult

[Type text]

to Melania because it is a reflection of that "trophy wife" mentality that these white boys (and black male celebrities and athletes) seem to adhere to and abide by.

Perhaps the answer can be found in the following excerpt:

> Donald Trump has previously turned to the women in his life to help counter claims that he is a misogynist. He frequently invokes Melania and his daughter, Ivanka, on the campaign trial, talking about how, behind the scenes, they are the ones urging him to behave "more presidential."m"Again, my wife: 'Darling, you're so brilliant, you're so bright. Act presidential. It's so easy for you,'" Donald Trump told a crowd Sunday night in West Allis, Wisconsin, mimicking his wife's breathy, accented voice. "I said, 'Darling, I've got to win first, you know? I've got to win.'" (Parker, 2016)

To begin with, if Melania told him he was brilliant and bright, she was either (1) running game on him; (2) bullshitting him so he would stop embarrassing the family and/or (3) telling him what he wanted to hear so he would get the hell away from her. But then again, she is no rocket scientist herself: remember that she dropped out of college after only one year!

Not only that, but Trump is such a pathological liar that he probably attributed quotes to Melania and Ivanka that they didn't even say. And what would they do about it? Nothing. It is clear that Trump hates people who have skin color and he hates women, in that order. It is a matter of record.

But nevertheless, when he needs a woman's voice, he can always rely on his whore/high priestess to bail him out:

> The decision to enlist Melania Trump comes as he has stumbled in recent weeks on issues that could damage him further with women, especially in a general election matchup against Hillary Clinton, who is trying to become the first female president.

The women who back trump are the Republican redneck hag-in-the-kitchen type who tote a Bible and do the bidding of their Wild Turkey swilling husbands. In other words: hicks. These red meat eatin' muthafuckas back Trump because he is a reminder that the "nigger" (meaning Obama) is no longer the President, hence the statement " Make America Great Again." As an example, when Ron Moore ran for the Senate in Alabama, despite testimony from a dozen or more women that he had sexually harassed them over the years, it was the Republican white woman who said they didn't believe it and formed a group to shout their stupidity to the world.

As Parker (2016) explains:

> Candidate spouses are often deployed as character witnesses, and the Trump operation believes that Melania Trump, 45, could help her husband as he has faced a barrage of unflattering news reports. She first made an appearance on the campaign trail in February in South Carolina, at a time when Trump was in need of some image softening amid criticism of his combative rhetoric. "She's exceptionally smart, very articulate," said Corey Lewandowski, Donald Trump's campaign manager. "She's a great asset to the campaign."

Let's look at the previous excerpt and, with my deep analytic abilities, show what this whole Trump marriage and its link to the misogyny that permeates American culture is really all about.

They say "like father, like son" and that may be true. In the case of Trump both Don, Jr., and Eric are equally as treacherous, greedy as prone to lying as their fat, orange father. But don't get it twisted: Ivanka flies under the radar but can there be any doubt that she's as big a slut as her mother Ivana and secondly, that she is as mendacious as her father? Parker (2016) writes,

> Ivanka Trump has also been a frequent surrogate for her father, appearing in how-to-caucus videos in Iowa and attending some of his rallies even while she was quite pregnant with her third child. For weeks, Donald Trump joked that his daughter was about to give birth in whatever state they happened to (Parker, 2016)

Like mother, like daughter. Ivanka somehow has three kids and is as thin as a rail and acts like she's a model. The clothes and shoes she designs are mediocre, at best, and yet because she has her father's last name, she can pawn her products off as high end merchandise. Just the fact that one of her promoting stores is Younker's should give you an idea of how low-end her products are.

Her husband, Jared Kushner, was a con man just like her father and she knew that before she tied the knot. He looks more like a bitch than she does and may be assume that role with some of the Russian "men" that he does business with. Who knows? Remember: we are talking about white men and those who crae power and are in need of financing —as both Donald Trump and Jared Kushner are — will bend over and do whatever it takes to remain "solvent."

[Type text]

Once you've paid 0ut as much money for companionship, sex and facical marriages as Donald Trump has, the women may not like you but they respect your status as a first-class "trick." And that is what he is regarded as. And these women bilked him for so much money that they became even more famous after he divorced them. Therefore, it should be no surprise that in their own respective ways, each of these trollups would sing his praises when and if he needed them to do so.

For instance:

> Even Donald Trump's first wife, Ivana, who is the mother of his three oldest children, is speaking up for her ex-husband, praising him in an interview published Sunday in The New York Post, which has long been friendly to him. In the interview, she said she still advised her ex-husband, wished Melania "all the best" and said Donald Trump "loves women" but is "not a feminist." (Parker, 2016)

What else can a white woman with a high school degree do other than mimic what she's told? She married "up" as far as her family was concerned and she spent her time making sure she didn't rock the boat. By saying that he "loves women" but is "not a feminist" doesn't mean a damn thing because its' vague. How can you "love" an entire gender just because they have tits and vaginas? That's sexism in and of itself. That's like white people who say that they're "color blind "meaning that they accept all people of color on WHITE terms. What else could it mean? Why would you have to be "blind" to the color in order to accept them unless the color you see is the one you prefer and the one you prefer is WHITE?

So "loving women" is a catch-all because this bitch knows the opposite is true, akin to Trump's claim that "nobody respects women more than me" right after he disgraced several women on national television. These kind of people speak in extremes because they have no emotional content; they have been "programmed" to do what it takes to have a relationship and they end up involved in alienated arrangements, not relationships. This is why what she said is a lie and proves that Trump is no "feminist" because few men really are. In order to give a damn about women you have to first of all accept them as human beings, and people of Donald Trump's ilk to not.

Moving right along:

[Type text]

> A spokeswoman for Ivana Trump, Catherine Saxton, said the interview was simply the result of good timing — The Post asked, and Ivana Trump was able to do it. (At one point during the interview Donald Trump even called his ex-wife.) Yet in a sign of Donald Trump's complicated relationship with women, Ivana Trump's staff later called the paper to say that Donald Trump was, in fact, a feminist, before calling again to say he was not — and then calling a final time to say he was, indeed, a feminist. (Parker, 2016)

Bullshit. Trump called his daughter (concubine?) and ordered her to "say something" and she did what daddy told her. What talent does she have that could sustain her if he took away all his money other than the talent between her legs? How would she survive with a husband like Jared Kushner who looks like a faggot and is up to his neck in loans and monetary debt? How could Donald Trump be a feminist and be caught saying the things he said during the 2005 Access Hollywood interview? How could he be a feminist and be documented espousing his disdain for women, especially when they "bleed" (see section on Trump's "menophobia')?

As I've written in other texts, the white woman is the new white man because the white man has assumed (created) a new class called meta-human or demi-god. She has taken over and has never made any bones about it: she's not saying "get off the throne of oppression"; she's saying "scoot over and I'll show you how it's done." Even now she is suing him up the ass for "sexual misconduct," which was conduct that she accepted in order to have access to the power that she wanted to be associated with. Now that she's got an inkling of it, it's time for payback.

As the new white man and new oppressor, the white woman can often appear to be one of the white man's biggest critics when it comes to outlandish manifestations of his various tactics and ideological predispositions. For instance,

> Katie Packer, the founder of an anti-Trump super PAC and the co-founder of Burning Glass, a firm that helps Republican candidates convey a conservative message to women, said it would take more than an appearance by Donald Trump's wife to help him attract female supporters. "You don't get special credit because your wife likes you," Packer said. "The rub on this guy that is commonly accepted now is that he's a sexist and a racist, and this isn't going to be fixed because he has one black guy who speaks ahead of him at a rally or because his wife comes out on the campaign trail." (Parker, 2016)

[Type text]

It sounds like a serious critique, doesn't it? But you have to always consider the source. The white woman is "the hand that rocks the cradle" and she is the one who trained those kids to say "nigger" and when those white people lynched us she was right there at the "lynching bees" cheering and applauding. When the white man was opposing busing and integration, not only was she there but she allowed him to use her image and promote a belief that, "The key to the classroom is a key to the bedroom."

The white woman and her cries of "rape" (most of them falsified) has closed down more black townships and villages than any other race of people (0ther than the white male). Rosewood was no exception; it was the rule. So when Packer talks about Trump being sexist and racist she's not condemning sexism and racism; she's condemning the way that Trump practices both: it is better to be subtle with your hate than to be highly visible and remove all doubt.

The article by Parker concludes with what I view as nothing more than another one of Donald Trump's setup scams. Check it out:

> But Donald Trump seems convinced of his wife's potential, both as a campaigner and as a first lady. Spotting a homemade sign at his rally Sunday night that read "Melania for first lady," Trump paused to praise his wife. "She'd be a great first lady," he said, gesturing to the sign. "That's beautiful. Thank you." (Parker, 2016)'

To begin with, I think the sign was contrived, printed and placed in a conspicuous place with Trump's pre-rally approval. Secondly, how would he know what kind of "first lady" she'd be? Simply because he said so?

She's a college dropout (after one year), a woman who plagiarized at least two of Michelle Obama's speeches, and someone who posed nearly butt naked for the world to see. You do the math.

Trump v. Mika and Joe of MSNBC's "Morning Joe"

Looking the way he does – orange skin, peroxide-dyed hair, pot gut and pale – you would think Donald Trump would be the *last* person to talk about other people's appearances. And yet, he rarely hesitates. In June of 2017 he again hurled insults at a woman, this one a TV talk show host, and then added that she was "crazy."

[Type text]

Let's look at the article that documented what took place and get yet another look at a grown man with an eight-year-old way of dealing with issues. Bykowicz (2017) writes:

> WASHINGTON — President Donald Trump ridiculed the looks and temperament of a female cable television host whose show he says he has stopped watching. In a series of tweets Thursday morning, the president went after Mika Brzezinski and Joe Scarborough, who have criticized Trump on their MSNBC show "Morning Joe." … (Bykowicz, 2017)

To begin with, why is Trump always watching cable television news? He lambasted Obama for spending too much time on the golf course (which Trump has since quadrupled) and other minor issues, but he's watching television and giving out "grades" on how women look. The fact is, "Morning Joe" has gone after Trump from the outset and exposed a number of Trump's mistakes, which is what he was REALLY going after. But since a woman was part of it, his misogyny got the best of him and he took on Mika Brzezinski (who is married to co-host Joe Scarborough, by the way) instead.

Continuing:

> "I heard poorly rated @Morning Joe speaks badly of me (don't watch anymore). Then how come low I.Q. Crazy Mika, along with Psycho Joe, came ... to Mar-a-Lago 3 nights in a row around New Year's Eve, and insisted on joining me. She was bleeding badly from a face-lift. I said no!" (Bykowicz, 2017)

How low can a person stoop? The President of the United States taking his time to attack is fellow white folks, his fellow elitists, just because they saw him for what he is? Only a white man could get away with this and Trump is not the first one to do so – he's just more callous and overt with his childish pranks and insults than his clones have been.

Mika was pissed and I made a point to watch "Morning Joe" for several mornings following Trump's insults. But as it was reported,

> Brzezinski responded on Twitter by posting a photograph of a Cheerios box that has the phrase "made for little hands." That was a dig at Trump, who has long been sensitive about the size of his hands. "It's a sad day for America when the president spends his time bullying, lying and spewing petty personal attacks instead of

> doing his job," NBC News spokeswoman Lorie Acio said in a
> statement. (Bykowicz, 2017)

And Mika, being a female, knew what she was implying about the hands. When all is said and done it is clear that Trump is either impotent or dickless. He spends too much time trying to convey a "mi mas macho" façade for there NOT to be something wrong in the genitalia department. White men tend to do that and have done it throughout history, especially when they are in the vicinity of men of color. Read Charles Herbert Stember's book, *Sexual Racism:The Emotional Barrier to an Integrated Society*, Joel Kovel's *White Racism: A Psychohistory* or Calvin C. Herton's *Sex and Racism in America* to gain more perspective on the phallic symbol psychosis that the white male has had for centuries.

White women know. But being the prostitutes that they are they settle for money, a home life and a family and they keep quiet. But among themselves they know what's going on and they compare notes. Many of them have screwed and sucked off black men while in college and therefore they have a point of comparison, one that they keep to themselves. But subtle longings often come out in the scripts by white male writers on some of the television situation comedies such as "Married With Children," "King of Queens" and shows of that ilk.

Trump's comments about Mika's "bleeding" is addressed elsewhere in this book. But Joe defended his wife and they struck back at Trump with facts:

> The White House did not immediately respond to questions about
> the tweets, including what it was that set the president off. On their
> Wednesday show, Brzezinski and Scarborough roundly mocked
> Trump for displaying in several of his golf resorts a fake Time
> Magazine cover featuring himself. "That's needy," Brzezinski said
> on the show. (Bykowicz, 2017)

How are you going to take a cover from Time magazine, splice your photo on it, enlarge it, and then post it in the lobby of your businesses. Even as he tells his backers that he is the greatest president ever, his own behaviors are the basis for America being laughed at all over the world. Because of American arrogance and hubris, the impotence and shallowness of most white people covers up how small most of them really are. Behind closed doors, in green rooms, in corporate board rooms and in closed quarters they get a chance to see how truly pathetic they are.

Joe and Mika stood up and continue to confront Trump, as do CNN and MSNBC, but make no mistake about it: this makes them no less racist because they

[Type text]

represent the Fourth Estate and the media is always going to be a key cog in the racist engine that keeps America sputtering along. At any rate,

> About 15 minutes before the president himself tweeted, White House social media director Dan Scavino similarly attacked the hosts. Trump was correct that the MSNBC hosts spent time at the president's Florida resort, a visit that Scarborough said was to arrange a Trump interview. The hosts confirmed they are engaged to be married earlier this month. (Bykowicz, 2017).

And so it goes. Let what is being documented in this book be a viable contribution to this country's own understanding of itself and its leadership, past and present. From George Washington's slaveholding and racist actions all the way through Obama currying favor to save a country that hated his guts to the election of the most backward and clownish president of all time, it is clear that when it comes to gooniness, pathological lying tendencies, intellectual impotence and outright ignorance, Donald J. Trump reigns without rival.

Trump Goes After Heidi Cruz, Wife of Sen. Ted Cruz

Trump was a long way from done in his campaign of insults against women. As DelReal & Johnson pointed out,

> Trump's gender problem flared again this week as he and Sen. Ted Cruz of Texas traded insults while Cruz's wife, Heidi, became the target of vitriol on social media from Trump and his supporters. At one point, the real estate mogul retweeted an unflattering image contrasting Heidi Cruz's appearance with his wife, Melania, a retired model.

And so it began. At the end of March in 2016, Trump went after the wife of one of his Republican opponents during the debates. As it was reported,

> Trump doubles down on Heidi Cruz attacks. Donald Trump has intensified his feud with Ted Cruz over the Republican presidential rival's wife after she slammed his statements for having "no basis in reality… Trump shared an image on Twitter around midnight Wednesday comparing his wife, Melania, a former model, to

Cruz's wife, stating, "A picture is worth a thousand words."
(Byrnes, 2016).

Trump is married to a woman who has the appearance of being an eastern European whore. She still looks and dresses that way. And yet he has the gall to point fingers at Cruz' wife? Cruz married a woman who has dyed her hair blonde so she looks like a trophy wife. Both Trump and Cruz are two ugly muthafuckas so they're lucky to have found women, period.

At any rate, Cruz was pissed off at what he saw as an underhanded shot byTrump and responded in vintage Captain America-like fashion:

> "Donald, real men don't attack women. Your wife is lovely, and Heidi is the love of my life," Cruz responded in a tweet of his own. Trump raised the specter of a lurid fight with Cruz with a tweet Tuesday night, amid primary voting in Arizona and Utah, that threatened to "spill the beans" on his rival's wife. (Byrnes, 2016)

Why tell Trump his wife is lovely? Lovely by whose standards? Because she's white and carries herself like a whore? How does Cruz think that made his wife feel? He's supposed to be pissed off at the fact that Trump insulted HIS wife and owes Trump no compliments in return. He's just telling Trump something that he (Trump) already must believe.

How did the feud start? One source claims that Cruz "cited an ad from an anti-Trump super-PAC that featured his wife Melania posing nude, claiming it was from Cruz, who said he has no connection to the group." (Byrnes, 2016) If Melania posed nude Trump already knew it. He likes sluttish women. Look at Marla Maples and Ivana – they have the appearance of sluts and that is what attracts white men more than anything else. Why? Because when they look like that it is most obvious that they can be bought, that they are for sale – because that is what prostitutes do. These bitches aren't slathering on all that makeup, puffing up their hair, padding their bras, jacking up their ass cheeks and walking about in 8-inch stiletto heels just for laughs! They are trying to, and succeeding at, selling pussy!

But Cruz didn't want to come off like a coward, so he came to his wife's "rescue":

> Cruz pushed back immediately, tweeting, "Donald, if you try to attack Heidi, you're more of a coward than I thought." He later knocked him in a series of interviews, saying the threat to go after his wife "should be beneath Donald" and suggesting it illustrated the businessman's character. (Byrnes, 2016)

[Type text]

So what? He's not telling Trump a damn thing that Trump doesn't already know. Every morning when Trump looks in the mirror, and has he's getting his hair done like some bitch in a beauty shop, he is looking into the face of a man who isn't worth a shit. He knows it. But he also knows it's his job to embarrass and debase America by duping and tricking them into lowering their standards and believing the lies that he continues to impose on them. Trump has no "character" and neither does Cruz: both men are political leeches, sucking off the teet of the American people in their own individual ways.

Heidi saw what Trump was about from the get-go as she said, "Most of the things Donald Trump says have no basis in reality, Heidi Cruz told reporters during a campaign stop Wednesday in Wisconsin, acknowledging Trump's threat to go after her publicly (Byrnes, 2016). Heidi could fight her own battles. The photo from Trump further set the stage as he compared Melania's photo with a picture of Heidi looking like she was having her ass flossed with barbed wire:

> "The images are worth a thousand words," read the caption on the
> photo that Trump retweeted to his 7.2 million followers. That
> message and others have prompted an outcry among Republicans
> and Democrats alike, while Cruz said Thursday that "real men don't
> bully women." . (DelReal & Johnson, 2016).

Cruz had the gall to act as if there were "rules" where Trump was concerned. Check it out:

> "Our spouses and our children are off-bounds," Cruz told reporters
> while campaigning in Dane, Wis. "It is not acceptable for a big,
> loud New York bully to attack my wife. It is not acceptable for him
> to make insults, to send nasty tweets." He added: "Donald, you're
> a sniveling coward. Leave Heidi the hell alone." . (DelReal &
> Johnson, 2016).

Who is Cruz to define any political parameters of what constitutes what is or is not "out of bounds"? These white men, Cruz included, have been "out of bounds" ever since the inception of this country. One of my Master's degrees is in Political Science and we learned that elections to the United States House of Representatives for the 1st Congress were held in 1788 and 1789, coinciding with the election of George Washington as first President of the United States. The dates and methods of election were set by the states. I further learned that this lily-white, all male "Congress" set the stage for a similar racial and gender makeup of what exists today: male and pale. A few white women who think just like their men, are sprinkled in, and a couple of coons who think that they're "Americans" have made it, but the end result is still the same: white supremacy is the foundation and ideology of the land.

Are these unbalanced facts "out of bounds"? Of course not. But when the assimilated Cuban Cruz makes the claim, he thinks that he's saying something deep and profound. He's a part of the problem. Two sick childlike white men attempting to "play the dozens" at the respective expense of their wives:

> "Meet Melania Trump. Your next first lady. Or, you could support Ted Cruz on Tuesday," the ad read. Trump, who went on to lose the Utah caucuses, excoriated Cruz and issued a threat via Twitter: "Be careful, Lyin' Ted, or I will spill the beans on your wife!" Trump — who wrongly alleges that Cruz was behind the ad — defended the tweet Wednesday on Fox Business Network, saying it was a "disgraceful" and "terrible thing" that demeaned his wife, "a very, very successful model."(Oliphant, 2016).

Trump calls his wife "a very, very successful model." If you take off enough clothes in that industry, success will find its way to you. That is after you jump through hoops and perform enough "stunts for bumps." And Trump "re-tweeted the "unflattering image of Heidi Cruz, setting off a fresh series of condemnations" (Oliphant, 2016).

And Trump finally won, Cruz faded and once Trump was president, Cruz was one of the first people to kiss his ass. But when it came to Heidi, Cruz made his shallow point rather well:

> "I have to say, seeing him go deeper and deeper into the gutter, it's not easy to tick me off," Cruz said at a news conference while campaigning in Dane, Wisconsin. "But you mess with my wife, you mess with my kids, it'll do it every time."Donald, you're a sniveling coward," Cruz said. "Leave Heidi the hell alone." .(Oliphant, 2016).

Another sellout Cuban, akin to Marco Rubio, continues to push the conservative Republican agenda and in doing so, promote white supremacy and the Neanderthal notions of people like DonaldTrump.

Trump's Attacks on ESPN's Jemele Hill

[Type text]

Jemele Hill, ESPN

Another black woman is punished because of her views on Trump. The white boy has a serious hatred for black people in general and black women, in particular (other than Omarosa). He called the wife of a dead soldier a liar and her mother as well. He called a black Congresswoman a liar although it was clear that he was the one telling a bald-faced lie. He dogged out Latinas, from judges to Salma Hayek and he even referred to Elizabeth Warren (who claimed she was part Native American) as "Pocahontas."

Now we come to ESPN sportscaster, Jemelle Hill. In September of 2017, Brittney Cooper penned an article in Cosmpolitan magazine titled, "Jemele Hill Called Donald Trump a White Supremacist. Where's the Lie?"

> Earlier this week, Jemele Hill, an African American woman and journalist at ESPN, <u>tweeted</u> that "Donald Trump is a white supremacist who has largely surrounded himself w/ other white supremacists." Given Trump's own racist rhetoric toward Mexicans, Muslims, and African Americans, the cozy relationship he has enjoyed with Steve Bannon, and the fact that <u>Ku Klux Klan endorsed him for president</u>, one is hard-pressed to find the lie in Hill's words. But what far too many white Americans hate more than racism itself is being called racist. (Cooper, 2017).

I like Jemele Hill and I watch the show she does on ESPN. But her statements about Trump, while true, were also foolish. How are you going to have that national TV show talking about sports and not remember that the white man is watching your every move? ESPN, like the other sports channels, obviously prefer white women to do their broadcasting, announcing and "mediating" (they sit between groups of white men talking about sports, wearing skirts up to their vaginas and breasts sticking out of their blouses). The sisters who are on the air are beautiful but are just window dressing. As Cari Champion if you don't believe it.

The article about Jemele's suspension seems to miss the important point:

> But here we are: with Donald Trump,with Donald Trump, a man who was accused of <u>refusing to rent to African Americans</u> in a 1970s lawsuit, a man who <u>questioned</u> a judge's ability to decide a case impartially because he is Mexican, serving as our president. Yes, these facts about Trump have been repeated so many times that you are probably tired of

reading them. The repetitive nature of their being said does not in any way diminish the egregious offense and error that these comments represent.(Cooper, 2017).

So what? What was Jemele Hill's spouting off general truisms gonna do? She has no solutions and if she did she was smart enough not to discuss them. She was just venting. And white people don't like it when the few blacks that they trust go on the air and "vent' without "permission." Look what they did to white-ass Jimmy "The Greek Snyder" when in January of 1988 he said, as a reporter working for CBS, the following:

> ``The black is a better athlete to begin with,`` you said. ``Because he`s been bred to be that way, because of his high thighs and big thighs that go up into his back and they can jump higher and run faster because of their bigger thighs, you see. . . .``````This goes back all the way to the Civil War when . . . the slave owner would breed his big black to his big woman so that he could have a big black kid. . . .`

What Snyder said was true in my book. But he didn't get permission and he "vented" just like Jemele did. CBS canned his ass right away. White people don't want the world to know about their racist past, which is why they spend so much money and time attempting to revise their history. And the product is a brainwashed public consisting of people like Alabama Congressman Roy Moore, who, during a special United States Senate special election in Alabama said that slavery was good for black families because it kept them together. This is what the American school system and its racist culture have produced.

What happened to Jemele:?

> After Jemele Hill's comments, press secretary Sarah Huckabee Sanders called her words "a fireable offense." ESPN opted not to fire Hill, but did indicate that her comments were inappropriate. On Wednesday night, Hill issued an apology to ESPN saying, "My regret is that my comments and the public way I made them painted ESPN in an unfair light. My respect for the company and my colleagues remains unconditional." (Cooper, 2017).

If her respect for ESPN are unconditional, then why did she do it? And why apologize if what she said was based on a heart and soul felt conviction? Unless she was FORCED to. White people love to get black people to apologize for

[Type text]

things, although Trump and his race members have yet to apologize for the wrongs they have heaped upon the heads of Black people.

Sarah Huckabee Sanders said that the words were a "fireable offense." That is the sword that white people hold over the heads of black people. And when you don't yield, you are punished. Look at what these cowardly muthafuckas did to Colin Kaepernick who spoke truth to power about white cops gunning down unarmed black men. A world-class quarterback he can no longer get a job in the National Football League. Coward ly white men, like Trump, made that decision. And remember that Trump referred to the athletes who knelt in protest as "sonofabitches." On TV, For the world to see.

Sanders spoke for Trump and he added on his own feelings. As Cooper (2017) cogently contended,

> The people who call out racism, by name and with proper definitions like white supremacy, are never the problem. Racists are and will always be the problem. Donald Trump is the problem. His hired "Yes Lady" Sarah Huckabee Sanders is the problem. Those on both the right and the left who act as cultural apologists for white racism are the problem. (Cooper, 2017)

Jemele is back on the air after being publicly shamed for telling the truth. As the quote that I used earlier made clear, *"To expect bad men not to do wrong is madness"* And to think that mouthing general truisms about a man who the entire world sees as a world class asshole is a waste of your time and energy.

<u>Punish Women Who Have Abortions</u>

When I initially heard this proposal from Trump, my mind raced back to the days of witch burning and how these white men didn't hesitate to accuse a woman of being a witch or delving into what they call "the black arts." But in reality, this is even worse.

An article titled, "Donald Trump, Abortion Foes, Eyes 'Punishment' for Women, Then Recants" appeared in the New York Times on March 31, 2016. Let's take a look at it and get an idea just how misogynistic Donald Trump is and why, in many ways, he represents the typical American male in many respects as it relates to deciding what women should do with their own bodies.

[Type text]

> Donald J. Trump said on Wednesday that women who seek
> abortions should be subject to "some form of punishment" if the
> procedure is banned in the United States, further elevating
> Republican concerns that his explosive remarks about women
> could doom the party in the fall. The comment, which Mr. Trump
> later recanted, attracted instant, bipartisan criticism — the latest in
> a series of high-profile episodes that have shined a light on Mr.
> Trump's feeble approval ratings among women nationally.
> (Flegenheimer & Haberman, 2016).

Maybe if he considered aborting one of those mannequin-looking freak sons of his (Don Jr., and Eric) or that daughter that he is having sex with, perhaps he would better understand that such a choice is the woman's and as such, she should not be punished. This goes back to that fear of "menstrual blood" that I discussed earlier in this book. This freak always wants to punish women when, in my view, three have already experienced the ultimate punishment: being married to HIM!

Continuing:

> In this case, Mr. Trump also ran afoul of conservative doctrine,
> with opponents of abortion rights immediately castigating him for
> suggesting that those who receive abortions — and not merely
> those who perform them — should be punished if the practice is
> outlawed. (Flegenheimer & Haberman, 2016).

Those who would "receive" abortions are, of course, women. And Trump, as a misogynist, uses his bully pulpit and policy-oriented powers to degrade and debase women every chance he gets. He has nothing good to say about women, other than the ones he randomly points out in audiences and claims to "love" them. And Trump made this statement in public. Take note of the following:

> The statement came as Mr. Trump appeared at a town-hall-style
> forum with Chris Matthews of MSNBC, recorded for broadcast on
> Wednesday night. Mr. Matthews pressed Mr. Trump, who once
> supported abortion rights, on his calls to ban the procedure, asking
> how he might enforce such a restriction. "You go back to a
> position like they had where they would perhaps go to illegal
> places," Mr. Trump said, after initially deflecting questions. "But
> you have to ban it." He added, after a bit more prodding, "There
> has to be some form of punishment." (Flegenheimer & Haberman,
> 2016).

What about punishment for dickless assholes who end up somehow fathering children and then raising them to be as corrupt as they are? Trump used to abuse Don Jr. and he (Trump Sr.) was sent off to military school by his own father who also abused him. Trump has been rejected at every turn and is mentally scarred in my view. A kid who grows up with disdain will grow up to show it toward others, and this is Trump's problem: he hates himself but doesn't know how to deal with it, so he takes Custer stands and does dumb shit so people can do as his parents did him: dump all over him and give him money to start a business so he would get the hell out of their faces.

But then, in vintage schizophrenic manner, Trump backtracked on his previous statement:

> Hours later, Mr. Trump recanted his remarks, essentially in full, a
> rare and remarkable shift for a candidate who proudly extols his
> unwillingness to apologize or bow to "political correctness."If
> abortion were disallowed, he said in a statement, "the doctor or any
> other person performing this illegal act upon a woman would be
> held legally responsible, not the woman." "The woman is a victim
> in this case, as is the life in her womb," he continued.
> (Flegenheimer & Haberman, 2016).

What would be know about life in a womb? He was never around. Barron spends far more time with Melania that he does with daffy Donald. This asshole is out on the golf course and interacting with bankers and financial people leeching for loan money.

The general problem goes beyond Trump – he is no exception, as I've argued. White men think they have the right to tell women what they can and cannot do with their bodies. This seems to me to be the thrust of the problem. These white boys have elevated themselves to "demi-God" or "meta-human" status, akin to their bullshit superheroes that now dominate the big screen and much of television. They really think that the "white way" is the "right way" and you can hear them to this day continuing to claim that they are the "moral leaders" of the rest of the world. And yet look at their views on abortion.

As I say, it's not just Trump:

> Mr. Trump's Republican rivals moved quickly to distance
> themselves from his initial comments as well. Gov. John Kasich of
> Ohio said, "Of course women shouldn't be punished." "I don't
> think that's an appropriate response," he told MSNBC. "It's a
> difficult enough situation." The campaign of Senator Ted Cruz of

[Type text]

> Texas said attention should be focused on providers of abortion,
> not the women who receive them. (Flegenheimer & Haberman,
> 2016).

In either the Cruz or Trump case, you still have white men making decisions for what women should do with their bodies. This is the white man's own doing: you create a society where everybody is "free-fuckin'" and what do you expect to happen? The "free love" movement of the 1960s cut loose a bunch of white women and there was a population explosion. In a kind of "technological fix," whitey came up with condoms and other birth control methods. These were not 100% effective. Then came "the final solution": abortion. And that is where America finds itself, which is why *Roe v. Wade* is hated so much by the fake ass Christian public.

In sum, Roe v. Wade was a major decision in 1973 by the Supreme Court. As Wood & Hawkins (1980) explain the case addressed,

> ... the constitutionality of laws that criminalized or restricted access
> to abortions. The Court ruled 7–2 that a right to privacy under
> the Due Process Clause of the 14th Amendment extended to a
> woman's decision to have an abortion, but that this right must be
> balanced against the state's interests in regulating abortions:
> protecting women's health and protecting the potentiality of human
> life.[1] Arguing that these state interests became stronger over the
> course of a pregnancy, the Court resolved this balancing test by
> tying state regulation of abortion to the third trimester of pregnancy.

Society's views on abortion, led by these white men, is a major controversy even to this day, and has become used as a kind of political football for decades. Again, Flegenheimer & Haberman (2016):

> A New York Times/CBS News poll this month had already
> demonstrated Mr. Trump's weakness with female voters, who
> favored the Democratic front-runner, Hillary Clinton, 55 percent to
> 35 percent. On Wednesday, Mrs. Clinton called Mr. Trump's
> comments "horrific and telling."

So Trump is blamed for the sexist legislation that nearly all white men endorse. As Ted Cruz put it, "Once again, Donald Trump has demonstrated that he hasn't seriously thought through the issues, and he'll say anything just to get attention … "Of course we shouldn't be talking about punishing women; we should affirm their dignity and the incredible gift they have to bring life into the world." (Flegenheimer & Haberman, 2016). But at the same time, this vulture-nosed sonofabitch Cruz doesn't respect women enough to recognize that it is their right to determine what they do with their body and what is inside of their body.

<u>**Trump and Daughter Ivanka: Innocence or Incest?**</u>

` One apparently unrelated article serves as a perfect lead-in for this section on Ivanka and her relationship with her father. According to Flegenheimer & Haberman (2016),

> In Mr. Trump's struggles, his Republican opponents seem to have sensed an opportunity. Even before the latest controversy, Mr. Cruz and Mr. Kasich had invoked their daughters while discussing Mr. Trump's treatment of women. Earlier on Wednesday, Mr. Cruz appeared in Madison, Wis., to introduce a "Women for Cruz" coalition. He was joined by his wife, Heidi; his mother, Eleanor Darragh, who is seldom seen on the campaign trail; and Carly Fiorina, a high-profile supporter.

As I mentioned elsewhere, I do not put Trump above incest. He has had three wives and none of them were born in this country. Why that is I have no idea, but I think it's because he knows that he can have more control over someone who is not familiar with American ways than he would one of these homegrown white women who would sue him for every cent he even thought about having.

At any rate, Ivanka is supposed to be his daughter. But in my view, he treats her more like his wife. In public, he treats her BETTER than he treats his wife, Melania.

One newspaper reported it like this:

> President Trump caused controversy when he said, "I don't think my daughter Ivanka would pose for *Playboy*, although she does have a very nice figure", which would have been a lovely compliment if he had left it there. However, he added, "I've said if Ivanka weren't my daughter, perhaps I'd be dating her". . (Chicago Tribune, 2006)

Perhaps he'd date his daughter if she weren't his daughter? He said this shit in 2006, meaning that he was 60 years old at the time, meaning that Ivanka, who was born in October of 1981, was only 24 or 25. This is the same shit that Roy Moore, the redneck from Alabama who is running for Congress and who is the same age as Trump, is being busted for: dating under aged women when they were in their twenties and he was an assistant district attorney and in some cases was married. He also dated 14 year olds. These are the white boys that are rarely covered in the media other than in the crime pages; but look at their history. During the days of the wild, wild west, they were marrying girls who were 14 and 15 years of age – as long as their parents consented. And in the days of George Washington they were often younger than that.

But this is this asshole's daughter. And some of the photos I've seen them in truly shows that he had an incestuous attraction toward her and it appeared as if she was liking it. After he made the comment about possibly dating Ivanka if she wasn't his daughter check out what the Chicago Tribune had to say about his public statement:

> His comments drew laughs from the audience, and prompted "View" co-host Joy Behar to crack, "Who are you, Woody Allen?"Trump's representative, Jim Dowd, told The Associated Press on Tuesday that Trump "was absolutely joking." "He was making fun of himself for his tendency to date younger women," Dowd said. "It's a sense of humor that people don't see [from him] all the time." Trump's 35-year-old wife, Melania, is expecting the couple's first child this spring. (Chicago Tribune, 2006)

Trump has said on more than ten occasions, all documented, that he is "a smart guy." If he is so damn smart, why would he use his own daughter as an example of the kind of "young woman" that he would date? There is an explanation: because he had done it and considered it before. In fact, I'll go one step further: I think Trump and Ivanka had sex on a regular basis, that they still do, and that Jared Kushner is just a front for a fake marriage and that Ivanka's kids are Donald's! I think Melania can sense that something's not quite right between Donald and Ivanka and that's why you rarely se the two of them (Ivanka and Melania) in any kind of family photo together). That's my theory and I'm sticking to it.

Trump as White Male Prototype: Control Freak

There is a book called *The Iceman Inheritance: Prehistoric Sources of Western Man's Racism, Sexism and Aggression.* Written by Michael Bradley (don't worry – he's white), the book offers some interesting views on the white race, views that I believe go directly to Trump's control freak tendencies and indeed, to the actions of far too many men who attain power and then appear to lose their damn minds.

I will quote from that book and apply the theories of Bradley to one Donald J. Trump (and the white males who are just like him). I will propose in this section of the book that the white race possesses an atypical level of aggression. Whether this characteristic is a "superiority" or an "inferiority" depends solely upon environmental conditions (Bradley, 1978, p. 28).

Is that the case or is it that the white man's savagery dictates that he be in a superior position whether he knows he's an inferior or not? For instance, take professional sports. Black men are in the majority in the major sports that generate the most revenue in college and in the professional ranks. The white man can't compete on the field, on the court or on the track. So what does he do? He trains himself to be a coach, a consultant, a manager, a stadium owner and so on. He is the one who signs the checks and in such a relationship, the superior black athlete becomes nothing more than a well-compensated thrall

Bradley, on the other hand, would rather engage in wishful thinking:

> It is my purpose to turn our Caucasoid prejudice back onto
> ourselves once we have seen that we do tend to differ from other
> kinds of men in at least one behavioral parameter: aggression.
> (Bradley, 1978, p. 33).

If only it was that simple. The white man's cold-blooded nature is combined with a number of his physical attributes, and that includes his colorlessness and we cannot forget his dicklessness. His tiny penis is the key to his racist ways and even Charles Herbert Stember wrote about that in his book Sexual Racism: The Emotional Barrier to an Integrated Society. Other white scholars have come clean over the years including Sigmund Freud who claimed that little girls were jealous because they didn't have dicks. Personally, I think it was Freud who was dickless and he was "projecting" (his term) that feeling of inadequacy off on others.

And yet Bradley wants to make racism and the way white men treat others as some kind of personality quirk. For instance, he writes:

> Not intelligence, nor morality , nor 'spirit,' but *aggression* is
> responsible for the white man's 'superiority.' Aggression is

> responsible for the expansion of Caucasoids, both geographically
> and culturally, at the expense of other races. We witness the final
> act of this expansion in our own time. It began when the glaciers
> retreated, when Wurm released the white race from his tutelage
> under fire and ice, when pathological temporal aggression was
> unleashed upon the world (Bradley, 1978, p. 26).

What "superiority"? Do you mean political superiority? Social superiority? Because the white man is in no way physically superior to anyone. If that was the case, the NBA and the NFL would be predominantly white, the way they were when the laws of the land excluded men of color. Once those ranks opened up, the white man's gooniness, clumsiness and physical inferiority was almost immediately exposed.

Bradley wants to talk about glaciers and the role that fire and ice played in "unleashing temporary aggression" upon the world. This might be good fodder for a science fiction movie, but Bradley is still not getting to the essentials. And maybe it's because he is a white man himself. But that's his problem. My role as a scholar is to get at the truth. The white man in general became a control freak because he wanted to do so. The rest of the world was ripe for the plucking and he jumped at the chance to use bombs, bullets and beastlike men to take over and then maintain that position of "white privilege." Just like Trump is doing even now and other white male presidents and white prime ministers in other countries did long before Trump.

Moving on:

> This higher level of aggression, which is merely an incidental
> result of glacial evolution, has fueled extreme manifestations of
> temporal assertion and defense among Caucasoids. Rampant
> technology, environmental pollution, resource rapine and the threat
> of nuclear war are the results (Bradley, 1978, pp. 26-27).

Incidental result of glacial evolution? Bullshit! "Rampant technology, environmental pollution, resource rapine and the threat of nuclear war" are the result of the white man being a control freak based on his deep-seated feelings of inadequacy, as Dr. Frances Cress Welsing taught. They feel little so they have to act as if they are big through the use of economic manipulation and brute force Just like Trump!

A control freak does not like the idea of being controlled and doesn't view "rules" as being worthy of being adhered to. As a megalomaniac and narcissist, he doesn't like rules. Look at the people I've analyzed in this book: all of them have

[Type text]

authoritarian personalities and will join or become a part of a political team with the ulterior motive of pushing their own agenda. It may take place from the outset or perhaps over time, but that personal agenda will raise its head eventually.

MSN.com's Katherine Krueger published a story with the headline, "CNN: Donald Trump Broke the Rules of Fox News' GOP Debate." The article, and my analyses, follow:

> Republican frontrunner Donald Trump violated the rules of Fox News' presidential debate on Thursday night by consulting with his campaign manager during a commercial break, CNN reported. According to a report from CNN Money's Dylan Byers, Trump consulted with campaign manager Corey Lewandowski during the first commercial break of Thursday's event, coordination that is explicitly banned by the network's debate rules. (Krueger, 2015).

Control freaks don't follow rules and anyone who interacts with these kinds of people know that to be the case. Trump doesn't have self-respect so why should he respect the rules of others? This kind of mentality has nothing to do with glaciers, icebergs or snowflakes: this is the white man running rampant through the global universe in order to seize control so he can disguise his own low self-concept and obvious dicklessness   !

And what is described above was not the only time during the debates:

> Citing "rival campaign sources," CNN reported that while Trump has broken the rules by communicating backstage with Lewandowski at multiple debates, the campaign manager met Trump directly on stage Thursday, which Byers characterized as "a new extreme." The campaigns were explicitly informed they were not allowed to communicate with the candidates during breaks, the sources told CNN. (Krueger, 2015).

And Trump would go on to hire Lewandowski before firing him. Once Trump became President, all the people that helped him cheat his way in were soundly rewarded – the way you reward a dog with a bone after it turns a flip. Control freaks USE people and that is what Trump learned from his father and grandfather. That is what their ancestors learned as they developed a capitalist system where there were going to be "haves and have-nots": the man with the gold makes the rules.

Once the rules are broken that means there are no rules. Lewandowski simply refused to get out of the way and the spineless white organizers at Fox News didn't want to stand up to him:

> An unnamed Fox News source said debate staff asked Lewandowski to leave the stage but he refused. Network representatives then told the campaigns for Sen. Ted Cruz (R-TX), Sen. Marco Rubio (R-FL), and Ohio Gov. John Kasich that they could consult with their candidates because Trump had broken the rules. (Krueger, 2015).

So then with no rules, these men were being "consulted" by others in what was supposed to be the chance for them to debate one another heads up. But the control freak took over the debates time and time again and once he became President, Trump continued this "I make the rules" approach to government. These white people are all in it together. Check out what took place next:

> While it wasn't immediately clear what Trump and Lewandowski spoke about, the billionaire did produce a report from the Better Business Bureau, which showed the rating for Trump University upgraded to an "A" grade, to hand over to the Fox News moderators during a commercial break. Fox News and the Trump campaign did not respond to multiple TPM requests for comment. (Krueger, 2015).

The Better Business Bureau gave Trump University an "A"? In retrospect we now know that Trump University was nothing but a scam. The grade from the Better Business Bureau is akin to those jacked up kudos and awards given by JD Powers – a system that you have to pay to join in exchange for a good remark and an award. This is what the white man's system has produced and what control freaks can pay for in order to use. It's been that way throughout recorded history.

Trump's "control freak" activities and words, what his white pals refer to as being "an alpha male," have been seen far longer than the election. He's always been an asshole, but the people who were around him thought it was cute. So cowardly were they that they figured that as long as he didn't direct his ire, insults and inhumanity toward THEM, then it was cool. Many of them even joined in with the Trumpian cacophony of emotive labeling.

Not all racists are control freaks but if a control freak gets into a position of power, he will inevitably display his or her racism. It is only in that way that they could have the guts to impose on black people. After all, racism is not just prejudice – it is a belief system (an ideology) which white people all directly or indirectly share in, it is a violent imposition, and you have to have some semblance of power in order to impose your will on those you hate, and it is an institutional arrangement. You have to have some semblance of institutional power.

With that having been said, let's take a look at the white control freak tendencies as demonstrated by one Donald J. Trump. On December 11, 2015 a website called Thinkprogress.org ran an article by Justin Salhani called, "Leaders Across the World Denounce Trump." Six nations were observed by the author and he printed what he found. I shall respond to each of these areas.

> Presidential candidate Donald Trump's recent comments about banning Muslims from entering the United States drew <u>criticism</u> across the political spectrum. Denunciations, however, also emanated from outside of these shores as Trump's name was stripped from real estate holdings, politicians gave him labels like "a dangerous fool", and one country's citizens even signed a petition to ban him entry. (Salhani, 2015).

This was in 2015 when Trump was but a candidate. Today we are at the end of 2017, Trump was elected President, and he still hates immigrants – brown ones, that is. This racist bastard is a prototype, but not an original. After the nasty peckerwoods staggered through Ellis Island after arriving on the shores of this country, there was anti-immigrant fervor and it was imposed especially hard on people of color. Some background is in order as this is a teaching moment.

According to Wikipedia (2017),

> The United States Constitution was adopted on September 17, 1787. Article I, section 8, clause 4 of the Constitution expressly gives the United States Congress the power to establish **a uniform rule of naturalization …** Pursuant to this power, Congress in 1790 passed the first naturalization law for the United States, the Naturalization Act of 1790. The law enabled those who had resided in the country for two years and had kept their current state of residence for a year to apply for citizenship. **However it restricted naturalization to "free white persons" of "good moral character".** (Emphasis added)

So they were ethnocentric and racist from the get-go. And yet the history courses in the high schools of America don't want to address these kinds of issues. As the old saying goes, "what goes in is what comes out." You cannot hate the root of a tree (in this case immigrants of color) and not hate the tree itself." Then came the punishments: "The <u>Naturalization Act of 1795</u> increased the residency

[Type text]

requirement to five years residence and added a requirement to give a three years notice of intention to apply for citizenship, and the <u>Naturalization Act of 1798</u> further increased the residency requirement to 14 years and required five years notice of intent to apply for citizenship." (Wikipedia, 2017).

So now you see the rules and regulations as well as the mandatory requirements and potential punishments. So let's fast forward to the coming of Chinese immigrants:

> After the immigration of 123,000 Chinese in the 1870s, who joined the 105,000 who had immigrated between 1850 and 1870, Congress passed the Chinese Exclusion Act in 1882 which targeted a single ethnic group by specifically limiting further Chinese immigration. Chinese had immigrated to the Western United States as a result of unsettled conditions in China, the availability of jobs working on railroads, and the Gold Rush that was going on at that time in California. The expression "Yellow Peril" became popular at this time. (Wikipedia, 2017)

So we have the same kind of name calling that Trump and those of his ilk are so guilty of. The only colorless race on Earth has the gall to have a name for every single person they come across who is different from them. Again, Trump is no exception – he is the racist rule.

And that is good enough for now because this book is not about immigrants per se. It is about how a white man who dyes his skin and his hair has the gall to show complete disdain-and-how-dare-you toward people of color. Today they call it "Border security," but the intent is still the same: screen people of color out of America and work like hell to return it to the white nation that was envisioned in the Constitution where it said – and let me remind you of the wording: "A restricted naturalization to "free white persons" of "good moral character".

Today he's still at it and his millions of supporters have grown the courage to voice their anti-immigrant views as well. Using the claim that "immigrants are taking American jobs," these peckerwoods never add that their fear is based on their (American) inferior work ethic, uncontrolled hubris and the lack of education as well as the decline in American technological know-how. Even Silicon Valley nerds pale in comparison (no pun intended) when compared to the work being put in by the Japanese, the people in India, the Chinese and the Middle East. America thinks that by selectively allowing a handpicked few of these types into American colleges, they can "upgrade." The selection process is, in itself, evidence of a "control freak" attitude and American policies reflect it.

[Type text]

Before he became president, the cowardly Trump worked to manipulate the tone of the Republican Presidential debates. An article by Laurie Kellman outlined a proposal for a 'softer' debate coming from a man whose loud mouthed vitriol paved the way for much of the verbal hatred that is even to this day in 2017 being hurled about in Washington and across the country.

According to the article:

> WASHINGTON — The chairman of the Republican Party has declared that he wants Thursday's Republican presidential debate to be "more of a G-rated" event than recent showdowns. And who doesn't — given the bullying, sexual innuendo and unintelligible yelling that has made 11 previous Republican face-offs something less than family-friendly? (Kellman, 2016)

Since that time, as we know, the gutless Republican Party has swallowed bucket after bucket of Trump's warm spit and have literally kissed his ass no matter how insulting he has been to women, black athletes, black women, Latinas, the gay community and so on. The white contenders literally took it up the ass while Trump embarrassed America on international television during the debates. Even after Hillary Clinton (a crook in her own right) kicked his ass in the three Presidential Debates, the white man still showed his dicklessness by standing back and staying silent while Trump appealed to the racist nature of the white American voting public.

For instance,

> Republican National Committee Chairman Reince Priebus, the take-no-sides chief fundraiser for the party, has been saying all week that he wants the whatever-it-takes "tone" of past debates to improve on Thursday's debate stage. On Wednesday, he described on CNN just how, saying he'd like to see "more of a G-rated debate" than "some of the things that have been said in the past."He said the RNC has spoken to the campaigns and to the sponsors about taking steps to "reduce the temperature" on the debate stage and in the audience. (Kellman, 2016).

Priebus was full of shit then and he remained that way – which is why the two-faced Trump canned his ass as soon as he won the Presidency. Nobody respects a coward, even the people that the coward purports to defend. That is the way of war, folks. The control freak dictates who is trusted aides will be and anyone who even remotely sounds like a critic will be ousted from the ranks.

When Florida's Marco Rubio slyly insulted Trump's lack of a penis, he paid dearly for it. Despite the fact that it was probably true, the majority of white men probably took it personally since their own sexual racism is a part of their lives and is well known by the women they date or marry. At any rate, Rubio caved like the true coward that he was then and is still to this very day:

> By Wednesday, Rubio himself said publicly on MSNBC that he's "not entirely proud" of slinging personal insults about Trump's tan, his hair and the size of his hands — which set off Trump's racy comment about his anatomy. Rubio said his own children were "embarrassed" by his actions. In a town hall with MSNBC, Rubio says he knows the attacks are "not what we want from our next president." (Kellman, 2016)

Why would Rubio's children be embarrassed about what he said about the size of Trump's hands, implying that small hands mean small dick? Didn't he think it through? Of course not. He's one of those assimilated Cubans, like Ted Cruz, who comes into the political fray appealing to upper class Cubans and the Jews who live in Florida. He gets into office and, as is the case of the control freak, begins to think that he's above the law. The only reason he showed regret for his statements was because the projections showed that Trump was kicking his ass and if that was the case, he didn't want to pick on a peckerwood who might one day be President.

But when you're a control freak, you can create your own realities, tell lies when you feel like it and make promises that you have no intention of keeping. For instance, during the Republican Presidential primaries, pay close attention to Trump's truth-claims:

> Trump has been speaking in recent days of softness, party unity and potentially presidential behavior. But he's qualifying it, too, by adding that he can't just stand there and let Rubio, Kasich and Cruz insult him or tell him to, "breathe." So watch whether he lets them push his buttons, yells back — or shows the discipline to stay commanding but above the often juvenile tone that Trump himself has set. (Kellman, 2016)

Now look back from today in 2017: everything you just read was a damn lie and he knew they were lies when he told them. He says what has to be said in order to dupe the gullible public. Remember elsewhere in this book where I quote the New York Times and the fact that Trump had told me than a thousand lies? Just like the forefathers did when they wrote that bullshit Constitution, just like the so-called "settlers" did when they broke all those Indian treaties, and so on. In America, telling a damn lie is as acceptable as breathing. How can you tell when Trump is telling a lie? When his lips are moving.

Then he had to drag his slag of a wife into the issue (like he always does when he feels the need to prove that he indeed has a woman in his life):

> Remember: Trump revealed last week that his wife, Melania, does not like when he uses bad language and had urged him to, "be presidential." But that was before he took the stage in Detroit and bragged about the size of his genitalia. (Kellman, 2016)

Just the fact that he would publicly state that his wife doesn't like it but he does it anyway shows his lack of respect for her, which is a reflection of his lack of respect for all women. It's his way of saying, "That bitch don't tell me what to do," which is the same attitude he has about anyone who dares to offer him any type of advice – except for his secret lover Vladimir Putin, that is.

Trump is America the way America doesn't want to see itself: vile, vulgar and devoid of values. He represents tens of millions of white folks who hold him up as a role model which explains why America is on the decline. When Trump said "Make America Great Again," what he really meant was "Make America GRATE Again." As you know, to "grate" something means to reduce it to small shreds by rubbing it on a grater, right? And another definition of grate is "to make an unpleasant rasping sound." To even her mention of the name "Trump" almost anywhere in the world literally grates on the nerves of most clear-thinking people. Only in America is he seen as someone with an active brain stem.

TRUMP AS PROTOTYPE: CRITICISMS AND COMMENTARY

If this book has offered nothing else, it has shown that when it comes to morality, ethics and any semblance of human decency, Donald Trump's distorted versions of all of these reigns without rival. But my point remains that he is not someone who is unique in attitude or ideology when it comes to disdain for the rules or the rights of blacks, women, and others. He is so dim-witted that he speaks out loud what I believe most white people believe and feel. Not only that, but his narcissism and egotism, as I hope to have shown, is a characteristic that is shared

[Type text]

with a number of those who have vied for the presidency and along with that power-mongering comes the heretofore mentioned lack of human decency.

Because space will not allow me to write thousands of pages documenting my accusations, let us cut to the chase using insights and information provided by a group that specializes in dealing with ethics (or the lack thereof) in Washington.

C.R.E.W.(Citizens for Responsibility and Ethics in Washington) and Trump Hotels/Properties

According to the CREW website,

> CREW uses aggressive legal action, in-depth research, and bold communications to reduce the influence of money in politics and help foster a government that is ethical and accountable. We highlight abuses, change behavior, and lay the groundwork for new policies and approaches that encourage public officials to work for the benefit of the people, not powerful interests.

They call themselves CREW and this is not to imply that these people are any less racist than any other group of white people that claims to be about "doing the right thing." History is replete with examples of the morality façade and the claims of being upright when, in reality, the groups are grant seeking charlatans who only deal with issues that are the most blatant violators of rules and regulations.

The group is supposed to be about "emoluments" that may or may not be a part of the Trump Administration's routine. For your information the emolument clause, according to the Heritage Guide to the Constitution reads thusly:

> Article VI of the Articles of Confederation was the source of the Constitution's prohibition on federal titles of nobility and the so-called Emolument Clause. The clause sought to shield the republican character of the United States against corrupting foreign influences

Trump has long been accused of using his hotels, golf courses and casinos as places where foreigners could pay and have access to him. There is actually a membership fee to "join Mar-A-Lago," which Trump increased from $100,000 to $200,00 a year.

[Type text]

O'Connell (2017) writes, "This is nothing Washington has ever seen. For the first time in presidential history, a profit-making venture touts the name of a U.S. president in its gold signage. And every cup of coffee served, every fundraiser scheduled, every filet mignon ordered feeds the revenue of the Trump family's private business." As written earlier, control freaks don't comply with rules or tradition; they get into power and then the establish rules, norms, and values of their own.

Susan Wright (2017) wrote an article titled, "Ethics Group Fought to Gain Access to Mar-A-Lago Visitors Log, and Won." This article provides an excellent opening to this section of the book that documents criticisms of Donald Trump. As has been reported,

> The government watchdog group, Citizens for Responsibility and Ethics in Washington (or CREW), have been trying to make the visitor logs for the White House, Trump Tower, and Mar-a-Lago made public. Beginning this fall, they'll see some progress to that end. On Monday morning, the group announced that the Department of Homeland Security will be turning over visitor logs for President Trump's Florida club, Mar-a-Lago by September 8, 2017. They, in turn, intend to make the information public.(Wright, 2017).

No one who wants "access" to President Trump can be up to any good. I say this because most people know Trump is no good. So they also know he is susceptible to blackmail, bribery and extortion. The Russians surely know. So CREW is seeking to find out if Trump and his Administration are in violation of the Emoluments Clause – cutting deals with foreign governments.

Continuing:

> CREW was one of several organizations that have sued to see just who the Trump administration is entertaining. The National Security Archive and the Knight First Amendment Institute have also been on a mission to gain more transparency from Trump. Mar-a-Lago is a start. DHS says there are no records of who visits Trump Tower, and Trump has refused to turn over visitor logs for the White House.(Wright, 2017).

But it is the general "use" of the hotels that has many people concerned about how Trump continues to pimp the system.

In an August 7, 2017 article titled, "How the Trump hotel changed Washington's culture of influence," Jonathan O'Connell of *the Washington Post* offered insights on how this white man has totally exploited Washington's elite, made money in the name of the Presidency, and is evidently getting away with it. According to the article,

> On a June morning, Romanian President Klaus Iohannis, President of Romania, thanked Trump the next morning for his "strong leadership." His office did not say whether he stayed at the hotel overnight and his wife enjoyed croissants in the lounge of the opulent hotel, a day before joining President Trump a few blocks away at the White House for a Rose Garden news conference.(O'Connell, 2017)

These men from those other countries can be hypnotized by the glitz and glamour of Mar-A-Lago. If Trump throws in free room service, that is an even more powerful inducement. And in this way Trump can skin and grin and lie and convince people like President Johannis of Romania that he (Trump) is their buddy and will do whatever they want – as long as he gets what he (and Putin) want.

Moving on:

> Downstairs that same day in the grand ballroom, hundreds of bankers discussed their industry's future under Treasury Secretary Steven Mnuchin and his wife enjoyed croissants in the lounge of the opulent hotel, a day before joining President(O'Connell, 2017)

Steve Mnuchin was a crook from the get-go and since like takes to like, Trump hired him to handle the duties of Secretary of the Treasury. He would turn around and use the private jet to fly around the country and the world with his blonde, former actress wife, who is as sick as he is. This is what Trump prefers because they kinds of ultra-rich people are just like him.

According to the article,

> The scenes illustrate a daily spectacle of Washington influence at 1100 Pennsylvania Ave., the city's newest luxury hotel that has quickly become a kind of White House annex. Since Trump's election, the Trump International Hotel has emerged as a Republican Party power center where on a good day — such as July 28 around 8 p.m. — excited visitors can watch the president share intimate dinner conversation with his just-named chief of

staff, John F. Kelly, and be the first to brag about it on social
media. (O'Connell, 2017)

And what you just read is totally by design. Where is CREW and those other watchdogs from Congress? Nowhere to be found. In the meantime,

> In conversations with The Washington Post, the hotel's
> management described its strategy to capitalize on the president's
> popularity. It markets the hotel to Republican and conservative
> groups that embrace Trump's politics but takes care not to solicit
> business from fringe groups that would embarrass the president.
> Trump supporters in red "Make America Great Again" caps get a
> chance to rub elbows with White House officials against an
> American flag backdrop at the Benjamin Bar, where a signature
> concoction of winter wheat vodka, oysters and caviar goes for
> $100. (O'Connell, 2017)

So there was a "strategy" which means that all of this activity was pre-planned. It is a direct violation of the emoluments clause. I don't care if Republicans are the ones doing the renting or membership joining; those assholes are worse than any "foreign entity." Trump just wants to make America the way it was during slavery and Mar-A-Lago is his headquarters; his golf courses are bastions of lily-white planning where only Uncle Toms like Tiger Woods are allowed, and his business tendency is based on a lie: he puts his name on buildings that people of color constructed and clean, and takes all the credit. That muthafucka is no more an architect or a real estate magnate than a menu is a meal.

It's always about the money with Trump. That's how he got his women, including that prostitute-looking Melania that he is now married to but hardly ever sleeps with. The people who voted for him knew what he was when they were casting their ballots. But after eight years of an intelligent African-American president who made them all look and feel inferior, they wanted "get things back to the way they were" which means "let's put black people in their place.' And that is what Trump is attempting to do.

Moving on:

> Business from foreign customers is brisk, the hotel says, but as an
> ethical precaution, it says it does not market directly to foreign
> embassies. Under an agreement signed by Trump, the hotel has
> promised to donate any profits made from foreign governments to
> the U.S. Treasury. An obscure constitutional provision known as
> the emoluments clause prohibits the president from profiting from

foreign governments without specific approval from Congress. (O'Connell, 2017)

They don't have to directly "market" to foreign customers. America is the most popular nation in the world and as such, so is the person who leads it. And if he leads it and his name is slathered all over hotels and golf courses, that is publicity enough! Not only that, but they can tell through their research that Trump is a greedy bastard who can be bossed, bought and bribed. Put the two together – access to Trump and Trump's own lack of character – and you have the perfect recipe. All these countries have to do is spread the word about what a sap Trump is. And that is exactly what is taking place even as I write these words.

Much of it is done in a roundabout manner. For instance, pay close attention to the following lie … oops! I mean "explanation":

"While we can't quantify how much business we have received because of politics, neither can we quantify how much we have lost," Patricia Tang, director of sales and marketing, said in an interview. It is difficult to see comings and goings at the hotel. There are no signs in the lobby to direct guests to daily events, velvet ropes block the public from meeting areas, and some groups holding conventions and banquets omit references to Trump's name in their promotional materials. Many decline to answer questions about why they chose the Trump hotel from the many similar luxury Washington venues. (O'Connell, 2017)

It's a scam, a den of sin for politicians. Trump buys pussy so he probably has a few call girls in the lobbies for those foreign brown-skinned cockhound who watch American TV and movies in their countries and come to the conclusion that white women are international whores. So they look for blondes and the like, eat up all of Trump's food at jacked up prices and maybe, just maybe, they might attend a meeting or two. They take some photos and then go back to their country singing the praises of the American president.

Why would these people refuse to answer questions about why they would choose to stay at a Trump Hotel in DC rather than any of the other luxury hotels. It is clear because Trump's hotels are no cheaper. It's because Trump is a piece of shit and so are most of those "dignitaries" that come to Washington DC seeking favors from the corrupt people in Congress. Trump is the pimp and all others are nothing more than willing thralls.

For instance:

> In July, about 300 Republican donors, paying $35,000 apiece,
> gathered at the hotel for a fundraiser headlined by the president.
> The event raised an estimated $10 million for Trump's campaign,
> the Republican National Committee and other GOP groups,
> according to news reports at the time. Money also has poured in
> from other Republican political committees that have chosen the
> Trump hotel as a venue for receptions. (O'Connell, 2017)

America is a whore that is about to get fucked for the final time. That is why this pimp-like individual, Donald Trump, should be the final chapter. He is a prototype that has been spliced together from the actions, policies and attitudes of dictators, kleptocrats, autocrats and plutocrats, past and present. That is why his speeches are permeated with stolen quotes from various rulers who dogged their people, casual references to Hitler and others and a blatant disdain for the "have-nots" which includes people of color, immigrants with a few white folks sprinkled in.

Violation of the emoluments clause is but the tip of the iceberg. Trump has violated every single tenet of the "human decency clause," in my book.

Trump's Struggle For Self-Preservation: Analysis

Just as I was about to put this book to bed and send it off to the publisher, an incredible article appeared on December 9th in the New York Times. Written by Maggie Haberman, Glenn Thrust and Peter Baker, the article was titled, "Inside Trump's Hour-by-Hour Battle for Self-Preservation," the article outlines what Trump is supposedly like behind closed doors. It is a sick portrait, one akin to that of a retired redneck sitting around all day long getting his news straight from the television set.

But let me not get ahead of myself. I am going to use the contents (with some exclusions due to repetition of what I already shared) of that article to offer a black scholar's viewpoint of this white man who became President. When I was young I learned that "all that glitters is not gold." I am not implying that there is anything glowing about Trump, but being the President means he attracts the one thing he apparently craves as much as money: attention. And this article clearly establishes that, as do some of the comments made about Trump's past.

The article begins, thusly:

[Type text]

> WASHINGTON — Around 5:30 each morning, <u>President</u>
> <u>Trump</u> wakes and tunes into the television in the White House's
> master bedroom. He flips to CNN for news, moves to "Fox &
> Friends" for comfort and messaging ideas, and sometimes watches
> MSNBC's "Morning Joe" because, friends suspect, it fires him up
> for the day. (Haberman, Thrush & Baker, 2017)

Several points to be made here.

First, he's sleeping alone. What does that say? He's not getting any sex action from Melania so he's suffering from erectile dysfunction, probably the reason why he got so upset when Marco Rubio made jokes about the size of his penis. So here you have a 72 year old pale white man who has to have a tan and get his hair done just the right way, including peroxide rinse. What I have just described is a female.

Second, watching "Fox & Friends" for the news is like watching "Deep Throat" if you want to learn about how to remove tonsils. That entire station is devoted to the conservative way of life and they don't give a damn about the truth. Their president was sued for sexual harassment, their leading talk show host, Bill O'Reilly, got sued for sexually harassment and so on. The entire network is rife with scum, including white bitches who wear skirts up to the cracks of their asses and learn how to cross their legs to attract viewers. So Trump is more likely looking for a boner than he is real news facts.

He watches "Morning Joe"? Why? He hates Joe Scarborough and I've already shared how he took swipes at both Joe and his wife Mika. But being the sick asshole he is, he may have a masochistic streak in him and likes to hear himself getting dogged: "beat me, I'm still conscious." Getting "fired up for the day" is not based on any television viewing; this asshole is on some form of drugs, and I'll elaborate on that later.

Moving on:

> Energized, infuriated — often a gumbo of both — Mr. Trump grabs
> his iPhone. Sometimes he tweets while propped on his pillow,
> according to aides. Other times he tweets from the den next door,
> watching another television. Less frequently, he makes his way up the
> hall to the ornate Treaty Room, sometimes dressed for the day,
> sometimes still in night clothes, where he begins his official and
> unofficial calls. (Haberman, Thrush & Baker, 2017)

So if the phone is "propped on his pillow," then that clearly proves that Melania's head is not there. He sleeps alone and she is just for show. And she intentionally keeps her distance from him when they're walking, they rarely hold hands and when they do it is clear that she is totally turned off.

The Treaty Room is probably where this butthead shoots up. They know he's taking some kind of dope. His doctor is a piece of shit who wrote some kind of note before the election claiming that Trump was "in perfect health," which is a damn lie. You can tell he's sick just by looking at him. Just a week ago he was giving a speech and started sounding like Sylvester the Cat (thuffering thucatash!) and had to take a swig of water. He's old, he's dying and he's too damn stubborn to admit either one.

The article then breaks into some facts which clearly proves that Trump wants to paint himself as some kind of wounded victim. Check it out:

> As he ends his first year in office, Mr. Trump is redefining what it means to be president. He sees the highest office in the land much as he did the night of his stunning victory over Hillary Clinton — as a prize he must fight to protect every waking moment, and Twitter is his Excalibur. Despite all his bluster, he views himself less as a titan dominating the world stage than a maligned outsider engaged in a struggle to be taken seriously, according to interviews with 60 advisers, associates, friends and members of Congress. (Haberman, Thrush & Baker, 2017)

Again, make it clear that Trump is no "original." He is just a different type of racist administrator. But black people and these white bitches who are going around talking about Trump as if he is "the worst" is like grabbing one rattlesnake out of rhumba of them and saying "this is the one that is the most problematic"! Trump is not "redefining" anything – he is personifying it. He is the personification of the same racism and callous disregard for human that other peckerwoods before him had, from Washington and Jefferson to Truman and Reagan. The only difference is that he focuses his ire on ALL groups and the others specialized and kept their eyes on people of color and women.

The article claims, "Despite all his bluster, he views himself less as a titan dominating the world stage than a maligned outsider engaged in a struggle to be taken seriously." What? This statement is wrong on both counts. First of all, he is no "titan." He is a mouse who stumbled into the presidency when the Electoral College gave him the election. Secondly, he is not maligned; but the truth is so insulting that it appears as if he is being castigated. He is so fucked up that to merely describe his daily antics, attitudes and statements would be considered an insult to the normal human being. He IS taken seriously: he is a serious pain in the ass and America will never recover from the fact that this orange colored oaf was in the Oval Office.

Continuing:

> For other presidents, every day is a test of how to lead a country, not just a faction, balancing competing interests. For Mr. Trump, every day is an hour-by-hour battle for self-preservation. He still relitigates last year's election, convinced that the investigation by Robert S. Mueller III, the special counsel, into Russia's interference is a plot to delegitimize him. Color-coded maps highlighting the counties he won were hung on the White House walls. (Haberman, Thrush & Baker, 2017)

How would the writers know what other presidents considered to be their priority? Did they ask them? Those presidents had one thing that Trump didn't have the sense to put together: a cabinet of professionals, a vice-president with a functioning brain stem and a cabinet of Eveready bunny-type peckerwoods ready to dig in and get to work. Trump has none of this: he goes it alone. And since he's an idiot, he is learning on the job and learning by trial and error. And he is wrong almost every single time.

Still obsessing on his election day ass kicking. He won the Electoral College, where basically 78,000 peckerwoods got him in. Hillary had more than 3,000,000 more votes – and she wasn't shit either. But he's so misogynistic and such a megalomaniac that like a baby, "him want to get kwedit for winning the game." What an asshole.

It gets worse:

> Before taking office, Mr. Trump told top aides to think of each presidential day as an episode in a television show in which he vanquishes rivals. People close to him estimate that Mr. Trump spends at least four hours a day, and sometimes as much as twice that, in front of a television, sometimes with the volume muted, marinating in the no-holds-barred wars of cable news and eager to fire back. (Haberman, Thrush & Baker, 2017)

What? A television show? Why would he tell them that? He had no control at NBC! He was a fuckin' flunky in a show where he intermittently appeared to bark out orders and then, at the end, tell someone "You're fired." In real life the cowardly muthafucka never had the guts to fire his own people. He didn't fire

Comey, he didn't fire Flynn and he didn't fire Manafort. He had somebody else do it.

He spends four to eight hours a day in front of a television set, sometimes with the volume muted? What's wrong with this muthafucka? TV is bad enough with the volume ON, but with it muted all you see is a bunch of pale faces talking into the camera. He is "eager to fire back" because he has the power to do so; but when you fire back it's always good to make sure you're not shooting blanks. And the more Trump "tweets" the bigger of an ass he makes of himself. One good thing about that is that all those tweets are a matter of public and historical record. So in about four years there will be enough material for a major comedy about the Trump presidency. It would have to be a comedy – unless Trump has dropped a nuclear bomb before then.

His lifestyle thus far seems to be that of a neurotic nincompoop. But people like Trump always want to claim to be the victim:

> "He feels like there's an effort to undermine his election and that collusion allegations are unfounded," said Senator Lindsey Graham, a Republican from South Carolina who has spent more time with the president than most lawmakers. "He believes passionatcly that the liberal left and the media are out to destroy him. The way he got here is fighting back and counterpunching. (Haberman, Thrush & Baker, 2017)

Lindsey Graham is a two-faced southerner who dogged Trump during the Republican debates but now that Trump is president, he's kissing his ass. He spent more time with Trump because, in my view, Graham is homoerotic. That's the kind of "men" Trump likes. And make no bones about it: the "liberal left" and the conservative right are all racist. The only difference is that one thinks black people are too stupid to do things for themselves (Hillary Clinton and the liberals) and the other side thinks black people ought to be lined up and shot (conservatives like Trump, Trent Lott, and the rest).

Then Graham has the gall to add, "The problem he's going to face "is there's a difference between running for the office and being president. You've got to find that sweet spot between being a fighter and being president." (Haberman, Thrush & Baker, 2017)

Notice the use of the term "sweet spot." In most cases that would refer to a woman's body. But when you're talking about Lindsey Graham and Donald Trump, it could be a political reference or it could be a reference to the underworld of a man's nutsack.

[Type text]

And the media, the one that hounds Trump and makes money with their reports on his antics, nevertheless give that asshole far more credit than he deserves. For instance, check out the following passage:

> Bracing and refreshing to his alienated-from-the-system political base, Mr. Trump's uninhibited approach seems erratic to many veterans of both parties in the capital and beyond. Some politicians and pundits lament the instability and, even without medical degrees, feel no compunction about publicly diagnosing various mental maladies. (Haberman, Thrush & Baker, 2017)

"From-the-system political base." "Uninhibited approach." Trump is acting like any other individual who is both neurotic and psychotic. And what is a neurosis defined as? According to one source it is, "a relatively mild mental illness that is not caused by organic disease, involving symptoms of stress (depression, anxiety, obsessive behavior, hypochondria) but not a radical loss of touch with reality." On the other hand psychosis is, "a severe mental disorder in which thought and emotions are so impaired that contact is lost with external reality." So in my view Trump ventures back and forth between neurosis and psychosis, but in the main, and in a vernacular that we can all understand, he's a god damned NUTCASE!!

You don't need to medical degree to see if a person is out of his damn mind. The Bible itself (which is no valid construct in my view), nevertheless claims that a man is the sum of his functions. If a man is always fucking up, then he's an asshole. And as the quote by Marcus Aurelius at the outset of this book makes clear, "To expect bad men not to do wrong is madness"

The article on Trump continues:

> After months of legislative failures, Mr. Trump is on the verge of finally prevailing in his efforts to cut taxes and reverse part of his predecessor's health care program. While much of what he has promised remains undone, he has made significant progress in his goal of rolling back business and environmental regulations. The growing economy he inherited continues to improve, and stock markets have soared to record heights. His partial travel ban on mainly Muslim countries has finally taken effect after multiple court fights. (Haberman, Thrush & Baker, 2017)

The key words from the previous excerpt are "the growing economy he inherited." That's right. He's taking credit for Barack Obama's work and is rolling back much of what Obama did. This is a political version of "ethnic cleansing" because the racists who back Trump – namely the Koch brothers and the Mercer family – hate people of color and are white nationalists through and through. This again proves that Trump is no prototype, but the rule. Every President who has been in power, including Obama, did the bidding of the people who spent the money that got them into office. Don't forget that Obama deported more Mexicans than anyone, saved the racist banking industry, bailed out the "hire few niggas" auto industry and killed more black men around the world than any other president. But he was black in terms of skin color so African-Americans gave him a pass – the same kind of pass that crackers, peckerwoods and rednecks are now bestowing upon Donald Trump.

Furthermore,

> Jared Kushner, his son-in-law and senior adviser, has told associates that Mr. Trump, deeply set in his ways at age 71, will never change. Rather, he predicted, Mr. Trump would bend, and possibly break, the office to his will … That has proved half true. Mr. Trump, so far, has arguably wrestled the presidency to a draw. (Haberman, Thrush & Baker, 2017)

The presidency wasn't shit to begin with. It was easy to change it because it was nothing more than a peckerwood sitting in a chair doing what the people around him "advised" him to do. Since Trump didn't want anyone around him who he couldn't control, he just transformed what was there in his own image and interests. And now America is seen in the same way that Trump is seen by most Americans: as a bloviating piece of shit that lies every time he opens his mouth. K

Jared Kushner, the effeminate-looking son-in-law, is supposedly married to Trump's daughter Ivanka. It is clear that Ivanka is a slut, just like her mother Ivana was and just like most of Trump's wives were and like most of the women he prefers. She claims to be a designer, but her clothing line is mediocre at best, benefitting only from the "Trump" name. She comes out every now and then and speaks on women's issues, but that bitch is just fronting: how could she be married to an international money launderer like the faggot-looking Kushner and then have the gall to boast about being a mother and someone committed to women's rights? Her father is one of the biggest impediments to women's rights that the country has seen and he is a reflection of an entire nation with a history of treating women like shit.

[Type text]

John Kelly came in supposedly to keep Trump under control. That's like asking Rocky to control Bullwinkle: Under a sub-heading called 'Time to Think', take note of the following:

> 'Time to Think'
> In the jargon of the military, John F. Kelly, a retired four-star general, served as a "wagon boss" for Marines crashing into <u>Iraq</u> in 2003, keeping his column moving forward despite incoming fire. As <u>White House chief of staff</u>, Mr. Kelly has adopted much the same approach, laboring 14-hour days to impose discipline on a chaotic operation — with mixed success. (Haberman, Thrush & Baker, 2017)

Have you noticed that all of these male assholes that Trump has brought on board are old geezers? I don't give a shit if their generals or presidents of corporations they are all old. From Mnuchin, Kelly, Tollerson and Ross to Mattis, Sessions and Perdue, these old farts are probably near their death beds and here they are getting paid all that money, jet setting all over the world carrying out Trump's orders and proving to the majority of the world's people – who are people of color – that America is a white nation, not only in its history and ideology, but also in its leadership priorities. They think all their talking, negotiating and meeting with world leaders is going to cancel out what people can plainly see.

Kelly is as big a coward as Trump, and it showed when Trump was confronted about the lies he told about the death of a black soldier. Kelly backed up Trump and then insulted the soldier's mother and a black Congress woman by calling their both liars. These basic actions are a testament to Kelly's character: once a racist, always a racist.

Continuing:

> In the months before Mr. Kelly took over last summer from his embattled predecessor, Reince Priebus, the Oval Office had a rush-hour feel, with a constant stream of aides and visitors stopping by to offer advice or kibitz. During <u>one April meeting</u> with New York Times reporters, no fewer than 20 people wandered in and out — including Mr. Priebus, who walked in with Vice President Mike Pence. The door to the Oval Office is now mostly closed. (Haberman, Thrush & Baker, 2017)

A disorganized mind reaps unorganized results. Trump didn't know what the hell he was doing and he had surrounded himself with mindless leeches that were there just to collect a paycheck. The plan was that Kelly would bring more order than the effeminate Priebus who was a serious politician but so scared of Trump that his fear showed every time he appeared in public. Like the spineless Sean Spicer and the punk he chose for vice-president, Mike Pence, these "boys" were just the kinds of people that Trump eats and spits out. After all, he had done it all his life to his minority employees, had he not?

Check out what the "plan" for Kelly was:

> Mr. Kelly is trying, quietly and respectfully, to reduce the amount of free time the president has for fiery tweets by accelerating the start of his workday. Mr. Priebus also tried, with only modest success, to encourage Mr. Trump to arrive by 9 or 9:30 a.m. (Haberman, Thrush & Baker, 2017)

Evidently Kelly is failing just as Priebus did. Trump is like the comic book character Richie Rich, spoiled and not beholden to anyone. You read what his day started off like: sleeping alone with a Diet Coke at his side. He's not having sex with Melania and he's got servants and 24l-hour service. He's a glutton who scarves down huge amounts of cake and loves his steaks well done, according to a recent report on CNN. He's a prime candidate for diabetes, but if he had it his white comrades would hide that point from the government. The same report said that two of the healthiest presidents were Barack Obama and George Bush. They said that Clinton used to pig out and didn't lose weight until he had heart surgery following his second term.

Surrounded by men – like some gerontological fraternity. None of them really qualified to do the jobs they were appointed to do by a man who didn't know what he was doing, either:

> The pace of meetings has increased. Beyond Mr. Kelly and Mr. Kushner, they often include Lt. Gen. H. R. McMaster, the national security adviser; Ivanka Trump, the president's daughter and senior adviser; Hope Hicks, the communications director; Robert Porter, the staff secretary; and Kellyanne Conway, the president's counselor. (Haberman, Thrush & Baker, 2017)

A veritable freak show while America teeters on the edge of poverty, increased depravity, ongoing racial problems and an economy that was rejuvenated by Obama that Trump is taking credit for. These clowns should be known as the "Injustice League" or "Anti-Justice Brigade."

Moving on:

[Type text]

> Mr. Trump, who enjoyed complete control over his business empire, has made significant concessions after trying to micromanage his first months in office. Despite chafing at the limits, the president actually craves the approval of Mr. Kelly, whom he sees as a peer, people close to Mr. Trump said. (Haberman, Thrush & Baker, 2017)

That is not true. Trump doesn't crave anything that has to do with someone else's role in addressing decisions that he (Trump) makes. He is such a liar and a false face that he may have duped the reporters into thinking that he approves of Kelly. But nothing could be further from the truth. Kelly became a near immediate lap dog for Trump during the murders of those four military officers in Niger, shifting the blame from Trump's lie about being the first to contact mothers of slain officers to the black women's complaints being bald-faced lies. Kelly, like the rest of Trump's coterie, appears to have fallen right in line with the orange-hued asshole.

Furthermore, according to the article

> He calls Mr. Kelly up to a dozen times a day, even four or five times during dinner or a golf outing, to ask about his schedule or seek policy advice, according to people who have spoken with the president. The new system gives him "time to think," he said when it began. White House aides denied that Mr. Trump seeks Mr. Kelly's blessing, but confirmed that he views him as a crucial confidant and sounding board. Mr. Kelly has also adopted some of Mr. Trump's favorite grievances, telling the president recently that he agrees that some reporters are interested only in taking down the administration. (Haberman, Thrush & Baker, 2017)

What happened is that Trump transformed Kelly into his way of thinking, using the same "I have confidence in you" bullshit that he used to seduce many of his flunkies … oops! I mean cabinet members. Kelly was a long time military person who was accustomed to barking out orders, telling people what to do and being the man in charge. He goes into Trump's office and within a few weeks he's acting like Stepin Fetchit: currying favor and dong what ever "the massa" tells him to do.

He became Trump's willing thrall. For instance, check out the following:

> At times, Mr. Trump has been able to circumvent Mr. Kelly. Over Thanksgiving at Mar-a-Lago, the president mingled with guests the

> way he had before the election. Some passed him news clips that
> would never get around Mr. Kelly's filters. And he dialed old
> friends, receiving updates about how they see the Russia
> investigation. He returned to Washington fired up. Mr. Kelly has
> told people he will try to control only what he can. As he has
> learned, there is much that he cannot. (Haberman, Thrush & Baker,
> 2017)

If there is so much that he can't control, and if Trump can "ditch" him the way a child who skips school gets around his parents not knowing, then of what use is Kelly? He's just an old fart getting a huge paycheck to give the "appearance" that Trump is working to do better. But nothing could be further from the truth. Kelly only "controls" those things that Trump wants him to control, and that's the way it's been from the beginning. Only those fairy tale ending white journalists who want to extend the news cycle and in doing so, provide increased readership and advertising revenue for their respective institutions, buy into this bullshit.

Now, earlier I wrote about how the white media is more committed to generating news stories than anything else. I also charged that they continue to give Trump the benefit of the doubt because he's white. Anyone else who did the shit Trump's done would have been run out of town – unless that person was a white male. Look at what they did to Hillary (who was guilty as sin); look how they avoided, alienated and castigated Barack Obama. But this fat peckerwood is always seen as some kind of "strategist" no matter how much he fucks up.

Case in point:

> For most of the year, people inside and outside Washington have
> been convinced that there is a strategy behind Mr. Trump's actions.
> But there is seldom a plan apart from pre-emption, self-defense,
> obsession and impulse. (Haberman, Thrush & Baker, 2017)

If there is "pre-emption," then that implies some kind of attack. If there is self-defense, then that implies that you plan on some sort of counter-attack. But if there is obsession and impulse, that cancels out both of the previous two. Obsession and impulse negate strategy because "a man without values is a man who is unpredictable." You need some predictability of behavior in order to stabilize yourself so that you can have a plan in the first place. Trump is like a kid who is surrounded with toys and has no one to play with. Bored to tears, he lashes out to get attention and destroys things so that he can feel good about himself. This is how Trump has lived his life. And the women who married him were as stupid as he is because they were gullible and willing to allow themselves to be subjected to Trump's daily degradation campaigns.

He craves attention in a noticeably childlike manner. For instance,

> Occasionally, the president solicits affirmation before hitting the "tweet" button. In June, according to a longtime adviser, he excitedly called friends to say he had the perfect tweet to neutralize the Russia investigation. He would call it a "witch hunt." They were unimpressed. (Haberman, Thrush & Baker, 2017)

The reporters have it all wrong. Trump is not seeking affirmation before he tweets. It only appears that way. It's like the wayward teenager who asks to borrow the car from his inattentive parents (fearful parents) and they say no, all the while knowing he has the keys to the car already and that his parents aren't going to be able to do anything more than gripe. Trump's tweets are going to be his own undoing because everything he transmits becomes a matter of public record and as such, is a matter of historical record. His pettiness, his misogynistic vitriol, his racist barbs and his callous insults are all a reflection of his lack of character and as such, are going to be laid squarely at the door of the Republican Party when all is said and done. How can the investigation be a "witch hunt" when you're staring directly into the eyes of the witch?

The media-induced alibis nevertheless continue:

> He has bowed to advice from his lawyers by not attacking Mr. Mueller, but at times his instincts prevail. When three former campaign advisers were indicted or pleaded guilty this fall, Ty Cobb, the White House lawyer handling the investigation, urged the president not to respond. If he did, it would only elevate the story. (Haberman, Thrush & Baker, 2017)

If Trump's "instincts prevailed" and he went after Mueller anyway – which he did – then he didn't "bow" to anyone's advice. Once again, these white people who are supposedly looking at "a day in the life" are engaging in and enwrapped in conjecture, wild coincidence and bullshit. Trump uses his "protectors" and attorneys as a smokescreen to do the dirty work of justifying, to the media, why he (Trump) is such a fuckup. Meanwhile, he just keeps fuckin' up. It's like a family that has the cops at their house questioning the parents about their son's theft of some property and while the cops question the parents the kid is outside stealing shit out of the police car!

[Type text]

Earlier the reporters used the terms "obsession" and "impulse." Both of these are signs of either mental instability or immaturity. With that being said, check out the following:

> Mr. Trump, however, could not help himself. He tweeted that the financial charges lodged against his former campaign manager, Paul J. Manafort, had nothing to do with the campaign and that investigators should be examining "Crooked Hillary & the Dems" instead. By the next morning, he was belittling George Papadopoulos, the campaign adviser who pleaded guilty to lying about his outreach to Russians, dismissing him as a "low level volunteer" who has "proven to be a liar." (Haberman, Thrush & Baker, 2017)

These are the keys to the colors: "Mr. Trump could not help himself." If this muthafucka is lacking in self control, then he shouldn't be president, nor does he deserve to be. This is the kind of shit that makes people believe that he's going to use those nuclear codes. This muthafucka is a mad scientist lacking in scientific background; he's Dr. Jekyll and Mr. Hyde without Dr. Jekyll. He's a "clear and present danger" and thcsc peckerwoods elected him and, like this news story, continue to print fluff and bullshit instead of calling it like it is: Trump is a full-blown mental case!

How can he have the nerve to call other people liars when the New York Times has documented more than 1,600 lies this asshole has told since January of 2017! In fact, during an October 14, 2017 segment of "The Last Word With Lawrence O'Donnell," he spoke with the New York Times' David Leonhardt , who counted (or attempted to count) the lies that Trump had told since taking office.

Leonhardt told O'Donnell called it a "definitive list" that wasn't mere exaggeration but an outright lie. He told a story about Genefal pershing executing Muslim terrorists. They scrsubbed Obama's stuff Trump told 103 distinct lies, Obama told 18 over eight years. That's about two a year. Jonahtan Capehart added that when others got caught in lies they admitted it. Trump keeps repeating the lie even when caught, he willfully lies to the American people. We have to fact check him in real time.

According to Leonhardt, the Times had to choose what constitutes a Trump lie. He lies to a degree that we've never seen before. He seems virtually indifferent to reality. Trump is trying to make truth irrelevant. An article titled "Trump's Lies vs. Obama's" by both Leonhardt and Stuart A. Thompson provides some context:

[Type text]

> Many Americans have become accustomed to President Trump's lies. But as regular as they have become, the country should not allow itself to become numb to them. So we have catalogued nearly every outright lie he has told publicly since taking the oath of office. **Updated**: The president is still lying, so we've added to this list, taking it through Nov. 11, and provided links to the facts in each case. (Leonhardt & Thompson, 2017)

America is a piece of shit and is slowly sinking into the commode of history. And Trump is the one who is going to flush it away and he's going with it. Anybody can see it, the world can see it, but these patriot oriented flag-blinded ass peckerwoods in America sit around hoping for the best. Hoping for the best? Shit in one hand and put some hope in the other and see which one fills up first. As the old saying teaches, "Dress a liar as you will/A liar is a liar, still."

Back to a day with Trump.

He surrounded himself with rip-off artist corporate types and people who were tight with his boyfriend Vladimir Putin. And slowly but surely, he's paying the price. For instance:

> He was calm at first when his former national security adviser, Michael T. Flynn, pleaded guilty. The next morning, as he visited Manhattan for Republican fund-raisers, he was upbeat. He talked about his election and the "major loser" in the Senate who had said his tax bill would add to the deficit (presumably meaning Senator Bob Corker, Republican of Tennessee). (Haberman, Thrush & Baker, 2017)

He was calm about Flynn because he knew Flynn was a sick asshole from the outset. When I saw that curmudgeon stand up in front of the Republican Convention and lead those "lock her up" chants against Hillary Clinton, I could tell right then and there he was a piece of shit. During that same presentation he said that if he had done "one tenth" of what Hillary did, he would be locked up. Well guess what? He did more than one-tenth. He was working for the Turks and for Russian, he wrote an editorial asking for renewed attention to Turkey, he made millions from giving Russia information about the U.S. and all the while Trump had to know. He was Trump's National Security Advisor – he knew everything and whatever he knew, Putin was able to find out about.

[Type text]

Trump was calm because he was getting ready to throw Flynn under the bus, which is why Flynn turned snitch. Even in that, Trump has already shown that he will pardon any of his cronies who get busted. Calling other people "losers" is a clear cut example of "transference"- Trump need only look at his personal life to know that his days are numbered. But a spoiled child only knows one way to deal with adversity: to ignore it. And that is what Trump does:

> By Sunday morning, with news shows consumed by Mr. Flynn's case, the president grew angry and fired off a series of tweets excoriating Mrs. Clinton and the F.B.I., tweets that several advisers told him were problematic and needed to stop, according to a person briefed on the discussion. (Haberman, Thrush & Baker, 2017)

The more he tweets, the more of his own shit he eats. And yet here he is being featured by the New York Times and on the covers of magazines. Even when caught in lies and clearly shown to be a pimple on the asshole of humanity, he keeps getting the one thing that he craves: publicity. He cannot get over the fact that Hillary got more than three million more votes than he did, so he lies about the electoral system being flawed. He cannot get over Obama being superior as a President, a leader, and a human being, so he works to eliminate Obama's record, a political version of "ethnic cleansing" in my book.

Moreover, he is surrounded by cowards who fear him:

> Once he posts controversial messages, Mr. Trump's advisers sometimes decide not to raise them with him. One adviser said that aides to the president needed to stay positive and look for silver linings wherever they could find them, and that the West Wing team at times resolved not to let the tweets dominate their day. (Haberman, Thrush & Baker, 2017)

These "aides" babysit and spoonfeed this old far. They are afraid of him and don't want to "make him mad." In a segment of "Deadline: White House" on MSNBC on December 14, they talked about the daily briefings that the president gets and the people who bring in the global news have to take care in how they mention anything about Russia and Putin. They have to ease into the bad news so that he would "go off the rails." While prodded by Jared Kushner and Rance Priebus to acknowledge Russian meddling in the 2016 election, he ignores it and continues to make excuses. On the other side of the world, Putin is saying similar things, claiming Russia had nothing to do with the election and that it's all a ruse to "get Trump" because he won. Two white men who stand for the same thing showing that Trump is no original. Both of these men are wannabe authoritarian kleptocrats.

According to the same segment on "Deadline" White House," it was stated that Trump sees any affront against Putin as a personal attack. Just like a boyfriend and girlfriend (you can decide who's who). Trump says that the U.S needs to get along with Russia. And the games of control continue.

Back at the White House:

> The ammunition for his Twitter war is television. No one touches the remote control except Mr. Trump and the technical support staff — at least that's the rule. During meetings, the 60-inch screen mounted in the dining room may be muted, but Mr. Trump keeps an eye on scrolling headlines. What he misses he checks out later on what he calls his "Super TiVo," a state-of-the-art system that records cable news. (Haberman, Thrush & Baker, 2017)

Like some abusive father with a "don't touch the remote" rule, Trump reigns that White House like the paternalistic control freak that he is. I watch a great deal of television because I am a scholar, a writer and a community organizer. Trump doesn't do jack shit. He can't even meet with foreign leaders without getting the information and logistics all fucked up. He has a staff that is equally bereft of cultural competency and therefore America has taken a giant step backwards since the days of the suave and knowledgeable Barack Obama. That's another reason why Trump is jealous of the former President. Barack was everything good that Trump is sorely lacking in and can never be. And white people know it.

Recording cable news may be a good idea if you're doing it for research. But Trump is just doing it to count the times that these pundits mention his name as they are on a never ending quest to see if they can "make" Trump change. A leopard can't change its spots and Trump can't transform from the asshole that he has always been.

Moreover,

> Watching cable, he shares thoughts with anyone in the room, even the household staff he summons via a button for lunch or for one of the dozen Diet Cokes he consumes each day. (Haberman, Thrush & Baker, 2017)

[Type text]

He sits in there watching television and "sharing thoughts." A person like Trump doesn't "share" anything. He imposes his thoughts, usually wrong and one-sided, with people who are too dependent and spineless to speak out in opposition. How could they? You've already read where these people do whatever Trump asks, so what would make you think that he would engage them in free and frank discussion? You've seen him during TV interviews: the interrupts the reporter, he changes the subject and shows that he has the attention span of a gnat.

As for those Diet Cokes, the question is: for what? That fat muthafucka ain't on no diet! His suits are tailor made so he can hide his fat, his ties extend all the way down past his scrotum, and he wears dark colors which tend to make a person appear thinner. This fat bastard is killing himself because Diet Coke is no healthy drink. Doctor after doctor will confirm the following five health problems associated with guzzling diet soda: (1) can harm your heart; (2) can present kidney problems; (3) can increase risk of metabolic syndrome and diabetes; (4) can increase waist circumference and (5) can alter moods.

Pay close attention to points 4 and 5. That fat bastard is getting fatter and he continues to lay around, eat and play golf. As I have said for decades, Golf is not a sport – it is a leisure activity for sorry ass white boys and sick negroes. And that waist line is going to get bigger and bigger because Trump strikes me as the kind of person who is too lazy to exercise. And as for altering moods, you can see it for yourself: one day he's bubbly, buzzing and asking questions that are not even being asked, and the next day his mouth is try and he's sounding like Yosemite Sam.

Moving on:

> But he is leery of being seen as tube-glued — a perception that reinforces the criticism that he is not taking the job seriously. On his recent trip to Asia, the president was told of a list of 51 fact-checking questions for this article, including one about his prodigious television watching habits. Instead of responding through an aide, he delivered a broadside on his viewing habits to befuddled reporters from other outlets on Air Force One heading to <u>Vietnam</u>. (Haberman, Thrush & Baker, 2017)

Fifty-one fact checking questions to a person like Trump? I realizes the reporters were attempting to interject professionalism into their story but come on! Trump is an idiot: you can't give him questions in written form! I have debated and destroyed hundreds of white graduate students during my quest and they all show a tendency to not the importance of study various seriously. They were the cream of the crop at their lily white schools, cruised through undergraduate level education with teachers the same race as they, and then they get to graduate school where you have to be able to read, think and write on a developed level. And in the classroom, during discussions, debates and seminars, I ate them alive. They learned what to think (white nationalist terms) but never HOW to think. I was engaged in critical thinking long before the white boy discovered it.

With that having been said, check out how Trump answered the questions about his TV viewing:

> "I do not watch much television," he insisted. "I know they like to say — people that don't know me — they like to say I watch television. People with fake sources — you know, fake reporters, fake sources. But I don't get to watch much television, primarily because of documents. I'm reading documents a lot." Later, he groused about being forced to watch CNN in the Philippines because nothing else was available. (Haberman, Thrush & Baker, 2017)

Lie after lie. Fake sources? He's the President and such sources would be open to violations of slander and libel. Fake reporters? He claims he's reading documents a lot but he doesn't name them. And in a somewhat related matter, he claims "I'm very smart" on a regular basis. He brags about being a good student and about his vocabulary. Trump is a typical white boy who screwed around and I believe PAID for that degree from Wharton College of Business. He and Melania are kindred spirits: she dropped out of an imaginary college after claiming she majored in architecture.

Pay attention to what follows:

> Before taking office, Mr. Trump told top aides to think of each presidential day as an episode in a television show in which he vanquishes his rivals. Here, he called journalists back into the Roosevelt Room in January to hear a union leader praise him. CreditDoug Mills/The New York Times(Haberman, Thrush & Baker, 2017)

That shit about thinking of each day as an episode in a television show is the same explanation that Omarosa gave in her "analysis" of Trump after she got her ass kicked out of the White House. These people think the same and they act the same and they all are expert liars. How then, can Trump be "an original"?

[Type text]

Another sub-heading in the article is "Aren't You Glad I Don't Drink?" begins like this:

> 'Aren't You Glad I Don't Drink?'
> To an extent that would stun outsiders, Mr. Trump, the most talked-about human on the planet, is still delighted when he sees his name in the headlines. And he is on a perpetual quest to see it there. One former top adviser said Mr. Trump grew uncomfortable after two or three days of peace and could not handle watching the news without seeing himself on it. (Haberman, Thrush & Baker, 2017)

The sign of a true megalomaniac. He has to see and hear his name, even though the vast majority of the time it is negative. And do you know what else has a similar tendency? The United States of America. These egotistical assholes have been the bane of the world's existence on a number of levels and in a myriad of arenas for centuries. That is why their media is so important. But positive or negative, when the decision makers read about the "good ol' US of A," they get boners. Their red, white and blue insignia and color scheme makes them feel an air of superiority. Just like Trump does when he sees his name emblazoned on those hotels and casinos.

And,

> During the morning, aides monitor "Fox & Friends" live or through a transcription service in much the way commodities traders might keep tabs on market futures to predict the direction of their day. (Haberman, Thrush & Baker, 2017)

In one of Richard Pryor's "Wino and the Junkie" skits, he has a line where the young junkie says, "Tell me some more of those lies of yours so I can stop thinkin' about the truth." This is similar to the thinking of Trump, which is why he tunes in to "Fox and Friends," one of the most deceptive TV news shows ever put on the air. When it comes to black people all of them are, but it is the mendacity of these people on "Fox and Friends" that keeps Trump pumped and continues to convince viewers that he's the best thing to happen to America since sliced bread.

It gets worse:

> If someone on the show says something memorable and Mr. Trump does not immediately tweet about it, the president's staff knows he may be saving Fox News for later viewing on his recorder and

instead watching MSNBC or CNN live — meaning he is likely to be
in a foul mood to start the day. (Haberman, Thrush & Baker, 2017)

Just like pacifying and catering to the needs of a child – a bad seed type of child at that. But what is worse is that the people around him are so spineless and so without character that they tolerate this kind of situation for the sake of a job title and a paycheck. They ingratiate themselves to Trump, the way black people did to the white plantation owners during the days of enslavement. These modern day white "Uncle Toms" are a joke, and Trump enjoys humiliating them. Every time they go on television to repeat his lies – from Kellyanne Conway, Sean Spicer and Sarah Huckabee to Paul Ryan, Trey Gowdy and the rest of the conservative curmudgeons, Trump feels like an emperor surrounded by willing thralls and court jesters.

More evidence of this description can be found in the following passage:

> Yet the image of him in a constant rage belies a deeper complexity
> for a man who runs in bellow-and-banter cycles. Several advisers
> said the president may curse them for a minor transgression — like
> bringing an unknown aide into his presence without warning — then
> make amiable small talk with the same person minutes later.
> (Haberman, Thrush & Baker, 2017)

That kind of on-again off-again behavior is known as schizophrenia. If you believe in astrology, then Trump was born under the sign of Gemini, which is symbolized by twins. In other words, two personality types. All the Geminis that I know are two-faced for sure, some of whom I am related to. So you never know what you're going to get with people born under this sign. And you never know what you're going to get when you deal with Donald Trump, either. But one thing you can bet on: whatever you get is going to be fucked up.

His hired lackeys make sure that Trump's on-going reign of error is rationalized on a regular basis. For instance:

> "He is very aware that he is only the 45th person to hold that job,"
> Ms. Conway said. "The job has changed him a bit, and he has
> changed the job. His time as president has revealed other, more
> affable and accessible, parts and pieces of him that may have been
> hidden from view during a rough and tumble primary." (Haberman,
> Thrush & Baker, 2017)

What you just read is an assessment from Kellyanne Conway, a rich blonde slut who has said some of the stupidest things ever uttered by a Presidential aide. She's the one who coined the phrase "alternative facts" and remember she sat on a couch with her boney legs gapped in a room full of black college presidents. Remember that? This bitch has no class, which is why she is often called upon following a Trump mistake to "explain" it to the media. And in most cases, her explanations only serve to make matters worse – such as the lie that she told in the previous excerpt.

Check out the following description of the fat, orange paranoid schizophrenic:

> Few get to see those other parts and pieces. In private moments with the families of appointees in the Oval Office, the president engages with children in a softer tone than he takes in public, and he specifically asked that the children of the White House press corps be invited in as they visited on Halloween. Yet he does little to promote that side, some longtime friends say, because it cracks the veneer of strength that he relishes. (Haberman, Thrush & Baker, 2017)

He engages with children because he is one himself! He can relate to children because in both cases you have people who are still in their formative years! Not only that, but Halloween is a holiday that these peckerwoods love because it is about the celebration of death, it involves promoting their children to be leeches and accept candy from total strangers, and it gives the adults and the kids a chance to do something that white folks love: dress up and pretend to be someone else! This holiday fits Trump like a glove, hence is ready willingness to celebrate it with young people. That doesn't make him sensitive; it makes him a sick fuck bordering on pedophilia.

Following is more propaganda that needs deciphering:

> Only occasionally does Mr. Trump let slip his mask of unreflective invincibility. During a meeting with Republican senators, he discussed in emotional terms the opioid crisis and the dangers of addiction, recounting his brother's struggle with alcohol. According to a senator and an aide, the president then looked around the room and asked puckishly, "Aren't you glad I don't drink?" (Haberman, Thrush & Baker, 2017)

[Type text]

When he talks about his brother's alcoholism he may sound emotional, but it's Donald Trump. He's just providing a window into the soul of how fucked up his family is and why, if he has any flaws, his upbringing – the same one that paved the way for his brother's addiction – is to blame. Trump will throw anybody under the bus, including his parents. And as cowardly as he is, Ivanka, Jared Kushner and his sons could be next in line.

The rather lengthy article then moves into an area that carries the sub-heading, "Don't Interrupt Me," and begins like this:

> 'Don't Interrupt Me'
> Mr. Trump's difficult adjustment to the presidency, people close to him say, is rooted in an unrealistic expectation of its powers, which he had assumed to be more akin to the popular image of imperial command than the sloppy reality of having to coexist with two other branches of government. (Haberman, Thrush & Baker, 2017)

What you just read is an over-simplification. Trump thought he could run government like he did his own businesses, and the multiplicity of other branches of government didn't matter to him. He ran his own businesses like some kind of dictator and felt that and still believes that he can do the same thing with government. He even goes so far as to compliment American adversaries while lambasting such American institutions as the legislative and judicial branches of government, the FBI, the military, Congress and so on. He is a double agent in my view. He is a traitor and he is betraying this country before our very eyes. But he's white and therefore the white majority continues to give him the benefit of the doubt.

Continuing:

> His vision of executive leadership was shaped close to home, by experiences with Democratic clubhouse politicians as a young developer in New York. One figure stands out to Mr. Trump: an unnamed party boss — his friends assume he is referring to the legendary Brooklyn fixer <u>Meade Esposito</u> — whom he remembered keeping a baseball bat under his desk to enforce his power. To the adviser who recounted it, the story revealed what Mr. Trump expected being president would be like — ruling by fiat, exacting tribute and cutting back room deals. (Haberman, Thrush & Baker, 2017)

A racist is a racist is a racist. It matters not what system you are functioning in. Since the ideological foundation is white supremacy, you have a blueprint laid out for you: dog out people of color, discriminate and insult women, and demand whatever it is you want and if you don't get it, blame everyone around you. This is what Trump has done for a full year as President and he has the entire world hating America and doubting its ability to lead. He's even managed to piss off large portions of the Jewish state, people who normally kiss America's ass.

Trump is a veritable loser whose claim to fame is that he is cutting and rolling back Obama's accomplishments. He is attacking black and brown people and lying on the former President and getting away with it. He has talked about grabbing women by the pussy and he's even gone so far as to make public comments about the way a woman looks. He is a piece of shit, but he is shielded by white (orange) skin and therefore in a white supremacist culture he benefits from white privilege.

The next sub-heading is "Morning Briefing" and is very interesting because Trump's daily habits reveal how lazy and inattentive he is:

> **Morning Briefing**
> But while he is unlikely to change who he is on a fundamental level, advisers said they saw a novice who was gradually learning that the presidency does not work that way. And he is coming to realize, they said, the need to woo, not whack, leaders of his own party to get things done. (Haberman, Thrush & Baker, 2017)

What you just read is a bullshit analysis of lies that were told to these reporters. That muthafucka is not going to change. Any modification of something that is essentially fucked up is still fucked up. He pretends that he is learning, he may say "oh wow, I didn't know that" or "gee, what a heavy concept." But deep down he's saying "get that shit out of here, I'm going to do it my way." Don't get me wrong: he will steal, plagiarize (like his wife did with Michelle Obama's speeches) and lay claim to ideas that are not his own, but he will never let anyone think for a minute that they actually taught him something. When he was running for office I heard him say during the debates that he knew more than the military generals that were sitting in the audience!

Trump is not "coming to realize" a god damn thing other than the fact that he is Putin's bitch. And having realized that he does not deny it or try to act in any other way. He goes out of his way to make phone calls, to shake his hand, to defend him and to put down anyone that dares to insult his "master." This guy has been bought and paid for and he wants that Russian money. And these white people in America are just as white as the ones in the Soviet Union. In other words there is a "racial bond," along with that white supremacist ideological bond, that can never be broken. Brothers may fight, but brothers will still be brothers.

The article informs us further that,

> During his early months in office, he barked commands at senators, which did not go over well. "I don't work for you, Mr. President," Mr. Corker once snapped back, according to a Republican with knowledge of the exchange. (Haberman, Thrush & Baker, 2017)

It is not as if Trump is going to whip anybody's ass, either. Barking orders is just something Trump did and still does out of habit. The saying teaches, "You've got to bring ass to get ass." Trump sells woof tickets that he can't back up. He's scared of that North Korean kid because he knows that Kim Jong-un doesn't play around. He's scared of Putin and he's scared of that Mexican president who told him on the phone, "I'm not paying for any wall." I attended school with cowards like these all my life: all talk, no action. And when you confront them, they turn beet red, wine like bitches and run and tell someone else.

Now we get to the purpose of the sub-heading mentioned earlier:

> Senator Mitch McConnell of Kentucky, the Republican majority leader, likewise bristled when Mr. Trump cut in during methodical presentations in the Oval Office. "Don't interrupt me," Mr. McConnell told the president during a discussion of health care. (Haberman, Thrush & Baker, 2017)

McConnell had it right but in recent days he, too, is kissing Trump's ass. Just like Speaker of the House Ryan is doing. Trump can't learn etiquette because in order for you to respect someone else you have to see them as a fellow human being. Trump has a God complex and thinks all other creatures on earth have to kiss his ass. Like the bad guy leader in "Superman II" ordered, "Kneel before Zod!"

But the idiots insist Trump is changing. Check it out:

> Mr. Trump may have gotten the message. After a bout of public feuding last summer, he and Mr. McConnell reconciled and began speaking most days. And as the president increasingly recognizes how much Congress controls his fate, Marc Short, the legislative affairs director, has sought to educate him by appealing to Mr.

> Trump's tendency to view issues in terms of personality, compiling
> one-page profiles of legislators for him, the congressional equivalent
> of baseball cards. (Haberman, Thrush & Baker, 2017)

It doesn't matter. Trump has insulted Congress time and time again, he's taken on individual senators, he's insulted Vietnam veterans who were prisoners of war, he's insulted female members of Congress, and he's basically isolated himself from them. But most of them are such ass kissers that they fear that Trump's "political base" will vote them out of office and those greedy peckerwoods want that status and those jobs! So they sell out the very people who they lie and purport to represent.

There is another mistake in the previous passage. The reporters contend that, "Marc Short, the legislative affairs director, has sought to educate him by appealing to Mr. Trump's tendency to view issues in terms of personality, compiling one-page profiles of legislators for him," What a joke. This implies that Trump gives a shit. To him, people are like Pringles: they are all to be treated (eaten) alike. And if he treats his fellow peckerwoods in such a hateful manner, you can imagine the low regard he has for people of color, a point made elsewhere in this book.

If Trump comes across something he knows he can't do (which is most things), he just writes it off that "nobody can do it." A case in point is alluded to in the following excerpt:

> While he is no policy wonk — "nobody knew that health care could
> be so complicated," he famously said at one point — he has shown
> more comfort with the details of his tax-cutting legislation. And
> aides said he had become more attentive during daily intelligence
> briefings thanks to pithy presentations by Mike Pompeo,
> the C.I.A. director, and a deeper concern about the North
> Korea situation than his blithe, confrontational tweets suggest.
> (Haberman, Thrush & Baker, 2017)

I am a former university and community college instructor. Over the many years in front of the classroom I can tell who is truly taking notes, paying attention and actually engaging in the learning process, and who is out there "faking the funk." Trump is one of those assholes who "pretends" to be taking in information but as he stares at the screen or looks at the information his mind is thinking about his next Diet Coke, about a mayonnaise sandwich, or about that woman he saw earlier whose tits he would like to grab. He is juvenile, sophistic, imbecilic and dense.

He pays attention to North Korea because it involves things that go "boom." He likes to see missiles flying and bombs going off. He likes to "play" with the idea of war because it makes him feel like a big man. He doesn't have any value for human life (just look at how he's fucked up his own), so hundreds of thousands of deaths doesn't mean a damn thing to this goony gunslinger.

Pay close attention to the following:

> "At first, there was a thread of being an impostor that may have been in his mind," said Representative Nancy Pelosi of California, the House Democratic leader, who has tried to forge a working relationship with the president. "He's overcome that by now," she said. "The bigger problem, the thing people need to understand, is that he was utterly unprepared for this. It would be like you or me going into a room and being asked to perform brain surgery. When you have a lack of knowledge as great as his, it can be bewildering." (Haberman, Thrush & Baker, 2017)

What was described above by Pelosi is only a small part of the problem. Not only is Trump unprepared but he's also a sociopath. So even if he had a hint of a clue about what to do, the end result, his motivations, would nevertheless still be totally fucked up. This is the part that his fellow whites, like Pelosi, seem to refuse to acknowledge.

It's not so much that he's "unprepared for this," as Pelosi says. It's that he doesn't give a shit about being prepared for it because he's too busy working to usher in an agenda of his own. And with that in mind the real issue is: is Congress prepared for Trump?

The effeminate Lindsey Graham is another high-ranking asshole who talks out of both sides of his mouth. Observe the following:

> Mr. Graham, once a fierce critic and now increasingly an ally, said Mr. Trump was adjusting. "You can expect every president to change because the job requires you to change," he said. "He's learning the rhythm of the town." But Mr. Graham added that Mr. Trump's presidency was still "a work in progress." At this point, he said, "everything's possible, from complete disaster to a home run." (Haberman, Thrush & Baker, 2017)

[Type text]

More cover-up related bullshit. Graham is talking about what "every president" does in terms of changing. Every other president had some experience. Every other president at least had some legal background of some kind. Every other president was involved in the political system and understood the Constitution. Every other president had a brain stem that was attached. Not Trump. So the rules don't apply. He is no exception to any racist rule – he IS the rule. And that is the only thing he has in common with his predecessors: a disdain for skin color.

Furthermore, Trump is no "work in progress" unless you are talking about the step-by-step process that he is undergoing to get closer and closer to the nuclear codes. Or unless you are talking about how he is gradually getting closer to uniting with his male fantasy Vladimir Putin. Other than that, Trump is just where he wants to be and is still shocked that he made it. But now that he has, in the words of Don Cornelius of "Soul Train," "You can bet your last money/It's all gonna be a stone gas, honey."

The daily play-by-play on the orange-colored oaf continues, beginning with another sub-heading, 'He Wears You Down'. What does that mean? Let's find out:

'He Wears You Down'

In almost all the interviews, Mr. Trump's associates raised questions
about his capacity and willingness to differentiate bad information
from something that is true. (Haberman, Thrush & Baker, 2017)

Say what? This is the asshole who boasted about how smart he was and about how he attended Wharton Business School and was a good student. If that is the case, how can he not be able to do something as rudimentary and fundamental as being able to differentiate bad information from something that is true? Nevertheless,

Monitoring his information consumption — and countering what
Mr. Kelly calls "garbage" peddled to him by outsiders — remains a
priority for the chief of staff and the team he has made his own.
Even after a year of official briefings and access to the best minds of
the federal government, Mr. Trump is skeptical of anything that does
not come from inside his bubble. (Haberman, Thrush & Baker,
2017)

Just like a child who is upstairs in his room surfing the internet for porn when he's supposed to be doing his homework. You can't trust him to do it because you know that he won't and the grades he gets reflect that he's a chronic fuckup. Just like Trump. He wants information from people who are as politically chauvinistic as he is, as narrow minded as he is. He wants to hear about trouble from troubled minds. That is how he maintains his image as a troublemaker.

Only those who are similarly as sick and wicked make statements that back up Trump's Neanderthal notions and asinine actions. For instance,

> Some advisers, like the Treasury secretary, Steven Mnuchin, consider this a fundamentally good thing. "I see a lot of similarities between the way he was running the campaign and the way he is as president," Mr. Mnuchin said. "He really loves verbal briefings. He is not one to consume volumes of books or briefings." (Haberman, Thrush & Baker, 2017)

Mnuchin is a charlatan himself and he and Trump share a number of similarly negative qualities. And, like Trump, he's married to a superficial bitch who is out of touch with reality. Like Trump he (Mnuchin) takes advantage of tax payers dollars and uses the private jet for his own personal use, and like Trump he is a very wealthy man. Like Trump he cannot write worth a damn, as the recent paperwork on the tax plan – consisting of one page – clearly points out. Like takes to like.

In my opinion Trump is mentally retarded. I don't care what you say about it. His thought process is surely lacking in anything even remotely approaching normal, and his application of ideas has always been ass backwards. According to the article, "Other aides bemoan his tenuous grasp of facts, jack-rabbit attention span and propensity for conspiracy theories. (Haberman, Thrush & Baker, 2017). You couldn't say any of these things about Obama, either of the Bush's, Clinton or Reagan. Well, maybe Reagan.

Moving on:

> Mr. Kelly has told people he pushed out advisers like Stephen K. Bannon and Sebastian Gorka, who he believed advanced information to rile up Mr. Trump or create internal conflict. But Mr. Trump still controls his own guest list. (Haberman, Thrush & Baker, 2017)

If Trump still controls the guest list then he is still in contact with both Bannon and Gorka by phone. He sneaks around Kelly to communicate with

[Type text]

whomever he wants to, including Putin. Kelly has no control over anything other than the low ranking menials who are competing with each other to see who can be the first on any given day to kiss Trump's ass. And the line of ass kissers is long, indeed. For instance,

> Jeanine Pirro, whose Fox News show is a presidential favorite, recently asked to meet about <u>a deal</u> approved while Mrs. Clinton was secretary of state that gave Russia control over some American uranium, which lately has become a favorite focus of conservatives. (Haberman, Thrush & Baker, 2017).

Jeanine Pirro is the female version of Trump except she is fine. But that bitch is crazy and does what she does for ratings points. She had a show on television similar to "Judge Judy" called "Justice With Judge Jeanine," which was also on Fox. Like Trump, she embellishes information, lies when she can, and has a tendency to shout. Her lies are convincing as the following excerpt implies:

> Mr. Trump, Mr. Kelly and Donald F. McGahn II, the White House counsel, met for more than an hour on Nov. 1 as Ms. Pirro whipped up the president against Mr. Mueller and accused James B. Comey, the former . <u>F.B.I.</u> director, of employing tactics typically reserved for Mafia cases, according to a person briefed on the meeting. (Haberman, Thrush & Baker, 2017)

Pirro is just another in a long line of white bitches who are doing the bidding of the white male. I have warned my readers about this for decades: "the hand that rocks the cradle rules the throne." She is just a pretender who wants to feign victimization and militancy in a way that the system uses "good cop/bad cop" tactics against those they arrest. Both cops represent the same racist system and have the same goals. But if one is brutal and the other offers you a Hostess pie while you're in the interrogation room, you are more likely to open up to the latter cop.

In the realm of political racism, the same thing works. The white woman has always been able to worm her way into corners of the world that the white man would not be able to. That is because when all is said and done, she's basically a slut, and has always been one. Of course she goes through the innocent years as do all females. But in the age of social media, mass-mediated culture and the like, she sees her image, butt naked, on billboards, on TV ads, in movies and almost everywhere. She has been duped into thinking that she is a goddess. In the South such an image was wrapped in "the myth of sacred white womanhood." So conservative white women are the new wave, a point that I highlight in my book, Transformers: Sex and Role Changes in America.

Trump's "harem of hos" is effective. From Kellyanne Conway and Hope Hicks to Sarah Huckabee Sanders, these white women aren't playing around. They're not telling the white man to "get off of the throne of oppression," they are saying, "Scoot over and let me share the throne with you." Jeanine Pirro is of that ilk.

She is able to irk Trump as the following point bears out:

> The president became visibly agitated as she spoke. "Roy Cohn was my lawyer!" he exclaimed, referring to the legendary McCarthy-era fixer who mentored Mr. Trump in the 1980s, suggesting that was the type of defender he needed now. At another point, Mr. Kelly interrupted. She was not "helping things," he said, according to the person briefed. Even Mr. Trump eventually tired of Ms. Pirro's screed and walked out of the room, according to the person. (Haberman, Thrush & Baker, 2017).

A "screed," the word used in the previous passage is, "a long speech or piece of writing, typically one regarded as tedious." In other words, the bitch was babbling on and on and it was getting to the point where Trump was probably about to snap. That is what immature minds do, and Kelly knew it.

Moving right along:

> Mr. Trump is an avid newspaper reader who still marks up a half-dozen papers with comments in black Sharpie pen, but Mr. Bannon has told allies that Mr. Trump only "reads to reinforce." Mr. Trump's insistence on defining his own reality — his repeated claims, for example, that he actually won the popular vote — is immutable and has had a "numbing effect" on people who work with him, said Tony Schwartz, his ghostwriter on "The Art of the Deal." "He wears you down," Mr. Schwartz said.
>
> (Haberman, Thrush & Baker, 2017)

That muthafucka is reading the newspapers because it is the newspaper that TV news stations like CNN, MSNBC and others use as their source material. So he's reading to see his name in print – it is doubtful if he reads entire articles.

[Type text]

As for that popular vote lie he keeps telling himself, he simply cannot accept defeat on any level. The popular vote is the one that the masses of people are in charge of. He lost to Hillary Clinton by over three million votes. That means that there are three million people who hate his damn guts. He knows that. He wants to lie to himself and pretend that he's popular. That's why he's always fishing for flattery and cruising for compliments. When Putin says something about how good the American economy is, Trump jumps for joy. Trump knows that because of his small support base, the only real people he represents are the illiterate rednecks who view him as the Second Coming.

Trump doesn't wear anybody down. He's just surrounded by lazy assholes who are too spineless to stand up to him. What wears them down is the amount of energy that they have to expend coming up with lie after lie defending this asshole. Then there is the energy they use up dodging the humiliating snickers, jokes, and statements they hear when they leave work, realizing full well that they are making asses out of themselves.

And check out the following:

> Mr. Trump spends at least four hours a day, and sometimes as much
> as twice that, in front of a television, sometimes with the volume
> muted, marinating in the no-holds-barred wars of cable news and
> eager to fire back. (Haberman, Thrush & Baker, 2017).

Watching television with the sound muted? In a white society where white faces dominate the viewing screen, he is just bathing in white nationalism for the most part. But when the volume is on that makes him have to process information, makes him have to actually think, and that is something that Trump is not good at. So he looks at a muted screen like a handicapped child with a coloring book telling his teacher, "See the pretty colors …. Pretty, pretty …."

The next sub-heading is titled, "Where the Hell Have You Been." In my view it lends itself to Trump's homoeroticism:

> 'Where the Hell Have You Been?'
>
> Some of the changes resulting from Mr. Kelly's arrival have been
> subtle. For the last decade, for example, Mr. Trump's most trusted
> aide was his longtime security chief, <u>Keith Schiller</u>, a bald, brawny
> former New York police officer who played an ambiguous role as
> protector, gatekeeper and younger brother to the president. An early
> warning system, Mr. Schiller tipped callers when the boss was in a

> bad mood and sometimes reached out to the president's friends to
> urge them to buck him up. (Haberman, Thrush & Baker, 2017)

This guy Schiller is another one of those "bromances" that Trump seems to have with bigger men. Putin is a runt so he is the exception. But Schiller is a brute and has no real credentials. Omarosa got canned because nobody could figure out what her duties were – the same can be said for Schiller. Schiller, like Omarosa, was a leech for the most part. Here is what one article says about him:

> In 1999, Schiller saw Marla Maples, Donald Trump's then-wife, at
> the Manhattan District Attorney's Office, accompanied by a
> bodyguard, whom Schiller judged as not being particularly imposing.
> Seeking side work to supplement his NYPD salary, Schiller asked the
> Assistant District Attorney to put in a good word with Trump, so that
> he could be employed as a bodyguard. The Trump Organization
> eventually brought him on for a one-month trial and later that year
> hired him officially. Schiller remained a part-time bodyguard until he
> retired from the NYPD in 2002. (Binder, 2015).

So Schiller didn't see the other bodyguard as being "particularly imposing." Is that one of the criteria? As a black man who went to school with white boys who were wrestlers, football players and steroid-taking genetic freaks, I have seen and been involved, in knocking out white boys left and right. They may be big but most of them are lacking in heart. I've seen small black guys beat the shit out of white boys who were one hundred pounds heavier. But in white culture, size is everything and that is what they go by: bigger is better. That only applies in dick length and we also have them beat out in that category. Ask their women if you don't believe it.

Trump's "attraction" to Schiller continued and,

> In 2004, Trump named him his Director of Security. Schiller made
> headlines in 2015 when he hit a protester outside Trump Tower ….
> He was appointed Director of Oval Office Operations after Trump
> assumed the office of the President in January 2017. In this role, he
> accompanied Jared Kushner to Iraq and sat in on meetings (Binder,
> 2015)

There is something that is weird about these relationships. There is no mention of Schiller having a wife and he seems to be desperate for a job and therefore right there at Trump's every beckon call. With Jared Kushner involved –

a gay looking man if there ever was one – who can say what is taking place behind Trump's closed doors when it's just him and Poopsie …. Oops! I mean Schiller.

Continuing:

> In August, Mr. Trump asked Mr. Schiller for a newspaper article he had heard about. After Mr. Trump mentioned the article to Mr. Kelly, the chief of staff dispatched two aides to investigate how it had gotten to the president without being cleared. Mr. Schiller acknowledged providing the contraband newsprint. Mr. Kelly thanked him tersely for coming forward, according to two people Mr. Schiller later told. (Haberman, Thrush & Baker, 2017).

Childish game-playing with Trump standing in the middle as two sides vie for his attention. This is going on while the world is in a shambles because of Trump's frequent fuckups and mis-statements. White America stands around with ear plugs blasting music, video games, movies and TV shows promotion hedonism and American hubris, while in reality brown people are kicking their ass in Afghanistan, Iran, Iraq, Syria and all over the world. A better script couldn't have been formulated by P.T. Barnam.

Trump was treating Schiller the same way he treated Omarosa. Check it out:

> To the surprise of aides, the president did not try to make clear Mr. Schiller's unique place in the Trump orbit. After some additional encounters with Mr. Kelly, Mr. Schiller <u>announced his departure</u>, a decision fueled primarily by a dislike for Washington and a desire to once again earn private-sector pay before retiring. (Haberman, Thrush & Baker, 2017)

The preceding could well be the story of Omarosa Manigault Edwards. She was also flitting about with no real job description, she also had some "encounters" with Kelly and she was then forced to "announce her departure" only after she had gotten canned by Kelly. Unlike Omarosa, Shiller left quietly but quite similar to her tactics, he immediately began seeking new sources of money.

Like star-crossed lovers, Trump is made to sound as if he lost a romantic interest. As the article states, "Since then, Mr. Trump has repeatedly expressed frustration at Mr. Schiller's absence, telling a visiting lawmaker that his Oval Office suite now seems "empty." The departure of other familiar faces has been equally unsettling." (Haberman, Thrush & Baker, 2017).

The following could well be insinuating about Omarosa as well:

[Type text]

> Once this fall, Mr. Trump lashed out at an aide he had not seen for
> weeks, asking, "Where the hell have you been?" When the aide told
> him that Mr. Kelly had limited the meetings he could attend, the
> president cooled off and said, "Oh, O.K.," according to an aide told
> of the exchange. (Haberman, Thrush & Baker, 2017).

In other words Trump doesn't have any understanding of what is taking place around him, who is supposed to be where and what they are supposed to be doing. He's out of it. And this is the asshole who these rednecks voted for to "drain the swamp" when, in reality, Trump is now the leading water moccasin in that swamp. White men, lacking in education, couldn't get jobs and got pissed off and as is the usual case, blamed it on black people. They wanted someone who they felt hated black people as much as they did – so they voted for Trump. It is as simple as that.

Again, let me make this clear: the key to the scam is to dupe the American public into thinking that "white supremacists" are the Klan, the Nazis and other ultra-right groups (known as "the Alt-Right") when, in reality, they are ALL white supremacists! Trump is an overt, dominative racist and Bernie Sanders is the liberal racist. Then there are the aversion racists but they all share a similar disdain and disrespect for black people when it comes down to it. They are all white nationalists on varying levels.

Back to "a day with Trump":

> If Mr. Kelly knows he cannot always control access, he is intent on
> at least knowing who is peddling what to his boss. He reserves the
> right to listen to calls coming to the president through the White
> House switchboard. To some callers, Mr. Kelly politely promises to
> forward messages. On calls he cannot monitor personally, Mr. Kelly
> or a deputy will usually double-back to debrief the caller on any
> promises the president may have made in unguarded moments.
> (Haberman, Thrush & Baker, 2017)

Running errands and interference for Trump because he's too immature to know how to handle serious business. This is the kind of person who is occupying the White House. He does what he wants to when he wants to. He goes down to Mar-A-Lago and parties, claiming that it's a "working vacation." He admits that he's grabbed women by the pussy and he called black men sons of bitches. He dogs out the handicapped, immigrants and Latinos. And what he's doing is acceptable by tens of millions of whites because, like spoiled brats themselves,

[Type text]

they got mad at the government, threw a temper tantrum and elected Trump to "teach American government a lesson."

While White House aides are working to chase the brat around the White House and keep him under control, the entire world is watching and laughing their asses off. America is a joke and the world knows it can no longer count on American leadership. This is the one thing positive that came out of the actions of Trump: the world is finally seeing America for the racist nation that it has always been but claimed not to be.

While the world is bracing for terrorist attacks, poverty, natural disasters and dictatorial takeovers, fat boy is in the White House thinking about what he's going to eat next:

> On weekdays, Mr. Trump's principal mode of blowing off steam is his nightly dinner in the residence. He has always relished gossiping over plates of well-done steak, salad slathered with Roquefort dressing and bacon crumbles, tureens of gravy and huge slices of dessert with extra ice cream. CreditTom Brenner/The New York Times

Trump is a dead man walking. Add to what you just read a dozen Diet Cokes a day, and this guy is walking around in a daze. He's 71 years old and how he's made it I have no idea. But you can believe one thing: there are some kind of prescription drugs involved. This can be seen by the kind of daffy doctor he's got, some loon who claimed in December of 2015 that "Trump has "extraordinary" stamina and physical strength and would be the healthiest person ever elected president" (Byrnes, 2015)

Healthier than Barack Obama? Healthier than George W. Bush? That is bullshit. The previous article added that, "Dr. Harold Bornstein, who has been Trump's personal physician since 1980, said that "over the past 39 years, I am pleased to report that Mr. Trump has had no significant medical problems." This guy is lying his ass off. And if he is willing to do that, then over that 37 year period he's also prescribed whatever drugs Trump needed, from Viagra to amphetamines.

The next sub-heading is, "'I Can Invite Anyone' and then proceeds to explain the following:

> Mr. Trump seeks release on the golf course on weekends. But on weekdays, his principal mode of blowing off steam is his nightly dinner in the White House residence, which begins at 6:30 or 7 p.m. with a guest list organized by the ever-vigilant Mr. Kelly.
> (Haberman, Thrush & Baker, 2017)

[Type text]

Golf is not a sport. It's a leisure activity for losers. The purpose of the golf course and the club house are for white boys to plan and engage in discourse about how they are going to move on a particular group or engage in a certain action on a certain project or program. It also serves to get them away from their big-mouthed trophy wives who they married for status reasons but now realize that if they divorce her she gets half their shit. So they pretend to love one another, sleep in separate bedrooms and remain together, they say, "for the kids' sake."

Trump is like this. He married three whores and then paid them and swore them to secrecy regarding his dicklessness. And each of the three looks the part. And when you're whole life is pimping, the way Trump's is, what other type of female would you be attracted to?

Like a child who wants other children to "spend the night" as a form of social control, Trump tells the reporters, "I can invite anyone for dinner, and they will come!" Mr. Trump marveled to an old friend when he took office. (Haberman, Thrush & Baker, 2017). Sure they will: leeches are always up for a free meal, even when the host is a bonafide asshole! In true bitch-like manner (in addition to the crush he has on Putin) check out the following:

> Mr. Trump has always relished gossiping over plates of well-done
> steak, salad slathered with Roquefort dressing and bacon crumbles,
> tureens of gravy and massive slices of dessert with extra ice cream.
> (Haberman, Thrush & Baker, 2017)/

Gossiping with his white friends, people who could probably care less about Trump but are there just for the status that Trump represents. Trump knows it and doesn't mind being used because he's shallow and doesn't really need friends. He needs control, and what better way to control people than through food? What comedian Chris Rock once said about women also applies to the effeminate Donald Trump: "There are only three things women need: food, water and compliments."

Also, at least according to the article,

> He needs support, a sounding board and, as a lifelong hotelier,
> guests. Mr. Trump is naturally garrulous, and loves to give White
> House tours. He has an odd affinity for showing off bathrooms,
> including one he renovated near the Oval Office, and enjoys pulling
> dinner companions into the Lincoln Bedroom or onto the Truman
> Balcony for the postcard view of the city he has disrupted.
> (Haberman, Thrush & Baker, 2017).

[Type text]

To begin with, being "garrulous" means more than just being talkative; it means being talkative especially when it comes to trivial matters. Keep in mind that these are top-notch reporters and wordsmiths so they choose their descriptions carefully. Trump talks just for the sake of talking, or so it seems. You've seen him wander from subject to subject during a nationally televised speech. Even when he's using a teleprompter he has to veer off script and add something utterly mindless and again, America becomes a laughing stock.

Giving White House tours – in other words showing off the way a child would do and of course, expecting "compliments" all along the way. But that's not all, folks:

> Over the summer, he invited four Democratic lawmakers and immediately peppered them with questions as they strolled through the Diplomatic Reception Room. "Who is going to run against me in 2020?" he asked, according to a person in attendance. "Crooked Hillary? Pocahontas?" — his caustic nickname for Senator Elizabeth Warren, Democrat of Massachusetts, who once claimed Native American heritage in a law school directory. (Haberman, Thrush & Baker, 2017)

What you just read is an example of the white nationalism collective that I alluded to earlier. This thing about "white supremacist" this or "white nationalist" that ludicrous. They're all in it. The Democrats and the Republicans are both white nationalist group, one that doesn't mind using "negroes" to do their bidding (Democrats) and the other one claiming to be "the party of Lincoln" while at the same time promoting invisible "no niggers allowed" signs (Republicans).

Check out the previous passage: four Democrats in the White House with Trump, none of them Black. They talk and converse and intermingle behind closed doors while pretending to be arguing and debating for the entertainment of the American public. Elizabeth Warren is no better: that bitch claimed to be part Native American so she could curry favor to get into law school. Yet she has the gall to act as if she is some kind of defender of the downtrodden, the same "social work approach" that Hillary Clinton used to use to win over sellout minorities.

The article claims that, "Senator Bernie Sanders of Vermont, the president opined, would definitely run — "even if he's in a wheelchair," Mr. Trump added, making a scrunched-up body of a man in a wheelchair. (Haberman, Thrush & Baker, 2017).

Let me tell you something about Bernie Sanders: he's a Jew first and a liberal progressive second. Jewish people have been ripping off people of color for

[Type text]

centuries, no matter where they are.They've been chased out of country after country and their outlandish usury fees on money they loan is all about land grabbing. And they occupy enough legal professions to push people out if they fall behind on their debts. That's how they make it. If they see something they want, they copy it and then sell it back to the people they stole it from. Ask Thomas Edison: they refused to pay his fees to rent materials to make films so they sent some people over to Europe, manufactured it themselves, and then came back to America and created Hollywood. That was the west coast while Edison's empire was on the east coast.

Bernie Sanders rips off people as well. All that "revolutionary" talk he's spewing is stolen almost directly from 1960s black radicals, from Stokely Carmichael and H. Rap Brown to Huey Newton. He's as power hungry and greedy as Clinton and Trump, only he shrouds it in a kindly old face and liberal sounding rhetoric.

Back to Trump:

> Mr. Trump still takes shots at Mark Cuban, a fellow rich-guy reality star, and expresses disappointment that Tom Brady, the New England Patriots quarterback, has distanced himself. But he spends much of his time now puzzling over political options and wrestling with the terrifying responsibilities of the presidency. (Haberman, Thrush & Baker, 2017)

Cuban is as sick and intrusive as Trump is. Because he owns the Dallas Mavericks NBA team, he thinks that makes him knowledgeable of the game. But when he made a comment about NBA player Kenyon Martin being a "thug" and then shouted to Martin's mother "that includes your won." When Kenyon heard about it, he was going to whip Cuban's ass but the billionaire quickly apologized for his statement. But this is one more example of the slave master mentality: Cuban felt because he owned the Dallas Mavericks that he could say anything about a black player, including one who played for the Denver Nuggets at the time.

How do you "puzzle over political options and wrestle with the responsibilities of the presidency"? He's in the office, having been voted in and having said a bunch of things during that campaign that made him sound as if he as Presidential. But once in office he realizes that he's bitten off more than he could chew. He's intimidated because he can't single handedly cheat and lie and steal his way to solutions and outcomes. So he's politically impotent. There is no vote-getting Viagra, no solution-oriented Cialis or leadership Levitra that you can take to attain an election erection or a bonafide boner!

According to the New York Times article,

> Even when Mr. Trump is in a lighthearted mood, hints of anxiety
> waft over the table like steam over a teacup. In September, he met
> with evangelical leaders to reassure them that he would still pursue
> their agenda despite a flirtation with Democrats. (Haberman, Thrush
> & Baker, 2017)

Evangelical leaders are nothing but Klansmen with crosses, bullies with Bibles and pimps with false piety. But they control huge numbers of weak-minded congregation members, and that is what politicians appeal to: buy off the people who, in turn, control large numbers of people using top-down control. If you control the leader of the church then you can control all the people who attend that church.

And it's quid pro quo:

> "The Christians know all the things I'm doing for them, right?" he
> asked, according to three attendees, who reported praising his
> positions on issues like abortion and Planned Parenthood.
> (Haberman, Thrush & Baker, 2017)

What happened to commitment to the U.S. Constitution? Doesn't the first amendment to the US Constitution make it crystal clear that, "Congress shall make no law respecting an establishment of religion, or prohibiting the free exercise thereof" The two parts, known as the "establishment clause" and the "free exercise clause" respectively, form the textual basis for the Supreme Court's interpretations ..."? But America is hypocritical and doesn't really give a shit about religion other than as a means of social control. That is why all these "Christians" in this "God fearing nation" can stand idly by and back racial segregation, rapes of Black women, lynchings of Black men, enslavement of African people, murders of Latinos and Asians and exploitation of women.

In the latter instance the issues of abortion and the attacks on Planned Parenthood are extensions of the Bible's own misogyny and sexism. Elsewhere in this book I document how the Bible stigmatizes women when they have their menstrual cycles! Trump seems to also have issues with women, from his own wives to Black women and to any woman who dares to voice an opinion. And yet he has the backing of these "Evangelicals".

Back to the article:

> When the guests depart, the remote control comes back out. He is less likely to tweet at this hour, when the news he would react to is mostly recycled from hours earlier. But he watches Ms. Pirro and her fellow Fox News hosts Sean Hannity and Laura Ingraham, and sometimes "hate-watches" CNN to get worked up, especially Don Lemon. (Haberman, Thrush & Baker, 2017)

Why "especially Don Lemon"? Because Don Lemon is the personification and embodiment of Trump's ire. Lemon is no "lemon" - he is handsome, he is Black and he is gay. Trump doesn't want to see anyone Black excelling at anything. That is why he is so hateful of Barack Obama. He knows that Ben Carson, the man he appointed to run the Department of Housing and Urban Development is not qualified because Carson is a neurosurgeon and Trump insulted him during the Republican campaign. But when a black man is qualified and admired, Trump can't take it. CNN has a number of anchors and reporters whose shows expose him, from Wolf Blitzer and Fareed Zacharia to Chris Cuomo and Anderson Cooper. But Don Nelson is the only one who is African-American.

Add to all that has been shared the fact that Trump is two-faced. He cannot be trusted. The saying teaches us, "Dress a liar as you will/A liar is a liar, still." With that in mind, note the following:

> In between, it is time for phone calls, to people he has fired like Corey Lewandowski and Mr. Bannon, old friends like Thomas J. Barrack Jr. and Richard LeFrak, and more recently Republican lawmakers, especially Representative Mark Meadows of North Carolina, the head of the conservative Freedom Caucus. This is when his fixations are unfettered: Russia, Mrs. Clinton, <u>Barack Obama</u>, the "fake news" media, his bitter <u>disappointment with Attorney General Jeff Sessions</u>. (Haberman, Thrush & Baker, 2017)

Truly sick – and I don't only mean Trump. The people who allow him to contact them after he's publicly humiliated them by firing them also need their asses kicked. In doing so these people – Lewandowski and Bannon – show how desperate they are. These white men are the best that the white race can produce, and white folks ought to be ashamed instead of running around chanting "Make American Great Again" and "Lock Her Up."

And these white people have the gall to put words like "Freedom" in the names of their fly-by-night organizations. White women, the co-signors of some of the worst atrocities to ever be imposed on the backs of black people, running around talking about being victims. America is trying to pawn itself off as freedom fighters the way black people were during the 1960s. While Black people kiss ass and scrounge to be recognized by a racist system that is hated the world over, the white folks are acting as if they are grass-roots revolutionaries. Every other commercial you see on television is boasting about a product being "revolutionary" on some level. This is social brainwashing at its best.

Now we near the end-game:

> In recent weeks, Mr. Trump's friends have noticed a different pitch, acknowledging that many aides and even his own relatives could be hurt by Mr. Mueller's investigation. As for himself, he has adopted a surprisingly fatalistic attitude, according to several people he speaks with regularly. (Haberman, Thrush & Baker, 2017)

When it comes to Trump, being "fatalistic" (accepting that all things are inevitable) and being realistic are one and the same. Trump cannot change and continually repeats mistake after mistake. I believe it was Albert Einsten who once said that the definition of "insanity" was repeating the same act and expecting a different result every time. Mueller is not going to "uncover" anything that Trump did not do; Trump is the sum of his functions, both lifelong and those directly associated with his relationship to Vladimir Putin. For the love of money Trump wanted money from Russia and wanted to build aTrump Tower there. He sacrificed everything, thinking he was above the law, and the Mueller investigation is showing that Trump is going to reap what he's sown.

But like a true nut, his response to his inevitable global humiliation and historically bad acts is a "que sera, sera" (what will be, will be) attitude:

> "It's life," he said of the investigation. From there it is off to bed for what usually amounts to five or six hours of sleep. Then the television will be blaring again, he will reach for his iPhone and the battle will begin anew. (Haberman, Thrush & Baker, 2017)

[Type text]

The "battle that begins anew" on a daily basis is Trump's battle with himself. But then again, white guilt is nothing new – America is filled with it. The difference being that most white folks can fake their way through it. But Trump is the prototype –he is not the "first" white man to pull the kinds of diabolical tricks that he has gotten away with. He is just the first to do so in such a public way.

CONCLUSION

I hope to have shown in this book that there is nothing that is exceptional about Donald Trump. He didn't build any of those skyscrapers or casinos, other people did it. And then in many cases after they built it, he wouldn't even pay them. And then he plastered his name on these structures and, after cutting shady deals with various city officials, developers and architects, raked in money and then wrote a book called The Art of the Deal. The fact is, he didn't even write the book, and the man who did write it exposed the fact that Trump tried to lie about it even though there was evidence that he (Trump) paid the man.

Now comes a Trump-Russia probe, but let me provide more relevant insights than what you will see on the white controlled media. Trump is guilty as sin for doing what white men have been doing for centuries: collaborating with other white men. It just so happens that in this case the "other" white men are Russian and the United States pretends to be at odds with them. But don't you get it twisted: these white people are in agreement when it comes to their hatred of people of color, from immigrants, migrants, Blacks, Latinos, Asians and others to even the mixed-breeds.

Even former FBI director Robert Mueller, who was assigned to look into the Trump-Russia connection, should not be trusted to do anything that is not going to benefit the white supremacy system. The on-going claim is that he is so "upright" and "moral," but we've heard that before, have we not? Remember the lie that Hilary Clinton was supposed to be the opposite of Donald Trump, and yet we come to find out that she was just like him, as greedy as he is and as big a liar. And remember one more thing about the FBI before we move on.

Those were the muthafuckas that were ordered to infiltrate the Black Panther Party – and they did it. They were the ones who were ordered infiltrate and work with Maulana Karenga's US organization. And they did it. They were the ones who set up the murders of numerous black nationalists under the orders of the cross-dressing J. Edgar Hoover. The FBI was the agency responsible for spying on groups like the Republic of New Africa, the Revolutionary Action Movement, the

Brown Berets, the Red Guard, the Students for a Democratic Society, the Student Nonviolent Coordinating Committee, Dr. Martin Luther King, Jr.'s civil rights movement and so on. They did what they were told to do by a white supremacist system. So don't come singing Mueller's praises to me because I know the history of his organization, whether he was there or not.

Let us look at an article on the appointment of Mueller and use that information as a bulwark for not only white supremacy, but how the "good cop-bad cop" approach continues to dupe and bamboozle millions of Americans. The article begins, thusly:

> WASHINGTON (AP) — The Justice Department on Wednesday appointed former FBI Director Robert Mueller as a special counsel to oversee a federal investigation into potential coordination between Russia and Donald Trump's campaign during the 2016 presidential election. "I accept this responsibility and will discharge it to the best of my ability," Mueller said in a brief statement. (Tucker & Gurman, 2017).

Since that appointment Mueller and his "team" have come up with a list of people that they have subpoenaed and they are getting closer to Trump. Trump is running scared, so he and his spineless Congress are working to make Mueller appear to be someone who is compromised and are whipping up stories in order to get him taken off the case. But in my view it's too little, too late. Trump's arrogance has left a paper trail that Stevie Wonder could follow, his bombast has alienated him (and America) from the rest of the world, and his love affair with Putin is becoming increasingly evident as the days and weeks pass.

And yet Trump , his attorneys, is lying ass kids and much of the Republican Party, continue to claim that there is no Trump-Russia connection:

> In a statement released by the White House, Trump said: "As I have stated many times, a thorough investigation will confirm what we already know — there was no collusion between my campaign and any foreign entity. I look forward to this matter concluding quickly." (Tucker & Gurman, 2017).

Lying bastard. In my view Trump's incessant appeals to build a major hotel in Russia, his need for money (since no sane bank in America would loan him any) meant that he was Russia-dependent. His worthless son-in-law, Jared Kushner was in debt up to his neck as well, and there were Russians running around all over Trump tower and even a few in the White House. The plot thickened and white people and the media stalled time by pretending that they were "taking their time" and "making sure that all the information was confirmed. The media was bleeding the story for all the ads and "specials" that they could possibly air, and trying to pretend to be detectives themselves.

Another thing the media does that shows that the white supremacist system is more committed to its whiteness than it is to any "ism" is how these cable TV talk shows try to justify or rationalize Trump's insanity. On December 11, 2017, CNN's Anderson Cooper 360 was the site of one such situation. Cooper had as his guests Michael D'Antonio, a man who wrote a biography on Trump and Christopher Ruddy, listed as a "friend" ofTrump. How are these two assholes credible? Their insights are slanted and biased in favor of Trump. It is their job to point out any actual or imagined "intricacies" behind Trump's thinking, as if all this callousness, buffoonery and stupidity is somehow the part of a "plan.

Let me tell you something before moving on: as black people, we know a racist fake-ass muthafucka when we see one. Those speeches he reads when he has to pretend to know something about people of color are as contrived and shallow as the Constitution and the Declaration of Independence. For instance, at the opening of the Civil Rights Museum in Mississippi (what a waste of snaps), he read about blacks fighting oppression and racism and then added, "those was great stuff. That was big stuff."

"Stuff," muthafucka? Black people in Mississippi died for the right to vote (don't ask me why) and to crawl into the white man's system. Black people gave America what little flavor and civilization it has. And here comes this mealy-mouthed sonofabitch calling actions of courage and confrontation,"stuff." The negroes on those cable TV shows glanced over general concerns but as usual, never get to the root of the problem. They know that if they show real courage, they will get the Jemele Hill treatment or the Colin Kaepernick treatment and their white master won't give them the money to make their next Mercedes Benz payment.

In the meantime,

> The appointment gives Mueller, who led the FBI through the Sept. 11 terrorist attacks and served under presidential administrations of both parties, sweeping powers to investigate whether Trump campaign associates colluded with the Kremlin to influence the outcome in his behalf, as well as the authority to prosecute any crimes uncovered during the probe. (Tucker & Gurman, 2017).

[Type text]

Those "sweeping powers" proved to be the beginning of the end for Trump. What he found was collusion between the Trump family and Russia, tens of millions of dollars exchanging hands between Trump's National Security Advisor Michael Flynn and Russia (as well as the Urkraine), Paul Manafort, Trump's former campaign manager working for the Russians and successfully getting the Republican campaign plank to eliminate a call for sanctions against Russia, which is what Putin really wanted all along. And the coast looked clear for drillings in areas of the world where Russia had been banned. Trump even lifted protections against America's state parks, leaving them vulnerable for drilling by his greedy oil speculator pals like the one he hiredRex Tillerson former President of Exxon, a man on record as saying that he wanted "a better relationship with Russian President Vladimir Putin.

Trump tried to cover things up by firing the FBI director because he couldn't get him to get rid of Mueller.

According to Tucker & Gurman (2017), Mueller was succeeded by Comey, who was fired May 9. The White House initially cited a Justice Department memo that criticized his handling of the Hillary Clinton email investigation, but Trump has since expressed frustration with "this Russia thing" and said he had already been thinking about dismissing Comey.

Things appeared to be unravelling.

But never fear. No matter what the outcome these white men will come out with clean hands. They will turn on each other, snitch and get a plea deal. The ones who are guilty, including Trump, will be "pardoned" in the same way that the clumsy and worthless President Gerald Ford pardoned the crook Richard Nixon.

So how could Trump be a prototype? How could he be an original? This stuff has been going on ever since the beginning of American government. These white men have stolen, lied, murdered, raped, cheated and done anything they could to retain their short- and long-term power. Trump learned from his ancestors and his predecessors.

So when I hear sick negroes and peckerwoods talking about Trump "making them sick" or how they are "depressed" because of something this fool did, I want to slap the shit out of them. Ever since these people were born, before their great parents were born, there were Trump-like white men in power to abused that power to the hilt. Trump is just one more in a long line of power hungry people who do what they want to do when they want to do it.

Pablo Freire once wrote, "Washing one's hands of the conflict between the powerful and the powerless means to side with the powerful, not to be neutral." America is going to hell in a handbasket and yet people talk about what they are "going to do" or about "wait until the next election." The more time they think they have the power corrupt Trump becomes and the closer this country comes to its inevitable end.

And the "Americans" have only themselves to blame.

REFERENCES

Abcarian, R. (2016, July 19). 'I put lipstick on a pig,' says Trumps 'Art of the Deal' ghostwriter, breaking a decades-long silence. *Los Angeles Times*. Retrieved from http://www.latimes.com/nation/

Badash, D. (2017, March 1). Trump's Speech to Congress Contained Dozens of Lies, Falsehoods, Inaccurate, or Misleading Statements. Retrieved from http://www.thenewcivilrightsmovement.com/davidbadash/trump_s_speech_is_being_heralded_as_presidential_but_it_was_filed_with_lies

Blinder, Rachelle (September 4, 2015). "Meet Trump's feisty head of security who smacked protester". New York Daily News. Retrieved February 8, 2017

Blumenthal, P. (2017, February 9). Steve Bannon Believes The Apocalypse Is Coming And War Is Inevitable. The Huffington Post. Retrieved from http://www.msn.com/en-gb/news/world/steve-bannon-believes-the-apocalypse-is-coming-and-war-is-inevitable/ar-AAmKhjJ
February 9, 2017

Bolshevik.org (1988-89, Winter). Jesse Jackson: Judas-Goat for the BourgeoisieDemocrats, Dixiecrats and Rainbows. *1917* no.5: Winter 1988-89. Retrieved from
http://www.bolshevik.org/1917/no5/no05jesse.html

Borchers, C. (2016, March 22). Donald Trump's campaign manager says he might sue BuzzFeed for libel. It would be tough to win. The Washington Post. Retrieved from http://www.msn.com/en-us/news/politics/donald-trump%e2%80%99s-campaign-manager-says-he-might-sue-buzzfeed-for-libel-it-would-be-tough-to-win/ar-BBqNr8O?li=BBnb7Kz&ocid=iehp

Bradley, M. (1978). *The Iceman Inheritance: Prehistoric Sources of Western Man's Racism, Sexism and Aggression.* New York, New York: Kayode Publications.

Brennan, W. (1995). Female objects of semantic dehumanization and violence. *Feminism and Nonviolence Studies*, 1,(3).

Bruney, Gabrielle (2017, December 23). 'The New York Times' Reports that Trump Made Blatantly Racist Statements About Immigrants. Esquire. Retrieved from http://www.esquire.com/news-politics/a14491687/new-york-times-trump-racism-immigrants/

Business Insider (2015, September 1). Donald Trump's ex-wife once said Trump kept a book of Hitler's speeches by his bed. Retrieved from http://www.businessinsider.com/donald-trumps-ex-wife-once-said-he-kept-a-book-of-hitlers-speeches-by-his-bed-2015-8

Byrnes, Jesse (2016, March 24) Trump doubles down on Heidi Cruz attacks. MSN.com. Retrieved from http://www.msn.com/en-us/news/politics/trump-doubles-down-on-heidi-cruz-attacks/ar-BBqRRY9?li=BBnb7Kz&ocid=iehp

Byrnes, Jesse (2015, December 14). Doctor: Trump would be healthiest president ever. The Hill. Retrieved from http://thehill.com/blogs/ballot-box/presidential-races/263146-doctor-trump-will-be-healthiest-president-ever

Byrowicz, Julie (2017, June 29). President ridicules female TV host's looks, calls her crazy. Minneapolis Star-Tribune. Retrieved from http://www.startribune.com/trump-ridicules-female-tv-host-s-looks-calls-her-crazy/431533533/

Chicago Tribune (2006, March 8). Trump: I'd date my daughter. Retrieved from http://articles.chicagotribune.com/2006-03-08/news/0603080162_1_ivanka-trump-donald-trump-woody-allen

Cirill, K. (2016, March 12). Agents rush stage to protect Donald Trump at Dayton rally. MSN.com. Retrieved from http://www.msn.com/en-us/news/politics/agents-

rush-stage-to-protect-donald-trump-at-dayton-rally/ar-
AAgHa7S?li=BBnb7Kz&ocid=iehp

Clarke, J.H. (1991, February). Introduction. In *The Iceman Inheritance*. Michael Bradley. New York, New York: Kayode Publications.

Cody, C. (2014, January 13). Majority In Congress Are Millionaires. NPR. Retrieved from http://www.npr.org/sections/itsallpolitics/2014/01/10/261398205/majority-in-congress-are-millionaires.

Condon, S. (2016, February 26). Marco Rubio suggests Donald Trump wet his pants, Trump hurls insults back. CBS News. Retrieved from http://www.cbsnews.com/news/marco-rubio-suggests-donald-trump-wet-his-pants-trump-hurls-insults-back/

Cooper, Brittney (2017, September 15). Jemele Hill Called Donald Trump a White Supremacist. Where's the Lie?: In this op-ed, Brittney Cooper argues that the ESPN journalist has nothing to apologize for. Cosmopolitan. Retrieved from http://www.cosmopolitan.com/politics/a12242564/jemele-hill-espn-trump-white-supremacist/

Costa, R. (2016, March 11). Washington Post. Ben Carson backs Trump, saying combative billionaire has 'cerebral' side. Retrieved from http://www.msn.com/en-us/news/politics/ben-carson-plans-to-endorse-trump/ar-AAgDCMp?li=BBnb7Kz&ocid=iehp

Cullen, Terence & Slattery, Denis. (2017, October 18). Trump did 'disrespect my son,' his wife and his family, slain Army sergeant's mother says. New York Daily News. Retrieved from http://www.nydailynews.com/news/national/trump-denies-telling-army-widow-knew-signed-article-1.3571173

Davis, Ethan (2008). "An Administrative Trail of Tears: Indian Removal". The American Journal of Legal History. **50** (1):

DelReal, J.A. (2016, March 12). 'Get 'em out!' Racial tensions explode at Donald Trump's rallies. The Washington Post. Retrieved from http://www.msn.com/en-us/news/politics/%e2%80%98get-%e2%80%99em-out%e2%80%99-racial-tensions-explode-at-donald-trump%e2%80%99s-rallies/ar-AAgF98g?li=BBnb7Kz&ocid=iehp

DelReal, J.A. & Johnson, J. (2016, March 25). Donald Trump can't stop saying nasty things about women. It could cost him. *The Washington Post*. Retrieved from https://www.washingtonpost.com/politics/donald-trump-cant-stop-saying-nasty-things-about-women-it-could-cost-him/2016/03/24/51a0ee82-f1d7-11e5-85a6-2132cf446d0a_story.html

DelReal, J.A. & Gearen, Ann. (2016, July 30). Backlash for Trump After he Lashes Out at the Muslim Parents of a Dead US Soldier. The Washington Post. Retrieved from The Washington Post https://www.washingtonpost.com/politics/backlash-for-trump-after-he-lashes-out-at-the-muslim-parents-of-a-dead-us-soldier/2016/07/30/34b0aad4-5671-11e6-88eb-7dda4e2f2aec_story.html?wpisrc=nl_most-draw6&wpmm=1

Easley, J. (2016, March 26). Anti-Trump forces seize on grim polls for Clinton match-up. The Hill. Retrieved from http://thehill.com/blogs/ballot-box/presidential-races/274317-anti-trump-forces-point-to-losing-match-ups-with-clinton

Estepa, Jessica. (2017, November27). Trump Trump calls Elizabeth Warren 'Pocahontas' while hosting Native American vets event. USA Today. Retrieved from https://www.usatoday.com/story/news/politics/onpolitics/2017/11/27/trump-calls-elizabeth-warren-pocahontas-while-hosting-native-american-war-heroes-event/898815001/

Edelman, Adam (2016, January 7). Donald Trump courted wife Melania while out on a date with another woman in 1998, she reveals in interview about GOP front-runner. New York Daily News. Retrieved from http://www.nydailynews.com/news/politics/donald-trump-wife-melania-tells-story-met-article-1.2488623

Fahrenthold, David A. (2016, June 28). Donald Trump has promised millions to charity, but records don't support claim. The Chicago Tribune. Retrieved from http://www.chicagotribune.com/news/nationworld/politics/ct-donald-trump-charity-20160628-story.html

Flegenheimer, Matt & Haberman, Maggie (2016, March 31). Donald Trump, Abortion Foe, Eyes 'Punishment' for Women, Then Recants. *New York Times*. Retrieved from http://www.msn.com/en-us/news/politics/donald-trump-abortion-foe-eyes-%e2%80%98punishment%e2%80%99-for-women-then-recants/ar-BBr9tP6?li=BBnb7Kz&ocid=iehp

Garver, Rob (2016, March 28). Donald Trump doesn't want to be president. Fiscal Times. Retrieved from http://www.msn.com/en-us/news/politics/ex-trump-insider-donald-doesn%e2%80%99t-want-to-be-president/ar-BBr2kwt?li=BBnb7Kz&ocid=iehp

Geobeats (2017, November 11). North Korea calls Trump a 'warmonger' who 'begged for a nuclear war' during Asia trip. Retrieved from https://www.aol.com/article/news/2017/11/11/north-korea-calls-trump-a-warmonger-who-begged-for-a-nuclear-war-during-asia-trip/23274275/

Glauber, Bill, et. al. (2016, August 17). Trump courts black voters in West Bend speech. Milwaukee Journal Sentinel. Retrieved from http://www.jsonline.com/story/news/politics/elections/2016/08/16/trump-addresses-milwaukee-unrest/88864016/

Gonen, Y. & Fredericks, B. (2016, March 11). Ben Carson endorses Trump at Mar-a-Lago, calls him 'a very intelligent man'. *Washington Post*. Retrieved from http://nypost.com/2016/03/11/ben-carson-endorses-trump-at-mar-a-lago-calls-him-a-very-intelligent-man/

Goodman, Amy & Shaikh, Nermeen (2017, March 23). Robert Mercer and the Dark Money Behind Trump and Bannon's Radical Vision. Democracy Now! Retrieved from http://www.truth-out.org/news/item/39968-jane-mayer-on-robert-mercer-and-the-dark-money-behind-trump-and-bannon-s-radical-vision

Graham, Bryan Armen (2017, September 23). Donald Trump blasts NFL anthem protesters: 'Get that son of a bitch off the field'. The Guardian. Retrieved fromhttps://www.theguardian.com/sport/2017/sep/22/donald-trump-nfl-national-anthem-protests

[Type text]

Haberman, M. & Sanger, D.E. (2016, April 9). Donald Trump's trial balloons are catching up with him. *New York Times*. Retrieved from http://www.msn.com/en-us/news/politics/donald-trump%e2%80%99s-trial-balloons-are-catching-up-with-him/ar-BBryIw4?li=BBnb7Kz&ocid=iehp

Haberman, Maggie,Thrush, Glenn & Baker, Peter (2017, December 9).Inside Trump's Hour-by-Hour Battle for Self-Preservation. .New York Times. Retrieved from https://www.nytimes.com/2017/12/09/us/politics/donald-trump-president.html

Hafner, Josh (2016, April 1). Trump says he's allow 'rich Muslims' to enter U.S. USA Today. Retrieved from http://www.msn.com/en-us/news/politics/trump-says-hed-allow-rich-muslims-to-enter-us/ar-BBrbWpG?li=BBnb7Kz&ocid=iehp

Hamburger, Tom, et. al. (2016, June 17). Inside Trump's financial ties to Russia and his unusual flattery of Vladimir Putin. *Washington Post*. Retrieved from https://www.washingtonpost.com/politics/inside-trumps-financial-ties-to-russia-and-his-unusual-flattery-of-vladimir-putin/2016/06/17/dbdcaac8-31a6-11e6-8ff7-7b6c1998b7a0_story.html?utm_term=.1308cde27391

Hellman, Jessie (2016, December 11). Bernstein says Trump's lies worse than Nixon's. *The Hill*. Retrieved from http://thehill.com/homenews/news/309874-bernstein-says-trumps-lies-worse-than-nixons

Hensch, Mark (2016, March 25). Carson: I'm why Trump is acting more 'presidential'. MSN.com. Retrieved from http://www.msn.com/en-us/news/politics/carson-im-why-trump-is-acting-more-presidential/ar-BBqVvM5?li=BBnb7Kz&ocid=iehp

Heye, Doug (2016, May 25). How Donald Trump's Attack on Susana Martinez Undermines the GOP–and Trump. Wall Street Journal. Retrieved from http://blogs.wsj.com/washwire/2016/05/25/how-donald-trumps-attack-on-susana-martinez-undermines-the-gop-and-trump/
May 25, 2016 5:29 pm ET

Hohmann, James (2016, June 22). The Daily 202: Reagan White House Viewed Trump and His 'Large Ego' Warily. The Washington Post. Retrieved from https://www.washingtonpost.com/news/powerpost/paloma/daily-

202/2016/06/22/daily-202-reagan-white-house-viewed-trump-and-his-large-ego-warily/5769f9e3981b92a22d278fa5/?utm_term=.9a7fdcf810e0

Horwitz, Jeff (2016, March 9). Trump received tax credit for middle class taxpayers. MSN.com. Retrieved from http://www.msn.com/en-us/news/politics/trump-received-tax-credit-for-middle-class-taxpayers/ar-AAgzPkx?li=BBnb7Kz&ocid=iehp

Indian Country Today (2017, February 16) Retrieved from https://indiancountrymedianetwork.com/history/genealogy/true-story-pocahontas-historical-myths-versus-sad-reality/

Indian Country Today (2017). Indian-Killer Andrew Jackson Deserves Top Spot on List of Worst US Presidents: Andrew Jackson tops list of worst presidents for Natives https://indiancountrymedianetwork.com/history/people/indian-killer-andrew-jackson-deserves-top-spot-on-list-of-worst-us-presidents/

Isadore, Chris (2017, March 3). Despite Trump promises, Keystone pipeline won't have to use American steel. CNN Money. Retrieved from http://money.cnn.com/2017/03/03/news/companies/trump-keystone-pipeline-american-steel/index.html

Isadore, Chris and Devine, Curt. (2016, December 22). Trump's vineyard is hiring – foreign workers. CNN Money. Retrieved from http://money.cnn.com/2016/12/22/news/companies/trump-foreign-workers/index.html

Johnson, Jason (2016, April 8). GOP exodus: Why are black staffers leaving the RNC? MSN.com. Retrieved from http://www.msn.com/en-us/news/politics/gop-exodus-why-are-black-staffers-leaving-the-rnc/ar-BBrrFYE?li=BBnb7Kz&ocid=iehp

Johnson, Jenna (2016, June 6). Trump says it's 'inappropriate' for ally Newt Gingrich to criticize his attacks on the 'Mexican' judge. Washington Post. Retrieved from https://www.washingtonpost.com/news/post-politics/wp/2016/06/06/trump-says-its-inappropriate-for-ally-newt-gingrich-to-criticize-his-attacks-on-the-mexican-judge/

Johnson, Jenna (2016, March 8). Trump: It's 'ridiculous' to compare his pledge to a Nazi salute. MSN.com. Retrieved from http://www.msn.com/en-us/news/politics/trump-it%E2%80%99s-%E2%80%98ridiculous%E2%80%99-to-compare-his-pledge-to-a-nazi-salute/ar-AAgwNtB?form=PRHPTP&ocid=iehp

Johnson, Jenna. (2016, March 12). Donald Trump demands that police arrest rally protesters. Washington Post. Retrieved from https://www.washingtonpost.com/news/post-politics/wp/2016/03/12/donald-trump-demands-that-police-arrest-rally-proteste
March 12, 2016

Just Jared . (2017, January 4). Omarosa Appointed To Donald Trump's Office of Public Liaison. Retrieved from http://www.justjared.com/2017/01/04/omarosa-appointed-to-donald-trumps-office-of-public-liaison/

Kaplan, Sarah (2016, March 14). Reporter who says she was manhandled by Trump campaign manager resigns from Breitbart. *The Washington Post.* Retrieved from http://www.msn.com/en-us/news/politics/reporter-who-says-she-was-manhandled-by-trump-campaign-manager-resigns-from-breitbart/ar-AAgKCRz?li=BBnbfcL&ocid=iehp

Kaplan, Rebecca. (2015, July 30). "Donald Trump: 'I'd get along very well with Vladimir Putin.' " CBS News. Retrieved from https://www.cbsnews.com/news/donald-trump-id-get-along-very-well-with-vladimir-putin/

Kellman, L. (2016, March 9). Viewer's Guide: 'Softer' GOP debate? So says Trump, maybe. Associated Press. Retrieved from http://www.msn.com/en-us/news/politics/viewers-guide-softer-gop-debate-so-says-trump-maybe/ar-AAgBIDN?li=BBnb7Kz&ocid=iehp

Kendricks, L. (2006, July 26). Are Al Sharpton and Jesse Jackson poverty pimps? New Pittsburgh Courier. p. A7.

Kessler, Glenn (2016, June 6). Trump says Elizabeth Warren Made 'Killing' in Foreclosures. The Washington Post. Retrieved from https://www.washingtonpost.com/news/fact-checker/wp/2016/06/06/trumps-claim-that-elizabeth-warren-made-a-quick-killing-in-foreclosures/?wpmm=1&wpisrc=nl_most-draw6

Kessler, Glenn.(2016, February 29). "A trio of truthful attack ads about Trump University." Washington Post Fact Checker.

Kessler, Glenn. (2o016, February 18). "Trump's truly absurd claim he would save $300 billion a year on prescription drugs." Washington Post Fact Checker.

Kessler, Glenn. (2015, December 6). "Trump's false claim that the 9/11 hijackers' wives 'knew exactly what was going to happen.' " 6 Dec 2015.

Krueger, Katherine. (2015, March 5). CNN: Donald Trump broke the rules of Fox News' GOP debate. MSN.com. Retrieved from http://www.msn.com/en-us/news/politics/cnn-donald-trump-broke-the-rules-of-fox-news-gop-debate/ar-BBqnNHL?li=BBnb7Kz&ocid=iehp

Krueger, Katherine (2016, March 16). Carson: I Didn't Really Want To Endorse Trump, But He Offered Me Position. MSN.com. Retrieved from http://www.msn.com/en-us/news/politics/carson-i-didnt-really-want-to-endorse-trump-but-he-offered-me-position/ar-BBquV5Q

Kuntzman, Gersh (2017, January 29). President Trump exhibits classic signs of mental illness, including 'malignant narcissism,' shrinks say. *New York Daily News*. Retrieved from http://www.nydailynews.com/news/politics/shrinks-break-silence-president-trump-exhibits-traits-m-article-1.2957688.

Lee, Matthew. (2016, March 20). Pro-Israel policy conference nervously awaits Trump speech. MSN.com. Retrieved from http://www.msn.com/en-us/news/politics/pro-israel-policy-conference-nervously-awaits-trump-speech/ar-BBqGWqY?li=BBnb7Kz&ocid=iehp

Lemire, Jonathan & Colvin, Jill (2017, August 18). Trump ousts Bannon, his influential, divisive strategist. Seattle Times. Retrieved from *http://www.seattletimes.com/nation-*

[Type text]

world/ap-sources-strategist-steve-bannon-leaving-white-house/?utm_source=The+Seattle+Times&utm_campaign=b92d9a29be- August 18, 2017

Leonhardt, David & Thompson, Stuart A. (2017, December 14). Trumps lies vs. Obama's. New York Times. Retrieved from https://www.nytimes.com/2017/12/14/opinion/trump-lies-obama.html?rref=collection%2Fbyline%2Fdavid-leonhardt&action=click&contentCollection=undefined®ion=stream&module=stream_unit&version=latest&contentPlacement=2&pgtype=collection

Love, David A. (2017, January 4). Here's the question: Is Megyn Kelly really a racist, or does she just play one on TV? And does it even matter?The Grio. Retrieved from http://thegrio.com/2017/01/04/megyn-kelly-is-a-racist/

Malveaux, Suzanne & Diaz, Daniella (2017, January 4). Omarosa to join Trump team, focus on public engagement . *St. Louis American*. Retrieved from http://www.stlamerican.com/entertainment/living_it/omarosa-to-join-trump-team-focus-on-public-engagement/article_da9801f2-d28d-11e6-b513-77f999401f58.html

Marcotte, Amanda (2015, December 28). Donald Trump is just exposing himself by roping in Bill Clinton's past infidelity into campaign. Salon.

Milbank, D. (2016, July 18). For Trump, it's white America first. Retrieved from http://elections.gatehousemedia.com/for-trump-its-white-america-first/

Miller, Zeke (2016, April 3). GOP Chairman Warns Of 'Consequences' for Trump Over Broken Loyalty Pledge. *Time magazine*. Retrieved from http://www.msn.com/en-us/news/politics/gop-chairman-warns-of-%e2%80%98consequences%e2%80%99-for-trump-over-broken-loyalty-pledge/ar-BBrhQxV?li=BBnb7Kz&ocid=iehp

Milwaukee Sentinel. (1992, July 14). Perot advisers at odds.

Moss, Candida (2015, August 10). From Eve to Megyn: Weak men like Trump have always feared menstruation. The Daily Beast. Retrieved from http://www.thedailybeast.com/weak-men-like-trump-have-always-feared-menstruation

MSN News. (2016, March 3). Fact Check.org.: FactChecking the 11th GOP Debate. Retrieved from http://www.msn.com/en-us/news/politics/factchecking-the-11th-gop-debate/ar-BBqkjbn?li=BBnb7Kz&ocid=iehp

Notable Quotes (2017). Lying quotes. Retrieved from http://www.notable-quotes.com/l/lying_quotes.html

O'Connell, Jonathan (2017, August 7). How the Trump hotel changed Washington's culture of influence," Washington Post. Retrieved from https://article.wn.com/view/2017/08/07/how_the_trump_international_hotel_changed_washington_8217s_c_o/

Pace, Julie & Swanson, Emily (2016, April 7). AP-GfK Poll: Americans overwhelmingly view Trump negatively. Retrieved from http://www.msn.com/en-us/news/politics/ap-gfk-poll-americans-overwhelmingly-view-trump-negatively/ar-BBru5xW?li=BBnb7Kz&ocid=iehp

Page, Susan & Raftery, Erin (2015, July 14). Poll: Trump leads the GOP field but falters against Clinton. USA Today. Retrieved from http://www.usatoday.com/story/news/politics/elections/2015/07/14/usa-today-suffolk-poll-republicans-donald-trump/30102255/

Parker, A. (2016, April 5). Struggling with women, Donald Trump turns to his wife. The Boston Globe. Retrieved from http://www.msn.com/en-us/news/politics/struggling-with-women-donald-trump-turns-to-his-wife/ar-BBrmBFA?li=BBnb7Kz&ocid=iehp

Parker, A. & Haberman, M. (2016, April 7). New hire signals a reboot in the Donald Trump campaign. New York Times. Retrieved from http://www.msn.com/en-us/news/politics/new-hire-signals-a-reboot-in-the-donald-trump-campaign/ar-BBruG3S?li=BBnb7Kz&ocid=iehp

Parker, K. (2016, April 23). Column: Black votes matter. Washington Post. Retrieved from http://www.thetimesnews.com/opinion/20160423/column-black-votes-matter

[Type text]

Peoples, Steve & Spencer, Terry (2016, March 29). Police charge Trump campaign manager with battery. MSN.com. Retrieved from http://www.msn.com/en-us/news/politics/police-charge-trump-campaign-manager-with-battery/ar-BBr4Whf?li=BBnb7Kz&ocid=iehp

Revesz, Rachael (2016, October 22). Salma Hayek says Donald Trump planted National Enquirer story about her height after she refused to date him. Independent. Retrieved from http://www.independent.co.uk/news/people/donald-trump-salma-hayek-refused-date-national-enquirer-height-2008-charity-auction-a7375321.html

Rayfield, J. (2011, October 11). Twelve Pretty Racist Or Just Crazy Quotes From Pat Buchanan's New Book. Retrieved from http://talkingpointsmemo.com/muckraker/twelve-pretty-racist-or-just-crazy-quotes-from-pat-buchanan-s-new-book

Reiss, J. (2016, March 22). Washington Post editor says Trump called her 'beautiful'. Boston Globe. Retrieved from http://www.msn.com/en-us/news/politics/washington-post-editor-says-trump-called-her-%e2%80%98beautiful%e2%80%99/ar-BBqL2eh?li=BBnb7Kz&ocid=iehp

Resnick, Gideon (2016, March 18). Carson's camp plots VP bid. The Daily Beast. Retrieved from http://www.msn.com/en-us/news/politics/carson%e2%80%99s-camp-plots-vp-bid/ar-BBqCG6q?li=BBnb7Kz&ocid=iehp

Resnick, Gideon (2016, March 3). Donald Trump wants you to know he's yuge. The Daily Beast. Retrieved from http://www.thedailybeast.com/donald-trump-wants-you-to-know-hes-yuge

Ricci, K. (2015, August 6). Watch Donald Trump Threaten Megyn Kelly After She Questions His Past Sexist Remarks. Uproxx. Retrieved from http://uproxx.com/tv/donald-trump-megyn-kelly/

Richardson, Bradford. "Trump calls 'highly respected' Putin's comments a 'great honor.' " The Hill. 17 Dec 2015.

Rosenberg, E. (2016, March 12). Trump Supporter Explains Why She Made Nazi Salute. The New York Times. Retrieved from http://www.msn.com/en-us/news/politics/trump-supporter-explains-why-she-made-nazi-salute/ar-AAgI63z?li=BBnb7Kz&ocid=iehp

St. Petersburg Times. (1992, July 14). Perot asks volunteers to sign loyalty oaths.

Salhani, J. (2015, December 11). Leaders across the world denounce Trump. Retrieved from http://thinkprogress.org/world/2015/12/11/3731183/how-the-world-is-reacting-to-donald-trump/

Sargent, Greg. (2017, January 2). Yes, Donald Trump 'lies' A lot. And news organizations should say so. *The Washington Post*. Retrieved from (https://www.washingtonpost.com/blogs/plum-line/wp/2017/01/02/yes-donald-trump-lies-a-lot-and-news-organizations-should-say-so/?utm_term=.b51a752b9f95

Schilling, Vincent (2017, September 9). The True Story of Pocahontas: Historical Myths Versus Sad Reality. Indian Country Today. Retrieved from https://indiancountrymedianetwork.com/history/genealogy/true-story-pocahontas-historical-myths-versus-sad-reality/

Schmidt, MichaelS., Apuzzo, Matt, & Habaaeerman, Maggie (2017, November 23). A Split From Trump Indicates That Flynn Is Moving to Cooperate With Mueller. New York Times. Retrieved from https://www.nytimes.com/2017/11/23/us/politics/flynn-mueller-russia-trump.html

Schmidt, W. E. (1987, May 19). Scandal in Atlanta: Heirs to The King legacy may be tarnished. *New York Times*.

Semuels, A. (2016, October 12). No, most black people don't live in poverty – or in inner cities. *The Atlantic*. Retrieved from https://www.theatlantic.com/business/archive/2016/10/trump-african-american-inner-city/503744/

Shan, Janet (2016, September 4). Trump surrogate Paris Dennard mocked on Twitter over his Black outreach. *Hinterland Gazette* . Retrieved from http://hinterlandgazette.com/2016/09/black-trump-surrogate-paris-dennard-mocked-twitter-over-black-outreach.html#ixzz4ZG4yE9TN

Sinderbrand, Rebecca (2016, May 13). The Daily Trail: Donald Trump Finds Out His Past Isn't Over. It isn't Even Past." *The Washington Post*. Retrieved from https://www.washingtonpost.com/news/post-politics/paloma/the-daily-trail/2016/05/13/the-daily-trail-a-surprise-blast-from-donald-trump-s-past-knocks-him-off-message/57362416981b92a22d77f8bc/?utm_term=.7bfe6274cd7c

Singer, Paul (2016, March 18). Trump's old blog shows very different views. USA Today. Retrieved from http://www.msn.com/en-us/news/politics/trumps-old-blog-shows-very-different-views/ar-BBqCL0m?li=BBnb7Kz&ocid=iehp

Stack, D. (2016, April 11). Trump: CIA director 'ridiculous' on waterboarding. USA Today. Retrieved fromhttp://www.msn.com/en-us/news/politics/trump-cia-director-ridiculous-on-waterboarding/ar-BBrCrQU?li=BBnbcA1&ocid=iehp

Stanglin, Doug & Madhani, Aamer (2016, March 12). Trump blames 'thugs' for canceling Chicago rally. USA Today. Retrieved from http://www.msn.com/en-us/news/politics/trump-blames-thugs-for-canceling-chicago-rally/ar-AAgHABO?li=BBnb7Kz&ocid=iehp

Szoldra, Paul (2016, March 18). The Anonymous 'leak' of Donald Trump's cell phone and SSN are nothing new , Retrieved from http://www.msn.com/en-us/news/politics/the-anonymous-%e2%80%98leak%e2%80%99-of-donald-trump%e2%80%99s-cell-phone-and-ssn-are-nothing-new/ar-BBqAQ6U?li=BBnb7Kz&ocid=iehp

Tatum, Sophia (2017, February 6). Trump defends Putin: 'You think our country's so innocent?' CNN. Retrieved from http://www.cnn.com/2017/02/04/politics/donald-trump-vladimir-putin/index.html

Trump, Donald J. (2016, July 21). Donald Trump's acceptance speech at the Republican National Convention. Retrieved from http://www.foxnews.com/politics/2016/07/21/donald-trumps-acceptance-speech-at-republican-national-convention.html

Tucker, Eric & Gurman, Sadie (2017, May 17). Former FBI director Mueller to lead Trump-Russia probe. Seattle Times.

Twohey, Megan, Buettner, Russ & Eder, Steve.. (2016, December 25). Inside the Trump Organization, the Company That Has Run Trump's Big World. New York Times. Retrieved from https://www.nytimes.com/2016/12/25/us/politics/trump-organization-business.html?mcubz=3

Uchimiya, E. (2015, September 9). Donald Trump insults Carly Fiorina's appearance. CBS News. Retrieved from http://www.cbsnews.com/news/donald-trump-insults-carly-fiorinas-appearance/

USA Today (editorial board). (2016, September 30). USA TODAY's editorial board: Trump is 'unfit for the presidency'. Retrieved from http://www.usatoday.com/story/opinion/2016/09/29/dont-vote-for-donald-trump-editorial-board-editorials-debates/91295020/

Variety staff. (2017, September 12). ESPN reprimands Jemele Hill for calling Trump 'White Supremacist'. Variety. Retrieved from http://variety.com/2017/tv/news/espn-jemele-hill-trumo-white-supremacist-1202556517/

Vinton, K. (2016, December 7). Meet Linda McMahon, Wife Of WWE Billionaire And Trump's Pick For Small Business Administrator. Forbes. Retrieved from https://www.forbes.com/sites/katevinton/2016/12/07/linda-mcmahon-wife-of-wwe-billionaire-vincent-mcmahon-is-trumps-pick-to-head-his-small-business-administration/#1fa00c901750

Wagner, M. (2016, February 27). Marco Rubio mocks Donald Trump's 'spray tan': 'He should sue whoever did that to his face.' *New York Daily News*. Retrieved from http://www.nydailynews.com/news/politics/marco-rubio-mocks-donald-trump-spray-tan-article-1.2546027

Warshaw, Anne (2016, February 19). Trump Offers No Solutions, But He Speaks For Those Who See Little Future. Bloomberg News. Retrieved from http://www.marketwatch.com/story/donald-trump-can-ride-the-wave-of-anger-all-the-way-to-the-white-house-2016-02-19

[Type text]

Washington Post (2016, August 17). The The Daily 202: What Trump's latest shakeup says about his flailing campaign. Retrieved from https://www.washingtonpost.com/news/powerpost/paloma/daily-202/2016/08/17/daily-202-what-trump-s-latest-shakeup-says-about-his-flailing-campaign/57b3ba48cd249a2fe363ba23/?wpisrc=nl_most-draw6&wpmm=1

Welsing, F.C. (1974, May). The Cress Theory of color confrontation and racism. *The Black Scholar*.

Welsing, F.C. (1991). *The Isis papers: The keys to the colors*. Chicago, Illinois: Third World Press.

Willhelm, S.M. (1973). Equality: America's racist ideology. In Ladner, J.L. (Ed.) *The Death of White Sociology*. New York: Vintage Books.

Wikipedia (2016). Ross Perot presidential campaign, 1992. Retrieved from https://en.wikipedia.org/wiki/Ross_Perot_presidential_campaign,_1992#Decline_and_withdrawal

Wilkie, Christina (2016, July 19). Melania Trump's Claims She Graduated From College Are About As Credible As Her Speech Last Night. Huffington Post. Retrieved from https://www.huffingtonpost.com/entry/melania-trump-college-claims_us_578dd95ce4b0c53d5cfac0dc

Wood, Mary & Hawkins, Lisa. (1980). State regulation of late abortion and the physician's duty of careto the viable fetus. Missouri Law Review, 394.

Woodward, Bob & Costa, Rob ert (2016, April 5). Trump would seek to block money transfers to force Mexico to fund border wall. The Washington Post. Retrieved from http://www.msn.com/en-us/news/politics/trump-would-seek-to-block-money-transfers-to-force-mexico-to-fund-border-wall/ar-BBrnpYD?li=BBnb7Kz&ocid=iehp

Wright, Susan (2017, July 17). Ethics Group Fought To Gain Access To Mar-A-Lago Visitors Log, And Won. Red State.com. Retrieved from https://www.redstate.com/sweetie15/2017/07/17/ethics-group-fought-gain-access-mar-lago-visitors-log-won/

Zuess, E. (2014, January 23). Ralph Nader Was Indispensable To The Republican Party. Huffington Post. Retrieved from http://www.huffingtonpost.com/eric-zuesse/ralph-nader-was-indispens_b_4235065.html